Sustaining Innovation

Paul C. Light

Sustaining Innovation

Creating Nonprofit
and Government Organizations
That Innovate Naturally

Jossey-Bass Publishers
San Francisco

Substantial discounts on bulk quantities of Jossey-Bass books are available to corporations, professional associations, and other organizations. For details and discount information, contact the special sales department at Jossey-Bass Inc., Publishers (415) 433–1740; Fax (800) 605–2665.

For sales outside the United States, please contact your local Simon & Schuster International Office. .

Jossey-Bass Web address: http://www.josseybass.com

 Manufactured in the United States of America on Lyons Falls Turin Book. This paper is acid-free and 100 percent totally chlorine-free.

Library of Congress Cataloging-in-Publication Data

Light, Paul Charles.
  Sustaining innovation : creating nonprofit and government organizations that
    innovate naturally / Paul C. Light. — 1st ed.
    p. cm. — (The Jossey-Bass nonprofit and public management
    series)
  Includes bibliographical references (p.   ) and index.
  ISBN 0-7879-4098-4 (alk. paper)
  1. Organizational change. 2. Public administration. 3. Nonprofit
organizations. I. Title. II. Series.
JF1525.073L54   1998
658.4'06—dc21   97-40025

HB Printing 10 9 8 7 6 5 4 3 2 1   FIRST EDITION

The Jossey-Bass
Nonprofit and Public Management Series

Contents

Preface

This book is about building nonprofit and government organizations in which the act of innovation is more natural and therefore more frequent—organizations in which innovation is ordinary good practice. Any organization, be it nonprofit, government, or private, can innovate once. The challenge is to innovate twice, thrice, and more.

Because this book is designed to inform the world of practice, it is filled with real success stories and practical lessons learned. It is written for practitioners who want to build organizations in which the act of innovation flows naturally from how the organization faces its environment, structures its bureaucracy, leads itself, and manages its internal management systems. Readers stuck in moribund agencies will find examples of how other organizations began the journey toward renewal; those at the midpoint will find counsel on how to survive the inevitable mistakes along the way; and those who are part of innovating organizations will find tools for keeping the edge, as they must if they are to continue innovating.

These lessons are based on the Surviving Innovation Project, a five-year research effort designed to ask how nonprofit and government organizations can increase the odds that innovation will occur and endure. Launched in 1991 with funding from the Ford, McKnight, and General Mills foundations, the project involved case studies of twenty-six Minnesota organizations in which innovation had become an expression of ordinary good practice. These Surviving Innovation organizations, as they will be identified throughout the book, were hardly perfect. Indeed, two of the twenty-six were essentially dead by the time this book went to press—one had gone out of business entirely and the other had been absorbed by a much larger state agency.

As a group, however, the twenty-six Surviving Innovation organizations suggest that innovation need not be an act of organizational defiance. Although innovation in the nonprofit sector and government will never be easy, if only because the public is so impatient for overnight success, it need not be so difficult either. Even as we celebrate and admire the heroic leaders who struggle against the odds to create innovation in spite of their organizations, we can also aspire to a future in which innovation is less dependent on such acts of organizational heroism.

For the Surviving Innovation organizations, innovation was less a job for heroes ready to do whatever it took than an act of ordinary good practice by people who were extraordinarily committed to mission. Much as Minnesotans might imagine themselves to be "all above average," as Garrison Keillor describes the residents of Lake Wobegon, most of the people in this book are not so different from the rest of us. They may care deeply about their work, but they also live balanced lives, raise families, have hobbies, celebrate holidays, take vacations, plant gardens, mow yards, and shovel snow pretty much like the rest of America, albeit with a colder winter and shorter summer. Take away the snowshoes, long underwear, and mosquito bites, and most of the people in Minnesota's innovating organizations will seem very familiar indeed.

There will always be jobs for heroes, even in Lake Wobegon. No matter how much we change our nonprofit and government organizations, innovation will still take place in hostile settings, rising in spite of public cynicism, top-heavy bureaucracies, careless leadership, and antiquated management systems. The point is that struggling against the odds is not always the right job for heroes. It is far better that they use their considerable talents to remake their organizations for the future than engage in mythic acts of defiance only to see their victories dissipated by the passage of time.

Before turning to lessons from the Surviving Innovation organizations, it is important to understand the research on which this book is based. Toward that end, this preface provides an introduction to the Surviving Innovation Project, a discussion of the central research questions posed, a set of basic definitions of innovation, and a description of the methodology used in selecting and studying the twenty-six organizations. The preface concludes with an outline of the book.

The Surviving Innovation Project

The Surviving Innovation Project began with the simple notion that a very high percentage of nonprofit and government innovation occurs against the odds, brought forth in organizations that are hostile to change. As a result of these environmental circumstances, many innovations die quickly, whether killed by accident (for example, a funding crisis), neglect (the departure of an organizational champion), or intent (a turf war).

These deaths are particularly troublesome because they occur not at the beginning of the innovation process, where one idea in a thousand might survive, nor at formal adoption, where one idea in a hundred might pass, but after all the arm-twisting, deal-making, and winnowing are done. It is one thing to abandon an idea at the sketchbook stage, when the investment is small, quite another to abandon one that has survived the arduous journey to implementation. It is particularly painful to see innovations of the kind celebrated in books such as David Osborne and Ted Gaebler's *Reinventing Government* (1993) and Lisbeth Schorr's *Within Our Reach* (1989) succumb so soon after launch.

Yet perish many of those celebrated innovations do. My own analysis of the thirty-five Minnesota projects highlighted in

Reinventing Government shows that roughly a third were either dead or near dead by the time the book came out in paperback. Several were dismantled by new administrations, several others ran out of money and momentum, and still others were only desperately clinging to life. At least for innovation in Minnesota state government, national visibility was clearly no guarantee of success (see Altshuler, 1997).

Although the private sector also loses a sizable percentage of its innovation after launch (see, for example, Maidique and Zirger, 1984; Cooper and Kleinschmidt, 1987), the costs of launching a nonprofit or government innovation are so high that even a one-in-ten failure rate may be untenable.

This does not mean all innovation should live forever, however. Indeed, the very term *surviving innovation* is something of an oxymoron. The longer an innovation lives, the more it should become the prevailing wisdom against which future innovations will emerge. The goal is not to create immortality but to improve the odds that innovation will become an organizational habit. When a new idea dies because it is poorly designed, badly timed, or simply cannot work, we have learned something that can be used to inform future innovation. When a new idea fails because the organization is poorly designed, badly led, or simply hostile to new innovation, we have learned mostly how to kill the next innovation.

Defining Innovation

The word *innovation* is one of the most overused, underdefined terms in organizational life. No one seems to be sure just what the word means. Is it merely something new to a given organization or a development that challenges the prevailing wisdom in a field? Is it an initiative that achieves a certain cachet as the fashion of the moment or something that actually changes the course of practice?

Although the "whatever is new to you" definition is by far the most common in studies of private-sector innovation, it fails to take account of the ultimate rationale for innovation in the public sector.

Whereas in the private sector an innovation merely needs to be profitable to be worth doing, in the public sector innovation must be about doing something worthwhile. If it does not challenge the prevailing wisdom, if it does not advance the public good, why bother? As Lawrence Lynn defines it, public innovation must be "an original disruptive act" (1992).

This definition provides much greater clarity about what innovation is and is not. First, nonprofit and government innovation involves *more than whatever is new to a given organization*. Public innovation is just too expensive to be defined as mere novelty. Instead, the word innovation should be reserved for acts that are original to an organization's field. Learning how to copy an innovative act from organization to organization in a given field is primarily a worry for experts on replication, not innovation.

Second, public sector innovation involves *more than simply doing the public's business well*. Much as Total Quality Management or employee empowerment might warrant celebration as an act of reinventing, it should not be considered innovation any more than an updated telephone or computer system should be. Peter Drucker makes a similar point about the effort to reinvent the federal government: "In any institution other than the federal government, the changes being trumpeted as reinventions would not even be announced, except perhaps on the bulletin board in the hallway. They are the kinds of things that a hospital expects floor nurses to do on their own; that a bank expects branch managers to do on their own; that even a poorly run manufacturer expects supervisors to do on their own—without getting much praise, let alone any extra rewards" (1995, p. 50). As I will argue at several points in this book, rigorous management is essential in an innovating organization, but it is certainly not one and the same as innovation. Most innovating organizations are very well run, but not all well-run organizations are innovating.

Third, nonprofit and government innovation involves *the broader public good*. The ultimate purpose of innovation is not to win awards, boost public confidence, or attract foundation support, but to create public value. This is not to argue that true innovation never wins awards, boosts confidence, or generates revenues. Rather, it is to suggest that these are only secondary effects of innovation. If a given act does not add public value, it should not be labeled innovation. To do so is to define innovation downward.

The creation of public value must be based on more than an abstract hunch that a given innovation will produce some benefit. Hard questions must be asked about whether the innovation is actually likely to work. As a general rule, innovating organizations take care to specify the goals of their work and the results by which they expect to be measured. They know they are creating public value not because their innovative acts are novel or win awards but because those acts have clear impacts (see Moore, 1995).

If we define innovation as an act that challenges the prevailing wisdom as it creates public value, an innovating organization can be said to be one that is structured and led to make such innovation more natural and frequent. It is important to note, however, that frequency alone is not enough to justify declaring a given organization innovating. An organization that has only one innovative act every decade might merit study as an innovating organization if it is able to keep that single idea at the edge of the field through frequent fine-tuning. By the same token, an organization that has one innovative act a week might be defined as anything *but* innovative if its ideas do not challenge the prevailing wisdom in the field.

The Surviving Innovation Data

This book is based on a five-year search for lessons about organizational innovation. The search involved twenty-six detailed case studies of Minnesota nonprofit and government organizations, more than two hundred face-to-face interviews, nearly a year of site visits, and a detailed analysis of the resulting data.

The twenty-six organizations were not picked at random, however. They were culled from an initial list of over one hundred nominees that emerged from focus groups with funders, practitioners, evaluators, and community leaders. To reach the final sample, each organization had to meet four criteria. It had to have a history of innovativeness—a criterion that could not be satisfied by one innovation every ten years. It had to show a commitment to innovativeness as a product of organizational design—that is, innovativeness could not take place in spite of the organization. It had to yield compelling stories on how other nonprofit and government organizations can become innovating organizations, which meant a capacity to teach important lessons. Finally, it had to be willing to participate in the Surviving Innovation Project by accepting a site visit of two to three days' duration.

An effort was also made to cover a broad portfolio of missions. The final sample included a Native American community development agency, a state zoo, a university extension service, a school for brain-injured children, a domestic abuse prevention center, a state community college, an adolescent treatment center, a puppet and mask theater, a seminary, a pollution prevention program, a county government, a Chicano/Latino social service agency, a sustainable agriculture project, and a rural elementary school. (See Appendix A for a complete list of the twenty-six organizations.)

In addition, the sample was designed to include a range of organizational types—from large state agencies to tiny nonprofits, from county governments to public schools, from relatively young agencies to long-established ones, from the highly visible to the nearly invisible, from the well endowed to the grant dependent, from urban to suburban to rural: in short, the gamut of public life. Every reader should be able to find at least one organization with which to identify. (A summary of the sample by sector, type of innovation, size, age, and primary field is offered in Appendix B.)

This sampling process was never intended to produce a list of the twenty-six *most* innovative organizations in Minnesota. Rather, it was designed to generate a collection of innovating organizations that could yield lessons across the spectrum of nonprofit and government activities, whether in the arts, housing development, environmental protection, education, or social services.

Questions of Validity

The immediate question for some readers may be whether lessons learned from twenty-six Minnesota organizations, however interesting, have any validity for other parts of the country. If Minnesota is, indeed, a place where everyone is above average, Minnesota organizations may be admirable but irrelevant to organizational life elsewhere in the United States.

The answer, I believe, is that these twenty-six organizations are similar enough to organizations elsewhere to warrant generalization. Having visited hundreds of organizations across the country, some well run and others in deep distress, I have come to believe that running an innovating organization in Minnesota is about as tough as running one anywhere. Dollars are just as scarce, pressures are just as intense, and although the public may be just a tiny bit more progressive, the "what have you done for me lately?" syndrome is always present.

Two patterns in the sample merit brief attention before we turn to the study design. First, nonprofit organizations outnumbered government agencies by a ratio of over two to one. The simple explanation is that government in general, and Minnesota government in particular, has been less successful than the nonprofit sector in building innovating organizations that fit the definitions stated earlier.

As if to prove the point, seven of the eight government organizations that made the Surviving Innovation sample actually behaved more like nonprofits than traditional public agencies. Three of the seven were state agencies (the Minnesota Office of Waste Management, the Minnesota Zoo, and the Minnesota Extension Service) that were barely recognizable as such. One Office of Waste Management employee remarked that the agency might as well have been flying the skull and crossbones instead of the Minnesota state flag. The other four were public schools that had reshaped themselves to meet the market pressure of public school choice or, in one case, had been launched as a charter school. For these seven institutions, becoming an innovating organization involved behaving like something other than a government agency.

Second, relatively small organizations outnumbered large ones by more than five to one, confirming the conventional wisdom that large organizations are more hostile to innovation. (See Dougherty and Hardy, 1996, for a similar conclusion about large private-sector organizations.) Although large organizations often provide greater resources for particularly promising ideas, they may have much greater difficulty cultivating those ideas in the first place and may require longer lead times to bring an innovation to fruition. Ultimately, as I have argued elsewhere, "What matters most is the distance an idea must travel before it reaches a champion who can supply the resources and political support needed to bring it to fruition against inevitable bureaucratic resistance" (1995, p. 70).

Study Design

The key evidence for this book was generated from site visits conducted during the winter, spring, and summer of 1994. In all, these visits involved 220 face-to-face interviews with a broad range of organizational employees and expert informants, including board members, frontline staff, funders, and clients.

These semistructured interviews covered virtually every aspect of organizational life. Each interview was used to deepen the portrait of the organization, meaning that some questions were asked of only one respondent during a site visit. After the site visits were completed, all the interviews from each site were collated into a single file, which was then *interrogated* for answers to eighty-four questions about the organization's environment, internal structure, leadership, and management systems. This *file interrogation instrument*, as it was labeled, ranged from simple, objective questions to much more impressionistic queries. (The questionnaire appears in the left-hand column of the data tables in Appendix C.)

This analysis of the files was designed to identify characteristics or preferences that might be essential to an innovating organization. Was the environment predictable? Was there a waiting list for services? Were there regular staff meetings? Had the organization been reorganized in the past five years? Was there evidence of high stress? Was there a single executive at the top of the organization (several had coexecutives and one used a team)? Was dissent encouraged? Did the organization as a whole enjoy its work? How were new ideas judged? Did the organization have merit pay? Did it have an innovation investment fund to seed promising ideas?

The study design has both strengths and weaknesses for distilling the lessons of innovating organizations. Its principal strength is depth. The information collected from the twenty-six organizations filled a file cabinet; the database generated hundreds of cross-tabulations; the interviews filled three loose-leaf binders. To the extent that one can know an organization after spending a few days in its embrace, this site-based research produced a rich and textured portrait of the sample. Moreover, a study of success is inevitably uplifting. In spite of the stress and conflict that appear to be inevitable in many innovating organizations, these were wonderful agencies to visit. They had a special energy and a commitment to mission that are all too rare in the public sector as a whole.

The main weakness of the study lies in the lack of a control group against which to compare findings. It is possible, for example, that all organizations, whether innovating or not, have flat hierarchies, high stress, and strong accountability systems. It may be that all encourage internal collaboration, employee participation, and teamwork. Lacking a control group of noninnovating organizations, one cannot know which of the lessons learned in this book are truly important.

Ultimately, the best that can be done with such a design is to generate what I will call *preferred states of organizational being*. Because we cannot know what is essential in an absolute sense, we must settle for what is preferred as a general state of organizational life. Other things being equal—for example, size and age—what do the twenty-six organizations suggest for relating to the environment, structuring the bureaucracy, envisioning the leader's work, and calibrating internal management systems? Some answers emerge from careful analysis of the data described in Appendix C, others from the detailed interviews, still others from my own observations. Moreover, there is more than enough variation among the twenty-six organizations to suggest that some lessons are more important than others.

In an unfortunate twist of fate that helped this project but clearly hurt the community, one of the Surviving Innovation organizations died in 1996. In succumbing, the Phoenix Group became a kind of informal control case against which to measure the other twenty-five organizations. The weakness of the Phoenix Group was not in its heart but in its general disdain for management, particularly strong financial controls. The organization subscribed to the myth that innovation is somehow incompatible with good management. Even for a group named after an Egyptian symbol of immortality, it was too great a myth to surmount.

Two caveats are warranted before proceeding to the plan of the book. In complete candor, I fell in love with most of the twenty-six organizations. I was often awed by their energy, commitment, and accomplishments. Although I believe I kept my objectivity throughout the project, readers are cautioned that this is very much a book about organizations I came to admire.

Second, although I can attest that the twenty-six organizations were *reputational* leaders in their fields, and can point to awards, commendations, and expert testimony that suggest they were clearly producing important results, I did not have the technical expertise to assure readers that these organizations were, *in fact*, producing truly innovative work. Lacking any training in neurology, for example, I cannot be absolutely sure that Chance to Grow was actually helping brain-injured children, even though the U.S. Secretary of Education seemed to believe so. Lacking more than passing familiarity with welfare programs, I cannot be sure that Anoka County was producing results through its innovative child support program, even though the Ford Foundation and Harvard University's Kennedy School of Government seemed to believe so in giving the county a $100,000 State and Local Innovations Award.

This caveat holds across all twenty-six organizations. I cannot be sure that the Walker Art Center was on the cutting edge of modern art, the Zoo was leading its field in wildlife preservation, the Domestic Abuse Project was successfully treating domestic abusers, or the Cyrus Math/Science/Technology Elementary School was producing better-educated grade-schoolers. These are judgments I had to leave to others, whether funders, evaluators, or external boards of one kind or another. Readers will simply have to trust that the Surviving Innovation Project asked the right experts in designing the initial sample, and, therefore, that the twenty-six organizations were both challenging the prevailing wisdom in their fields and generating public good.

Overview of the Chapters

This book is designed to provide a set of accessible, well-illustrated lessons about building innovating organizations. Some of the lessons can be easily applied, whereas others involve longer-term reform, but all are offered against the encouraging background of twenty-six nonprofit and government organizations that actually improved the odds for innovation.

Chapter One provides the basic compass for my search for preferred states of organizational being. It begins with a brief review of the literature on innovation. Those who search that literature for practical lessons learned will be quickly frustrated by the lack of agreement on even the most basic issues, not the least of which is what constitutes innovation in the first place. Chapter One strikes out from that literature by focusing less on the demand for absolute truths and more on the search for preferred states of being. It is a search that involves four different components of organizational life:

the environment in which an organization resides, its internal structure, its leadership, and its management systems.

Chapter Two argues that the first step in creating an innovating organization is to remove the barriers and debunk the myths that so often discourage innovation. Assuming that creativity is evenly distributed within organizations, removing barriers and debunking myths should increase the likelihood of innovation. Although larger and older organizations will have more barriers than smaller and younger ones, all innovating organizations share a common concern for keeping the barriers low. They also struggle constantly with the myths that are created to discourage change.

Chapter Three deepens the discussion of preferred states of being by examining the preferred environment of an innovating organization. None of the twenty-six Surviving Innovation organizations accepted its environment as a given—that is, as something to either take for granted or hunker down against. Rather, all faced themselves into the environment and harnessed the enormous vitality that comes from introducing market pressure into their daily organizational lives. It was in *harnessing* the market that these twenty-six organizations improved the odds of innovation.

Chapter Four turns to the preferred internal structure for an innovating organization. Although the Surviving Innovation organizations certainly tried to stay as thin as possible (keeping the distance minimal between top and bottom), they also structured themselves to create greater freedom to imagine. Whether nonprofit or government, all worked to enhance the opportunities for internal collaboration, and they primed the pump for new ideas by putting real resources (dollars, time, additional staff) at risk. They also moved away from top-down, autocratic leadership systems toward more participatory approaches.

Chapter Five turns to the preferred leadership of an innovating organization. The central question of the chapter is simple: What is the leader's work in an innovating organization? The answer, according to the Surviving Innovation organizations, is to create the conditions for others to succeed. This involves, among other things, creating a bias for experimentation, giving permission to fail, communicating to excess, keeping faith and intuition alive—but not actually having every last innovative idea. Indeed, the leader's work may be precisely *not* to serve as the center of ideas. Rather, it appears to involve letting others generate innovations while the leader plays a much more prominent role as a teacher.

As we shall see, innovating organizations must know when to say no to promising or lucrative ideas and why to say yes. Reminding the organization of why it exists and whom it serves is very much a leader's role. As we shall also see, knowing when to leave is also part of the leader's work, although it is very seldom discussed as an important lesson of innovating organizations.

Chapter Six continues the search for preferred states of being by focusing on internal management systems. As we shall see in Chapter Two, far too many organizations believe that pay, personnel, training, financial management, accounting, strategic planning, and evaluation systems are barriers to innovation. For most of the Surviving Innovation organizations, however, these systems were not only seen as essential to innovation, they were embraced as essential accelerators of good ideas.

Chapter Seven encourages organizations to fit the list of preferred states to their realities. Not all the organizations in the Surviving Innovation Project were created equal. Some were government organizations; most were nonprofit; some were big, others small; some were young, others older. Part of tailoring the lessons learned from this sample to one's own organization involves an analysis of how the twenty-six organizations differed from each other. Chapter Seven provides that needed comparison.

Chapter Eight concludes the search for preferred states of being with a discussion of the core values that help innovating organizations know what fits and what does not. After all is said and done, the question is how to know what is right for your organization. The answer, I believe, is rooted in four core values: trust, honesty, rigor, and faith. The organizations that I came to admire were trusting of themselves, their employees, and the people they served (whether called audience, customers, clients, or just plain citizens), honest in assessing ideas and giving feedback, rigorous in challenging themselves with the facts about what would and would not work in achieving their missions, and confident in their faith about the future.

A Brief Note to Noninnovators

Although this book is written for people who want to build innovating organizations, many of the lessons apply to high-performing organizations in general. Almost by definition, all innovating organizations are high-performing. They have well-oiled financial management systems, strong internal leadership, relatively flat organizational hierarchies, and close contact with the outside world—all features of high-performing organizations in general.

Although all innovating organizations may be high performers, not all high performers are innovating. The difference resides in certain characteristics that reflect an organization's interest in new ideas—for example, innovation investment funds, a high tolerance for mistakes, and incentives for external and internal collaboration. It is my hope that readers from both kinds of organizations, innovating and noninnovating, will find lessons of value in the following pages. The leap toward innovation should depend entirely on how innovation helps or hinders an organization's mission. After all, innovation is a means to an end, not the end itself.

Acknowledgments

Acknowledgments have always been my favorite part of writing a book. I never write them until they can be savored as a final sign that a book is truly finished and, therefore, when I can actually reflect on all the people who helped bring an idea to fruition.

Writing the acknowledgments for this book is a particular pleasure, for I can now thank a number of friends and colleagues who had the faith to make this book possible.

First among them is Lisa Hinz, my research associate on the project and a linchpin in its success. Lisa made just about everything in the project better by her dedication and creativity. She was a key sounding board for my ideas, a talented analyst of data, a proficient interviewer in her own right, and a crucial supporter at every step of the project. This book could not have been written without her.

Sharon Anderson and her colleagues at the Humphrey Institute's Reflective Leadership Center were also central to this book, providing a safe haven for me to try out core themes and never wavering in their enthusiasm for the project. Sharon was a constant source of affirmation in her belief that I could and should do the project, and I will ever be grateful for her confidence.

Others at the Humphrey Institute gave their support as well. John Brandl engaged me in a four-year conversation about the sources of innovativeness in organizations, Judy Leahy provided unyielding friendship throughout, Harry Boyte struggled to teach me a bit about the role of the citizen in public work, and a host of students and colleagues permitted me to blather on about this finding or that. For all of their patience, indeed faith, in this effort, I am thankful.

My funders never wavered either. Carol Birde and Michael O'Keefe at the McKnight Foundation provided the key funding to get this project started in the first place and to bring it across the finish line when I needed extra funds to complete the analysis. David Nasby at the General Mills Foundation provided an injection of support and enthusiasm as well, and the Ford Foundation gave me the funding to begin the journey that eventually brought me to launch the Surviving Innovation Project.

Thanks also go to my colleagues at The Pew Charitable Trusts, particularly Rebecca W. Rimel, our president, and Nadya Shmavonian, our executive vice president, who both allowed me to carve out the time needed to write the book, and my staff in the Public Policy unit, who shielded me as I worked and reworked the manuscript. I could not have had a stronger team than Caitlyn Frost, Jennifer Bolton, and Betsy Hubbard. Nor could I have had a more supportive family than my wife, Sharon, and my children, Kate, Max, and Wheeler. Finally, I could not have had a more enthusiastic and helpful editor than Alan Shrader at Jossey-Bass, and I would also like to thank the production team led by David Horne, who smoothed the process more than I could ever have hoped for.

Ultimately, this book depended on the graciousness, patience, and persistence of the twenty-six organizations that consented to be part of the Surviving Innovation sample. What a joy it was to study them and what a gift they gave me in return. They gave me energy to persevere in my own work and showed me how I could live my life with greater meaning. I give them credit for all that is good in this book and accept all blame for everything else.

Merion, Pennsylvania　　　　　　　　　　　　　　　　*Paul C. Light*
December 1997

The Author

Paul C. Light earned his B.A. degree with highest honors, summa cum laude from Macalester College in 1975, and his M.A. degree and Ph.D. degree from the University of Michigan in political science in 1980. He has taught at the University of Virginia, George Washington University, and Georgetown University, and was associate dean and professor of planning and public affairs at the Hubert Humphrey Institute of Public Affairs at the University of Minnesota from 1988 through 1992. He is currently director of the Public Policy Program at The Pew Charitable Trusts in Philadelphia, where he is responsible for a new funding program designed to renew civic life in America.

Light arrived at the Trusts after spending roughly half his career in academia and half in the practice of public affairs. In 1982–83, he was an American Political Science Association Congressional Fellow, serving with Rep. Barber B. Conable Jr. on social security reform, and with John Glenn's then-nascent presidential campaign.

After serving as guest scholar at the Brookings Institution in 1983–84, he joined the National Academy of Public Administration as director of studies, where he was responsible for strengthening the Academy's research program. He left the Academy in early 1987 to return to Capitol Hill as a senior staffer to the U.S. Senate Governmental Affairs Committee under the chairmanship of John Glenn. He was responsible for general oversight of executive branch management, budget reform, and presidential transitions legislation.

Light left the Senate in 1988 to become a senior adviser to the National Commission on the Public Service, chaired by former Federal Reserve Board chairman Paul Volcker. He served in an identical role with the National Commission on the State and Local Public Service, chaired by former Mississippi governor William Winter, in 1992. Light drafted both final reports.

Light wrote nine books before turning to this project, including *The President's Agenda, Vice Presidential Power*, the award-winning *Artful Work: The Politics of Social Security Reform*, and *Thickening Government: Federal Hierarchy and the Diffusion of Accountability*, which won the National Academy of Public Administration's highest award for research on public management. His ninth book, *The Tides of Reform: Making Government Work, 1945–1995*, was published in 1997 by Yale University Press. Senator Daniel Patrick Moynihan (D-NY) has called Light's trilogy of books on making government work "wonderfully explanatory, and equally unsettling. . . . No regime lasts long enough for anything to be learned from it; little wonder the citizenry despair. But there *is* hope, and it resides in the work of this inspired activist and analyst."

Light is a member of Phi Beta Kappa and was elected a Fellow of the National Academy of Public Administration in 1994. Until joining The Pew Charitable Trusts, he was a senior fellow of the Washington-based Governance Institute and visiting fellow at the Brookings Institution.

Sustaining Innovation

1

Preferred States of Organizational Being

When Kathryn Roberts arrived as its executive director in 1986, the Minnesota Zoo was as far from being an innovating organization as possible. Granted, the zoo was perfectly located for big attendance, within easy reach of the Twin Cities and only twenty minutes south of what would later become the Mall of America, the nation's largest indoor mall and a huge tourism engine. Granted, too, the five-hundred-acre zoo was spectacular, with its bison, Siberian tigers, and timber wolves roaming free in their natural habitats, viewable from a walking/cross-country ski trail or a monorail.

Nevertheless, for all intents and purposes, the zoo was in serious trouble. Attendance was flat, the zoo's 250 state employees were demoralized, and the organization seemed doomed to a life of mediocrity, maintaining a modest core of loyal visitors and hosting occasional school field trips, but never igniting public interest in learning more about the environment or the protection of endangered species, the zoo's ultimate concerns. Since opening as the first state-run zoo in the country in 1978, it had added only one new exhibit.

Roberts needed more than a few crowd-pleasing exhibits to succeed, however; she had to turn the zoo into a locus of excitement. If the zoo was to survive and prosper, innovation had to be constant. It also had to take place in an organization where high value was placed on healthy animals, friendly staff, clean bathrooms, and good food and ice cream. In short, the zoo needed an overall makeover that would turn it into a place where people wanted to spend their scarce entertainment dollars.

Remaking the organization was no small challenge. Although Roberts came with impressive management credentials, having been director of the Minnesota Department of Administration's management analysis division, she was not a zoologist and had no experience running a zoo. "In retrospect," she would later tell the *Minneapolis StarTribune*, "I was probably pretty naive about it. I didn't realize how many masters I had to work for: the zoo's thirty-member board, the legislature, the governor, the public, and the zoo profession itself."

Whether prepared or not, she confronted a series of tough choices that tested her strength immediately, not the least of which was her highly controversial decision to give the zoo's beloved but ailing beluga whales, Big Mouth and Little Sister, to San Diego's Sea World rather than risk their death in Minnesota. Within a year of Roberts's arrival, attendance was at a record low, the *Minneapolis StarTribune* was celebrating the zoo's tenth anniversary with a story titled "Trouble Shadows Minnesota Zoo," and the legislature was beginning to wonder if the zoo was worth its annual operating appropriation. All Roberts had to show for her "baptism by fire," as she described it, was an empty beluga tank.

To save the zoo, not to mention her job, Roberts had to break the *bureaucratic paradigm* that dominated virtually every corner of the zoo (see Barzelay and Armajani, 1992, for a discussion of the bureaucratic paradigm and its postbureaucratic antidote). It was a way of being that basically did everything by the rules, took cover against the outside world, and never risked a mistake. In the existing culture, employees celebrated the good old days and the way things were; if the institution was to survive, they would have to focus instead on the way things should be. In the existing culture, they focused on how to say no; to survive, they would have to focus on solving problems and satisfying zoo visitors. Finally, in the existing culture, employees protected their bureaucratic turf by enforcing the rules; to survive, they would have to focus on improving every facet of the organization so that visitors would not only go home happy but bring their dollars back to the zoo again and again.

That Roberts succeeded in making a new zoo out of the old is undeniable. By 1991, attendance was at a record high, new exhibits were coming on line throughout the zoo, the beluga tank was now occupied by a family of dolphins and a coral reef exhibit was open nearby, Koala bears had taken up residence near the Northern Trail (where the deer and the antelope truly do play), a new amphitheater was host to the zoo's bird shows, and plans were in place for a $25 million marine science center, complete with a shallow "please touch" shark and ray tank. The fast food was better, too—french fries were hotter, burgers fresher, and a new Minnesota Moose ice-cream bar a big seller. Only three years after worrying about the zoo's future, the *Minneapolis StarTribune* (1991) editorialized about a zoo "on the move": "Surely the zoo still has problems; sure it always will. But while lots of people weren't looking, the Minnesota Zoo seems to have turned an important, post-beluga corner. Well done!"

As we shall see later in this book, Roberts succeeded largely by concentrating her considerable energies not on dreaming up new exhibits herself but on building an organization that would produce innovation naturally; not on greeting every visitor with a smile, but on teaching the organization as a whole the value of return business; not on imagining ways of attracting new visitors, but on lowering the internal barriers to having good ideas rise to the top. Lacking a magic recipe for reform, she simply started changing the way things worked, from expanding her board to hiring a full-time fundraiser, from removing incompetent staff to figuring out how to win freedom from particularly onerous state rules.

Looking back, one can see a method to her approach—bringing market pressure to bear on the zoo, flattening the hierarchy, being clear about who makes decisions, and building rigorous internal management systems. But at the time, it was very much a piecemeal affair as Roberts tried to stay afloat in a sea of crisis.

Readers will learn more in coming chapters about how Roberts and her Surviving Innovation peers succeeded in building innovating organizations. For now, however, it is important to understand how a book on preferred states of organizational being might be useful to those who work in other "zoos," whether literal or figurative. The explanation deals in large measure with what is missing in current scholarship on innovation.

Reading the Field

Imagine for a moment that a nonprofit or government organization leader, say Kathryn Roberts, had somehow been able to tap into today's literature on innovation to help craft her first-year strategy back in 1986. What practical advice could she have gleaned from reading in the field that would have helped her design an innovating organization in time to avert disaster? The answer, to be blunt, is "not much."

Reading the Whole

Her search would not have been frustrated by a lack of material. Public fascination with innovation is unrelenting—a simple Alta Vista Internet search for the word produced approximately 400,000 hits in mid-1997—and the scholarly literature is vast and growing.

Innovation scholar Richard Wolfe counted 1,299 journal articles and 351 dissertations on organizational innovation from 1989 to 1994 alone, and another 6,244 journal articles and 1,336 dissertations during the same period on innovation more generally (1994, pp. 425–426). Although the majority of this research deals with private-sector innovation, where a single new product can mean a life of profits, Roberts would have found a growing body of research on nonprofit and government innovation, much of it stimulated by the Ford Foundation's State and Local Innovations program (see, for example, Altshuler and Behn, 1997).

Nor would Roberts's reading have been discouraged by a lack of scholarly enthusiasm for innovation. To the contrary, there is an unmistakable "pro-innovation bias in the field," as Robert Drazin and Claudia Bird Schoonhoven say (1996). Innovation is often presented as the solution for all that ails organizations, be they private or not. In a financial slump? Invent a new product. Public cynicism got you down? Invent a new program. Losing customers? Get a megamouth shark (good luck!). Even "stick to your knitting" authors such as Tom Peters, of *In Search of Excellence* fame, have joined the innovation bandwagon. Peters now recommends to corporations, "Get Innovative or Get Dead," writing that "I've become obsessed with innovation of late. I even dream about it. (Yuk!) Looking back at the turmoil of the eighties, all ten bloody years, set me off" (1990, p. 9).

Rather, Roberts's search for information would have been frustrated by the lack of even the simplest agreement on virtually any key question in the field. As Wolfe argues, "the most *consistent* theme found in the organizational innovation literature is that its research results have been *inconsistent*. The current state of the literature thus offers little guidance to those who want to influence organizational innovation" (1994, p. 405).

To date, the field has yet to establish a common definition of *innovation*, let alone reach agreement on what interventions might make an organization more innovative. Some say innovation is whatever is new to the organization, while others put the focus on true breakthroughs. As Wolfe concludes, "The underdeveloped state of the innovation literature, in spite of the substantial number of studies and reviews conducted across numerous disciplines, suggests that the challenge rests in the complex, context-sensitive nature of the phenomenon itself" (pp. 405–406).

This is not to suggest that the literature provides no practical counsel for struggling innovators. A leader such as Roberts would have been particularly intrigued by recent scholarship on converting older, noninnovative organizations into product innovators. "Most organizations can produce a successful new product occasionally," write Deborah Dougherty and Cynthia Hardy in an introduction eerily (and accidentally) parallel to the one that opens the preface of this book. "IBM's PC and General Motors' Saturn are good examples. The question is whether they can sustain or repeat what they did." The answer, according to their study of service and product innovations in fifteen large private firms, is to change the organization: "We found that most of these firms were not organized to facilitate innovation: occasionally innovation did occur, but it occurred in spite of the system, not because of it" (1996, p. 1121).

Despite its occasional insights, Roberts might well have felt dazed by the innovation literature. Lacking a common definition of terms and a common basis for inquiry, scholars bask in the extraordinary diversity of the field, leaving practitioners wondering what, if anything, might apply to their particular circumstance.

Reading a Part

Having started her search for practical lessons by reading the entire field, Roberts would then likely have done what any good public manager would do: she would have narrowed her search to government, leaving the private sector behind.

She would have found plenty of encouragement for doing so among scholars who argue that the public and private sectors are fundamentally alike in all unimportant respects (see Allison, 1983; Rainey, 1991). Despite occasional skeptics such as Barry Bozeman (1987), who offers a compelling argument that all organizations are public to some degree, students of nonprofit and government innovation have largely ignored the private-sector literature. Readers paging through the breakthrough articles on government innovation over the past decade (for example, Behn, 1988; Golden, 1990;

Levin and Sanger, 1992, 1994), will find few, if any, lessons drawn from the private sector.

Unfortunately, even if narrowed in focus to nonprofit and government organizations, Roberts's search still would have been frustrated by the lack of insights on organizational design. Generally speaking, the literature is not about designing organizations for innovation but rather about bringing single acts of innovation to fruition. At least three trends in the research on public innovation might have suggested to Roberts that her success depended on anything *but* organizational design.

First, the literature on nonprofit and government innovation literature has generally accepted the structure of government as a given. Simply put, government is seen as a hostile context in which to innovate (see Holdaway, Newberry, Hickson, and Heron, 1975; Perry and Rainey, 1988). According to Alan Altshuler, a professor at Harvard University's Kennedy School of Government and director of the Ford Foundation's Innovations in State and Local Government program, innovators in government face three distinct problems: "First, while government agencies face urgent problems, passionate claimants, and muckraking journalists, they face little direct competition. Second, the political arena is characterized by high conflict; there is no analogue of profitability as a consensual criterion for appraising public-sector innovations. Third, there is nothing that people in government fear more than newsworthy failure" (1997, p. 2).

Not only is the political climate often hostile, but innovators in government face the natural barriers that come with dense organizational structures, scarce resources, reluctance to delegate authority, and high levels of internal scrutiny—none of which has been characterized as beneficial to innovation (see Aiken and Hage, 1971; Pierce and Delbecq, 1977). The more these conditions are described as an immutable fact of life, however, the less likely that talented leaders like Roberts might see the value in attacking the obstacles. Although few would argue that the obstacles will ever disappear entirely, this book will suggest that nonprofit and government organizations can make significant progress in changing the organizational context of innovation, thereby creating a new definition of innovation as an act of ordinary practice.

Second, the nonprofit and government innovation literature has traditionally been much more concerned with the single act of innovation than with the organizational settings in which those acts take place. (For an exception, see Bozeman and Straussman, 1990.) Scholars have learned a great deal about how public entrepreneurs might grope their way to success, use old stuff in new ways, and turn bright ideas into innovation, but relatively less about how those same entrepreneurs might reshape their organizations to support innovation as a more natural act.

This focus on the single success makes perfect sense given the current political climate. As Ford Foundation president Susan Beresford states, "The Innovations in American Government awards program reminds us that people who work in government can and regularly do create effective solutions to important social problems" (Beresford, 1996, p. 6). For a public convinced that government causes more problems than it solves and that almost anything government does is bound to be wasteful and inefficient, single acts of innovation provide needed proof that public institutions, be they nonprofit or government, can actually succeed from time to time.

Moreover, single acts of innovation may be the best that most public agencies can do in a climate of intense hostility and scarce resources. "Yes, innovations exist within the federal government," Vice President Al Gore argued in the first report of the National Performance Review in September 1993, "but many work hard to keep their innovations quiet. By its nature, innovation requires a departure from standard operating procedure. In the federal government, such departures invite repercussions. The result is a culture of fear and resignation. To survive, employees keep a low profile. They decide that the safest answer in any given situation is a firm 'maybe.' They follow the rules, pass the buck, and keep their heads down" (Gore, 1993, pp. 2–3). It is no wonder that scholars would dwell on the single act of innovation when the single act of innovation is so miraculous.

Interestingly, some of the very best work on managing single acts of innovation comes from business school scholars like Harold Angle and Andrew Van de Ven. The focus is hardly surprising. After all, what matters most to a successful private firm is not its reputation for innovativeness but its ability to bring profitable ideas to market. Although overall innovativeness is clearly important to the bottom line, private firms exist in markets in which a single idea such as Intel's Pentium processor can make the difference between long-term success and failure. For scholars of process theory research, as it is labeled, it matters little whether a given idea emerges in a moribund agency or a vibrant start-up. Both require the same ingredients for success. Although those ingredients may be in greater supply in a start-up company, even the most reluctant organization can innovate.

Few scholars have made the argument more effectively than Angle and Van de Ven, whose research is designed to give "the innovation manager a road map that indicates how and why the innovation journey unfolds and what paths are likely to lead to success or failure" (1989, p. 663). Like any good road map, Angle and Van de Ven's has a beginning, a middle, and an end, or, as they describe it, "(1) an initiation period, in which events occur that set the stage for launching efforts to develop an innovation; (2) a developmental period, in which concentrated efforts are undertaken to transform the innovative idea into a concrete reality; and (3) an implementation or termination period, in which the innovation is either adopted and institutionalized as an ongoing program, product, or business, or is terminated and abandoned" (p. 665). Wherever the journey takes place, whether in a hostile setting or in relative calm, it is only by managing each stage of the process well that the innovator can maximize the probability of success. The focus, therefore, is not on the setting but on the management of the idea.

This focus on single acts of innovation in basically unchangeable settings fits with the third and final research trend that might deflect Roberts's findings away from organizational design as the path to innovativeness: most of the literature on nonprofit and government innovation focuses on the importance of the individual actor in making innovation occur. Organizations do not innovate, entrepreneurs do.

This is certainly the message from Martin Levin and Mary Bryna Sanger's *Making Government Work: How Entrepreneurial Executives Turn Bright Ideas into Real Results* (1994), the best book currently available on managing the innovation journey in government. "Success in the public sector depends on skillful executives; management matters," Levin and Sanger declare at the outset, "and, as this book argues, executives are key to innovation" (p. ii). Government will not get more innovative until its "ordinary public managers" get more entrepreneurial. To these innovators-to-be, Levin and Sanger say, "Just do it," providing simple, accessible advice on how to beat the odds against innovation: capitalize on crisis, scan the environment, make subordinates do what you want them to do, seize a good idea, and build momentum for implementation. This focus on the potential role of individual managers in challenging the prevailing wisdom is the book's greatest strength.

It is also the book's single weakness. If innovation is the job of entrepreneurs, the best way to foster more innovation is to mold ordinary managers into entrepreneurs. If, however, innovation is a characteristic of organizational environments, structure, leadership, and internal systems—if, for example, it comes from creating and embracing competition, flattening hierarchies, giving permission to make mistakes, and establishing learning systems—then the key to stimulating innovation lies in the more mundane work of organizational reform.

The relative impact of entrepreneurs versus organizations is far from resolved among scholars who study nonprofit and government innovation, largely because the field serves two very different audiences. One audience is composed of *today's* students and managers, many of whom desperately need a single innovation now. Members of this first audience are well served by *Making Government Work* and the research tradition it represents. Their legislatures and boards may second-guess them, a new governor or president may fire them, and they will likely burn out soon, but there is ample evidence that Levin and Sanger's advice will help them get that one innovation through.

The other audience is composed of *tomorrow's* students and managers, all of whom deserve a better fate than to wind up in most of today's organizations. Today's managers have no other choice but to struggle mightily against the odds, but pity the poor students who find themselves in such organizations tomorrow. Members of this second audience are less well served by *Making Government Work*. Although Levin and Sanger briefly touch on the issue of organizational design, their readers may conclude that there is nothing that can be done to help ideas rise faster, resources flow more smoothly, internal boundaries lower more easily, and management systems operate better, even though such changes are not only possible but essential for sustaining innovation.

Like many of today's nonprofit and government executives, Roberts represents both audiences. Much as she would have been cheered by the success stories on which books such as *Making Government Work* are based, and much as she would have been pleased to learn that innovation can grow in any soil, she would have been frustrated that the literature spends so little time on organizational design.

Unfortunately, Roberts needed much more than one innovation to succeed and certainly could not have done all the entrepreneurial work alone. Though she might have learned how to nurture a flower on a rocky crag, she would have found little information about how to till the organizational soil to let a thousand flowers bloom. And a thousand flowers is just what her zoo needed. (See Kanter, 1988, for a catalogue of organizational reforms that might have been useful to Roberts had she been in the private sector.)

The Search for Preferred States of Being

By now, it should be clear that it is impossible to write in absolutes about designing innovating organizations. As Wolfe concludes, "there can be no *one* theory of innovation, as the more we learn, the more we realize that 'the whole' remains beyond our grasp" (1994, p. 406). Given the current state of the literature, the best one can hope for is a set of reasonably helpful preferred states of organizational being. Simply defined, a *preferred state of being* describes a condition that favors innovativeness, *other things being equal*.

Other things being equal, for example, one would recommend that innovating organizations hire entrepreneurial leaders. That much is clear from the nonprofit and government innovation literature. At the Minnesota Office of Waste Management (OWM) in St. Paul, however, other things were definitely not equal in the 1980s. Even though the agency would later make the Surviving Innovation sample, OWM's leadership had been shuffled more times than a deck of cards. Moreover, several of its directors were appointed precisely because they opposed the small agency. The fact that OWM was able to innovate in spite of its leadership hardly recommends frequent turnover and hostile executives as a preferred state of being. Other things being equal, such leadership is a liability in an innovating organization.

The Surviving Innovation Project was anything but random in searching for the forty preferred states of being that form the core of this book. As Figure 1.1 illustrates, the project imagined a kind of ecosystem in which an organization's innovativeness depends on four factors that ignite and sustain new ideas: (1) the external environment in which a given organization exists, (2) its internal structure, (3) its leadership, and (4) its internal management systems. Before turning to the preferred states of being in each category, readers may find it helpful to review the four sources of innovativeness in greater detail.

Figure 1.1. The Search for Preferred States of Being

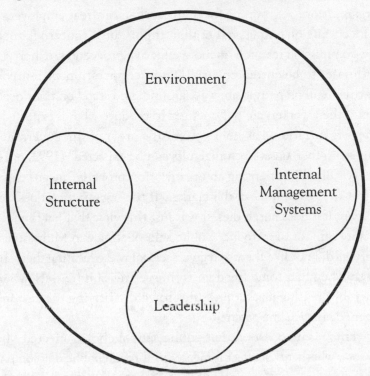

The External Environment

Scholars of organizational life have long agreed that the external environment shapes what organizations do. After all, the external environment contains the customers, competitors, resources, and costs that determine whether a firm lives or dies (see, for example, Hannan and Freeman, 1984; Haveman, 1992; Pfeffer and Salancik, 1978; Ruttan and Hayami, 1984).

Where scholars differ, perhaps, is in their view of what organizations can do to alter their environments. Some scholars view the environment as a mostly immutable force that exerts unyielding pressure toward efficiency. As my Humphrey Institute colleague John Brandl argues, managers can do little right if they are not in sync with their environment: "They can proclaim a mission for their organization, get training for their workers, entreat employees to concentrate on outputs rather than inputs, urge concern for quality, commission research on more effective procedures, exhort subordinates to be entrepreneurial, favor cooperation with private entities, call on patriotism, walk around, and stand on their heads. But if their workers are not oriented to produce what is expected of the organization—as they generally are not in government bureaus—then unsatisfactory results can be expected" (1992, p. 14).

For Brandl, "orienting an organization properly" means exposing it to the full force of the market. If the organization does well, it lives; if it does not, it dies. It was just this view that led Brandl as a state senator to introduce public school choice in Minnesota. If parents did not like the way a given school was educating their children, they had some freedom to move the children elsewhere, thereby creating market pressures toward satisfying the customer (here defined as the parent).

There is no question that public school choice affected Minnesota, whether that effect is measured through public opinion polls or the performance of selected schools, four of which made the Surviving Innovation sample. But not all schools exposed to the market have done equally well. Some have felt the sting of the market, particularly if they happen to be located in rural areas, whereas others have survived essentially unchanged.

This uneven performance suggests a different view of the environment. Rather than a powerful hidden hand that works its will in sometimes mysterious ways, the environment (and the market that resides within it) can be seen as something to be managed, exploited, even manipulated by the organization. Just as air and water are affected by the organisms within them, so too is the ecosystem of innovation affected by the organizations and ideas that compete for survival within it. The environment is not static and inflexible, but pliable and responsive.

As such, it contains at least five factors that favor or frustrate innovating organizations. The first is *turbulence*, simply defined as the level of external uncertainty besetting an organization. As Chapter Seven shows, some public organizations, mostly nonprofits, inhabit a turbulence approaching what one observer calls "permanent white water" (Vaill, 1996), whereas others, mostly government agencies, face a more stable world.

The second environmental factor is the level of *shocks* in the system. A shock can be viewed as an extreme event of some kind—for example, a budget crisis, the resignation of a key advocate, or a scandal. Whereas turbulence exists more or less unchanged over time, shocks are intermittent and far more noticeable. Organizations can become accustomed to remarkably high levels of turbulence; shocks to the system provoke an immediate focus.

The third factor is external *support/encouragement* for innovation. Some organizations exist in environments that are ready and willing to absorb innovation; others exist in more complacent settings. The degree to which the market greets a new idea with enthusiasm is no small determinant of that idea's survival, particularly if the market is willing to pay for the idea through subscriptions, donations, or other expressions of tangible support.

The fourth factor is *collaboration* within an organization's field. As we shall see shortly, many public organizations believe that innovation is best done in solitude, yet collaboration is often the key to success. Some organizations simply cannot collaborate because of high barriers within their environments; these barriers may result from a perceived need to maintain distinctions from other organizations in the field.

The final factor is the availability of external *support for innovation*, which many organizational scholars call *slack*. Slack simply refers to the level of resources available for discretionary investment. Some organizations exist in environments where every last dollar of support is already invested, whereas others seem to be able to find a few dollars (or, in many of the Surviving Innovation cases, a supply of committed volunteers) that provide the needed lift to an innovative idea.

Internal Structure

Scholars have long been interested in the link between internal structure and innovativeness. Indeed, this relationship is the oldest theme in the study of private-sector innovation, dating back to the work of Tom Burns and G. M. Stalker (1961) among electronics firms in England and Scotland. Such studies have consistently described innovation as the product of relatively loose organizational structures (see also Lawrence and Lorsch, 1967; Hage and Aiken, 1967; Zaltman, Duncan, and Holbeck, 1973).

There is no question, therefore, that such a link exists and, if it were well understood, could be exploited to increase the frequency of innovation. As Fariborz Damanpour argues, "The challenge for executives is to build congruent organizations both for today's work and tomorrow's innovation. Organizations need to have sufficient internal diversity in strategies, structures, people, and processes to facilitate different kinds of innovation and to enhance organizational learning" (1991, p. 92).

Unfortunately, the field has yet to determine exactly what would be congruent. Even a cursory reading of the literature on the role of internal structure in innovation yields the same kind of contradictions seen in the literature as a whole. Organizations are supposed to be simultaneously loose (that is, decentralized into relatively autonomous units) and tight (strongly controlled from the top); big (possessing extra money for good ideas) and little (with everyone having a stake in the organization's success); young (characterized by new people and new ideas) and experienced (stocked with seasoned professionals who know what they are doing); highly specialized (with individual employees and units focused on narrow pieces of the organization's overall job) and unified (with everyone sharing in the mission).

Some scholars have resolved this tension by arguing for different organizational structures at different stages of the innovation process—a point dating back to Gerald Zaltman, Robert Duncan, and Jonny Holbeck's 1973 classic, *Innovation and Organizations*, which argued that "the organization must shift its structure as it moves through the various stages of innovation; at the earlier initiation stage a more-organic or less-bureaucratic structure seems most appropriate. Then, as the organization moves to the implementation stage, more-bureaucratic structure becomes appropriate" (p. 155). Scholars of government innovation now know better, of course. It is not quite that easy to switch back and forth from bureaucratic to organic structure.

Even where there is solid evidence describing a clear link between structure and innovation at a specific stage of innovation, it is often so conditional that it cannot be applied to actual circumstances. Research suggests, for example, that innovation is more likely when organizations are composed of specialists rather than generalists; when employees know precisely who they work for and therefore where to go with a good idea; and when organizations are decentralized into many roughly autonomous units rather than centralized around a single leader. However, this evidence varies across types of innovation (administrative versus programmatic), scope of innovation (big versus limited), and sector (government versus nonprofit versus private).

Lacking much certainty about what kinds of structure work best under which circumstances, the organizational designer is best advised to pay attention to five features of bureaucracy that appear to affect innovativeness. The first is the *shape* of the organization, which is easily discerned by simply looking at the organizational chart. Is it a traditional pyramid, with more people at the bottom delivering services than at the top; a pentagon, with more people in the middle than at the bottom; or a circle, with almost no one actually delivering services?

For innovation, what matters most is not so much whether an organization looks like a pyramid or a blimp but how many people touch an idea going up or a message going down. The easiest way to check is to select the most important frontline jobs in an organization—say, the intake officer at a chemical treatment facility, the air traffic controller at the Federal Aviation Administration, the swimming guard at the local pool, or the teacher at a school—and ask who supervises that person, then who supervises that supervisor, and so on all the way to the very top, usually the board chair or elected official (governor, mayor, county executive).

The answer can be startling, as I found in my research on the federal government hierarchy (Light, 1995). At the Veterans Administration in 1992, for example, there were forty-one supervisors who had some say about what a hospital nurse did by way of clinical practice and another sixty-three who had some control over his or her budget. The obvious question, of course, is whether those people added to or subtracted from the patient's care.

The second facet of structure affecting innovation is *demographics*. Here, one can imagine a number of characteristics of both the organization and its workforce—for example, age, size, and diversity—that might alter the prospects for new ideas. (The age and size of an organization are both discussed in Chapter Seven.) My hunch going into the Surviving Innovation project was that diversity was an essential, if often neglected, source of innovativeness: the more points of view, the better. However, as we shall see later in this book, many of the Surviving Innovation organizations simply did not act that way, missing important opportunities for significant gains in innovativeness.

The third factor is *internal turbulence*, which can come from many sources, including frequent reorganizations and high staff turnover. Some experts even suggest that such turbulence is conducive to innovation, either because it breaks down walls between departments or because it brings new blood into the organization. The question is, How much turbulence is too much? Even if organizations need some turbulence to sense the need for innovation, there may be some point at which the resulting volatility is so great that employees do little else than worry about their prospects of holding on to their jobs.

The fourth factor is *internal boundaries*. Boundaries get erected for a host of reasons, not the least of which is the traditional desire to have everyone in their proper organizational place (for example, all accountants in the finance department, all planners in the planning department). Once specialists are separated into their own units, however, they tend to speak such different languages that they may be unable to talk with each other. Zoologists may be unable to talk with engineers about how to design better living quarters for zoo animals; social workers may be unable to talk with educators about how to train new immigrants in English; physicians may be unable to talk to community organizations about preventing AIDS. Heaven forbid that a finance employee ever be seen talking to a program person, that a zoologist ever meet with an engineer!

The final factor is *internal resources*. The question here is what extra internal resources an organization can place at the disposal of those promoting new ideas. Although the common focus is on money, organizations have other forms of internal slack they can bet on a good idea, including time, staff, office space, even a new computer. Sometimes, it does not even matter what the slack is as long as some tangible signal of organizational support is forthcoming.

Leadership

Innovation scholars probably know more about how organizational leaders affect innovation than they do about any other characteristic (see, for example, Kanter, 1988; Van de Ven, 1986; Behn, 1993). Leaders play a central role at virtually every stage of the innovation process, from initiation to implementation, particularly in deploying the resources that carry innovation forward.

Leadership is so important that some scholars see it as the sole factor in success. "To achieve public purposes," writes Robert Behn in a broad claim for leadership, "leadership counts. What influences the quality of the education in an elementary school? Leadership by the principal. What determines the quality of life in a prison? Leadership by the warden. What affects the performance of a welfare, training, and employment program? Leadership by the department's top managers" (1993, pp. 216–217).

The question is not so much whether leadership counts—the point is so obvious that it borders on a truism—but when and how. Here, scholars of private-sector innovation have made the greater headway, largely by specifying the role of leadership at various stages of the innovation process. At the initiation stage, leaders can harness the shocks and turbulence that give rise to ideas. They can also control the resources needed to move a particular idea from sketchbook to prototype to program. (See Mintrom, 1997, for a discussion of the role of policy entrepreneurs in the diffusion of innovations from state to state.)

At the developmental stage, leaders can provide the continuity as idea people are moved out of the way to make room for implementation specialists. They can also manage the changing human emotions involved in bringing an idea to fruition, which Angle and Van de Ven describe as euphoria at the beginning, frustration at development, and a search for closure at the end, together reflecting "some of the most gut-wrenching experiences for innovation participants and managers" (1989, p. 679). Leaders handle the natural mistakes and setbacks encountered along the way and help face the organization toward the outside world as an idea reaches what might be called *launch velocity*.

At the implementation stage, leaders can help link the new idea with the old (often, according to Levin and Sanger, by using old stuff in new ways). Leaders can also make the critical decision about when to *stop* innovating, and they can offer key interpretations of success and failure. These evaluations have an extraordinary impact in shaping the organization's future commitment to innovation, not to mention the careers of key innovation participants.

The leader's work clearly changes over the life of the process, shifting from sponsor to critic, institutional leader to mentor, as the stages succeed one another (Angle and Van de Ven, 1989, pp. 679–681). Because no single leader can play all four roles equally well, Angle and Van de Ven rightly argue that successful innovations demand a mix of leaders, often counterbalanced against each other to protect the organization as a whole. "The innovation sponsor runs interference for the project at corporate levels, while the mentor provides direct supervision, coaching, and counsel to the innovation," they write. "The counterbalancing role to this coalition is the critic, who is responsible for reality testing of the innovation against hard-nosed criteria" (p. 681). In turn, the critic must be checked by the institutional leader, whose overall responsibility is to assure a balance of support and restraint for a given idea. Being what they are, critics will second-guess every new idea to death.

At least in this book, the term *leadership* generally refers to the actions of institutional leaders, the individuals (and in several of the Minnesota cases, small teams) who are responsible for the overall direction of the organization. As was the case for Kathryn Roberts, they are not required to come up with the new ideas. Rather, they must work to create the conditions that will advance a good idea to formal launch. This book also sees the leader not just as an overseer of the innovation process but as the principal architect of organizational life. Simply put, it is up to the institutional leader to help his or her organization achieve the preferred states of being needed to create and sustain innovativeness.

Seen in this context, leadership in an innovating organization involves five components. The first is the leader's innovative *vision*. Leaders want to innovate for a host of reasons: some push for innovation as a means to an end, others as an end in itself; some see it as an essential aspect of mission success, others as a novelty of sorts.

The second component is *temperament*. One can imagine a number of personality traits that might enhance the prospects for innovation (see, for example, Angle, 1989), including intellectual curiosity, self-esteem, patience, generosity, even faith. If innovating organizations are more flexible places to be, their leaders must be more flexible, too. On the basis of an exhaustive battery of tests (California Personality Inventory, Myers-Briggs Type Indicator, and the Loevinger Sentence Completion Test), Nancy Roberts and Paula King suggest that innovators also need to be highly intuitive, action-oriented, creative, critical, and analytical, with well-integrated personalities (1996, pp. 144–145).

Whether innovating organizations also demand entrepreneurial instincts is not clear. As we shall see in Chapter Five, nonprofit and government organizations most certainly have the same need for leaders who can sell new ideas to potential funders and consumers. But it is not so clear that such organizations require quite the same level of ingenuity in surmounting barriers.

The third component is *communication*. To what extent, for example, does the leadership send regular, clear communication about what it values? To what extent does it keep secrets from the organization that might actually help inform innovation? Communication is an essential link between a leader's vision of innovation and the organization's overall commitment. It is also an essential tool for helping the organization relate to the outside world, whether in selling new ideas to the market or in explaining the market to those who work inside the organization.

The fourth component is *durability*. Leading an innovating organization is not an impossible task, but it does take physical and emotional endurance. If not yet defined as a personality characteristic per se, *stick-to-itiveness* appears to be part of the equation for innovation in any setting.

The fifth component is *innovation skills*. As noted above, there is an emerging science of sorts on how to nurture a good idea as it moves through the innovation process—that is, from invention to research and development to formal launch and fine-tuning. Part of the leader's work is to help innovation move efficiently through this life cycle, and this calls for some skill in knowing when to invest and how to move an idea to market. It also requires an ability to sense when to accept defeat. (See Delbecq and Mills, 1985, for a further discussion of innovation management.)

Internal Management Systems

Management systems provide an important link between the three other parts of the innovation ecosystem. They simultaneously act as a kind of cartilage that holds the skeleton of bureaucracy together and as a kind of nervous system that helps the organization center itself in its environment. These systems also help the organization keep track of the innovation process and are essential for managing the risks inherent in challenging the prevailing wisdom in a field.

Although scholars most certainly know that management systems are important to what organizations do, they rarely link the mundane world of pay, personnel, and finance to innovativeness. Many simply take rigorous management as a given. They assume that organizations cannot innovate without good systems and focus on more esoteric questions of creativity, leadership, or process.

Others are so interested in the single act of innovation that all else pales in comparison. Organizations and the systems within them are only relevant to the extent that they might provide funding for innovation, not because they have the human resource policies, employee involvement opportunities, education and training, performance measures, and so forth that might create a bias toward innovation in the first place.

The Surviving Innovation Project is based on a different view. Rigorous management systems cannot be taken as a given and are essential for sound innovation. They also make the single act of innovation less an act of courageous defiance and much more a natural act central to achieving an organization's mission. Consider at least six management systems that contribute to an innovating organization's success.

The first is *mission management*. This may not be a subject yet in most public management curricula, but it is a central issue within organizations, involving formal efforts to define, communicate, and fine-tune an organization's mission. The purpose of mission management is not to develop the perfect mission statement. Rather, it is to establish whom the organization serves, what it values, where it is headed, and how it will know when it gets there. Mission management therefore involves elements of strategic planning (see Bryson, 1996), forecasting of the future, evaluation, and external contact with the organization's environment.

The second management system is *pay and personnel*. There is no question that pay can act as a motivator for organizational performance, particularly if it comes in very large amounts. How it might increase innovativeness is less clear. Are bonuses for innovative acts the answer? If so, how much is enough to turn heads in a government or nonprofit agency? Should the money be provided to individuals or teams? For individual ideas or overall patterns of innovativeness? The lack of clear answers reflects a general lack of theory on how pay might actually improve performance (see, for example, Perry, 1986).

Money may not be a sure motivator for innovativeness, but its absence is most certainly a demotivator. As we shall shortly see, frustrations over pay often act as a barrier to performance. So do frustrations with promotions, job descriptions, complexities, and time delays so common to public sector personnel systems.

The third management system is *learning*. All organizations learn to one degree or another. They may not learn the right things and may not learn quickly, but learn they do. The challenge is to accelerate learning about the right things. (See Senge, 1990, who argues that building learning organizations is the leader's new work.)

Here it is important to distinguish the learning organization from learning systems. The term *learning organization* refers to attributes of the organization as a whole, including the environment, bureaucracy, leadership, and systems. The purpose of the learning organization is to learn and, in doing so, increase performance. In contrast, the term *learning systems* refers to a specific set of formal and informal activities that help the organization learn. (On the learning organization, see, for example, Marquardt, 1996; Senge, 1990.) The purpose of learning systems is to inform organizational decisions through a number of instruments, including libraries, intranets, training programs, formal evaluations, and sabbaticals.

These systems can also involve informal opportunities for people to talk in the hallways.

The fourth system is *idea generation*. Organizations do not have to wait for new ideas to rise by accident. They can establish formal systems for provoking ideas, including suggestion boxes, strategic planning efforts, and formal competitions for new ideas. They can also establish formal systems for culling ideas from their audiences, customers, and clients. And they can create *stovepipes* to ease the movement of ideas from the bottom directly to the top.

The fifth system is *budget*. Money is an essential commodity in all organizations, whether innovative or not. Therefore, shepherding money is an essential task of organizational life. However, innovating organizations must balance the pressure to protect their assets and the need to make investments in risky ventures. This means at least some effort to create fail-safe mechanisms that might stop innovative acts before they so drain organizational resources as to threaten survival.

The final system is *accountability and governance*. Here, organizations have several choices for assuring that individuals are accountable for their actions. The traditional approach of most public organizations is to use a compliance-based model of accountability (see Light, 1993), which puts its faith in carefully written rules against which to measure behavior. A second option is capacity-based accountability, which invests in the people and technologies of the organization as a way to assure that jobs are properly executed. A third option is performance-based accountability, which puts its faith in outcomes as the test of how the organization and its employees are doing. The choice of one option over another reveals a great deal about how an organization operates.

Conclusion

The preferred states of being described in this book are no guarantee of success. Luck also has something to say about innovation. After all her work raising the money and building support for the

Minnesota Zoo's $25 million Discovery Bay marine science center, Kathryn Roberts watched helplessly as all six sharks in the new shark pool died just two weeks before the spring 1997 opening. Some unknown toxin had seeped into the pool.

Even with the empty tank, Discovery Bay opened on time to capacity crowds, drawn in large part by two very playful dolphins in the 500,000-gallon main pool. "Everyone wants a simple reason for the sharks' deaths," Roberts told the *Minneapolis StarTribune*, "and each day we try to take into account every possible variable, but at some point, you have to move on." In making the decision to open, Roberts confirmed at least two of the preferred states of leadership: give permission to fail and keep faith alive.

Even though chance will always play a role in innovation, the preferred states of being described in this book can increase the odds that an organization will be able to exploit the good luck and minimize the effects of the bad. Thinking of innovativeness as the product of preferred states clearly changes the leader's work. It is the leader's job to design the organization, not the innovation; to build the culture, not the prototype; to create rigorous systems, not manage every detail. Innovation becomes less the product of the heroic leader and more the natural result of a tight alignment between the environment, internal structure, leadership, and internal systems. Where this innovation ecosystem is running well, it is the leader's job to protect it; where it is contaminated with barriers and myths, it is the leader's first duty to clean it up.

Luckily, there is no shortage of talented leaders in the nonprofit sector and government. The fact that innovation occurs at all in these organizations reflects extraordinary innovation management skills. Contrary to conventional business school wisdom, the private sector actually has a great deal to learn from these heroic nonprofit and government innovators about how to manage ideas to the point of fruition. Who better to do the teaching than successful public-sector champions who have learned the tricks of groping their way, fine-tuning, and using old stuff in new ways? They are the ones who have defeated hostile bureaucracies and antiquated systems. If they can bring innovation forth from the typical government agency and the increasingly top-heavy nonprofit, surely they can coax it out of private firms that have a bias toward innovation in the first place.

Nor is there any doubt that these leaders are often entrepreneurial. As Levin and Sanger describe them, they "opportunistically pick up resources lying around, opportunistically seize advantages (even in crisis), and take risks." They create highly personal visions of the future, rarely entering office with a "discrete mandate or even much guidance." They are entrepreneurs who exploit "by-products and excesses" and make "virtues out of necessity." They have a bias for action, emphasizing "rapid and visible success and concrete and measurable outputs." Most important for understanding the heroic misalignment, they consciously underestimate, even ignore, the bureaucratic and political obstacles to innovation. "If I had known what I was doing at all times," former Environmental Protection Agency hero William Ruckelshaus once remarked, "I might not have done all of it" (Levin and Sanger, 1992, pp. 108–112).

Finally, there is no question that these innovators produce results. The list of innovative acts is clear and their awards well deserved. The question is what happens when these innovators leave after their relatively short tenures, as they invariably do. Do they bequeath an organization still dependent on heroism for the production of innovation? Do they produce lasting changes in bureaucracy and systems that might make future innovation easier? The answers have too often been no. Like a heavy stone thrown into a pond, the innovator creates a big splash and large waves that inevitably settle down. The culture is disturbed for a memorable moment, but the future mostly remains unaltered.

The reality is that too many of America's most talented nonprofit and government innovators are working against, not with, their organizations. Although they are acutely sensitive to their environments, these innovators are either unwilling or unable to take on their bureaucracies or internal systems. They produce innovation more through exhortation and example than through lasting changes in the ways their organizations operate, focusing on the individual idea rather than the organizational ecosystem, staying very much in the near term and often ignoring the long term.

The innovators I have come to admire are just as action oriented as the ones described above. They exploit opportunities and are acutely sensitive to the environment. They are skilled managers of innovation who confirm Levin and Sanger's portrait of risk taking and evolutionary tinkering. They violate the solitary innovator model in two respects, however. First, they focus on breaking down barriers to innovation that other innovators consciously ignore. Second, they think a bit more of the long term. They struggle to stimulate innovative acts even as they reshape their organizations to make future acts easier. They see their organizations' long-term success in terms of aligning environment with bureaucracy, systems, and leadership. As we shall see in Chapter Five, they are ecologists of a sort who work to both create and nurture the conditions in which others can succeed.

Before turning to these and other lessons from the Surviving Innovation cases, it will be useful to inventory the barriers and myths that currently block innovativeness in many public organizations. In a sense, innovators are quite right to ignore the obstacles with an almost foolhardy bravado. The obstacles are many and the myths powerful. Hence, the first preferred state of being for an innovating organization is a willingness to remove barriers and debunk myths.

2

Removing Barriers
and Debunking Myths

The first step toward innovating naturally involves a simple question: Are new ideas the special gift of the few or randomly distributed across the organization? If the former is correct, there is no reason to build an innovating organization at all. All organizations need to do is find the gifted few in whom creativity resides and give them the resources to get the innovations out. If, however, the answer is the latter, there is every reason to concentrate on allowing new ideas to rise naturally (see Woodman, Sawyer, and Griffin, 1993).

The founders of the Phoenix Group, a Minneapolis economic development agency, clearly believed that creativity was randomly distributed, not just in the organization but throughout the neighborhood it served. Located in one of the Twin Cities' poorest neighborhoods, Phoenix opened itself to ideas from every quarter. "Every person who walks in the door can change the place," said one of the founders. "We are that flexible." It was a person off the street, for example, who convinced Phoenix to open an auto repair shop, and it was a person off the street who made the case for an upholstering business.

Phoenix created a steady flow of ideas simply by unlocking the front door. Operating out of a plain family house, Phoenix was one part organization and the other part living room. People were constantly moving through the space, stopping for a bit of conversation here, a cup of coffee there, dropping ideas and opinions along the way from the front porch to the kitchen. Both literally and figuratively, there were no barriers to the flow of good ideas and very few myths about their source. Phoenix was an innovating organization largely because it never had the barriers and myths that stymie so many nonprofit and government organizations.

This chapter explores the dominant barriers and myths that currently undermine innovativeness in nonprofit and government agencies. (Argyris, 1993, provides a tool kit for spotting barriers.) The underlying assumption of this chapter is simple: the first preference in building an innovating organization is to do as much as possible to release creativity. Although the absence of barriers and myths is by no means a guarantee of innovativeness, their presence is most assuredly a threat. If creativity is indeed randomly distributed within the organization, a simple first step toward innovativeness is to unlock the door.

Confronting Barriers

Imagine, for example, the worst possible circumstances for sustaining innovation—what one might call the unpreferred states of organizational being. Start with the external environment, where we would create unrelenting turbulence and unending shocks. We would keep our nonprofit and government organizations constantly guessing about the next crisis, thereby increasing the risks associated with investing whatever scarce resources they might have in innovation.

We would also foster public cynicism toward nonprofits and government, whether through petty scandals, constant bureaucrat bashing by candidates for elective office, a campaign finance system that turns elections into auctions, or media consumed with the failures of our agencies rather than their genuine successes. We would discourage collaboration among organizations by pitting one against another through categorical funding programs and by reducing the discretionary dollars for true experimentation.

After locking the door on the outside world, we would then create impermeable internal structures: we would add layer upon layer of needless management to already towering organizations, creating so much distance between top and bottom that ideas had no chance to bubble up. We would divide our organizations into small fiefdoms populated by specialists who would protect their turf at all costs. We would encourage high turnover at every layer of the organization—except among employees who valued security above all else—driving good people from our organizations at just about the moment they learned how to manage the innovation process.

We would also create enormous internal stress by reorganizing as frequently as possible, never providing a moment's peace from the latest fad. We would deny money for good ideas, forcing each proposal to fight for ever-scarcer resources in the outside world (which we would have already made impossibly inflexible). Finally, we would define diversity in the narrowest terms possible, ensuring that our organizations would never see the alternative perspectives as paths to higher performance but rather as burdens of social conscience easily dismissed at the next crisis.

After also locking the door on structure, we would cultivate a class of leaders who approached innovation solely as a tool of self-aggrandizement. We would set up a system of rewards under which only these leaders' personal ideas would have a chance of success, and everyone else's would fall victim to the not invented here syndrome. We would create a climate in which mistakes were intolerable, information was treated as a precious secret, and communication was discouraged.

Even if we could find leaders with the skills and commitment to create lasting reform, we would grind them down under a wheel of impatience and criticism, eliminating them as quickly as possible.

And even if we could find leaders with the intuition and judgment needed to bring innovation to fruition, we would undermine their vision with an excess of analysis and second-guessing.

Finally, after locking the door on leadership, we would create a set of internal management systems that would defy comprehension in their complexity. We would make sure that our mission would serve the systems, not vice versa—in part, by never talking about mission. We would create pay and personnel systems that yielded the least flexibility and the longest delays in filling critical positions. We would build our training curricula on the prevailing wisdom, thereby virtually guaranteeing that no one would learn enough to challenge it.

We would also create a budget system in which information was available in anything *but* real time, thereby increasing the risk that a given innovation could weaken, if not destroy, the entire organization. Because we could not track dollars, we would never give our frontline employees authority to spend money, thereby depriving them of incentives to try new ideas. Finally, we would build a shrine to rules as the essence of accountability, piling one regulation on top of another as a substitute for genuine discussion of mission.

Together, these unpreferences would create nonprofit and government organizations in which innovation was as difficult to achieve as possible. In these settings, just about the only way to innovate would be through heroic acts of defiance and personal sacrifice.

The problem, of course, is that this imagined ecological disaster is not imaginary at all but is, in fact, the reality for the vast majority of organizations, be they nonprofit or government. Despite the efforts of reinventors across the country, and despite obvious exceptions to the rule—organizations that are moving away from fossilized obduracy—the sad truth is that many of us would find stark parallels between this worst case and our own organizations. No one is perfect, of course, nor is perfection essential in building an innovating organization. But some organizations are so imperfect that innovation will always be an act of extraordinary defiance and courage.

Fortunately, there are many nonprofit and government organizations that are not quite so far gone. Although they have accumulated barriers, those barriers can still be lowered or eliminated. The Surviving Innovation organizations addressed them one at a time, eventually opening the way to innovativeness.

Before taking the first swing at a barrier, however, it is useful to know where to aim. The following pages will examine the dominant barriers that threaten innovation in the environments, internal structures, leadership, and internal management systems of organizations.

Environmental Barriers

The external environment contains some of the greatest barriers to innovation. We know, for example, that external turbulence will not abate anytime soon. The federal government will continue to shovel responsibilities downward to the states, which in turn will continue to push those responsibilities further down to counties and cities and out to nonprofits. The *devolution revolution* will continue regardless of who controls Congress. Devolution is the only means by which the federal government can resolve its budgetary challenges.

We also know that shocks are likely to continue. The 1996 decision to abolish Aid to Families with Dependent Children is only one example. Nonprofit and government organizations can expect continued upheavals in both the policies they must administer and the society they serve. Unlike private businesses, which can leave a market that turns sour, nonprofit and government organizations must persevere. Nonprofits that provide services under government contracts will experience persistent cost pressure, with occasional sharp cuts as elected officials confront shortfalls. Neither will government and nonprofit agencies be able to insulate themselves from downsizing or dodge the effects of changing public priorities as money is moved from program to program to program.

This white water, as Vaill calls it, is not a passing condition of organizational life. To the contrary, it is permanent. "Permanent white water consists of events that are surprising, novel, messy, costly, and unpreventable," Vaill writes. "Permanent white water conditions are regularly taking us all out of our comfort zones and asking things of us that we never imagined would be required. Permanent white water means permanent life outside one's comfort zone" (1996, p. 14).

As we shall see in the next chapter, the challenge for nonprofit and government organizations is handling the white water. Will they hunker down against the surf, holding on for dear life, or will they turn into it, harnessing the power it contains to take control of their own destiny? This book argues for the latter course.

The white water comes at a time when the public is ambivalent about innovation. On the one hand, Americans love innovation and the cost savings it often brings. On the other hand, the public remains addicted to the war on waste and is reluctant to give government agencies greater freedom from the onerous rules that put a brake on so much innovation. According to a 1996 survey by the Pew Research Center for The People & The Press, 61 percent of Americans said the federal government is almost always wasteful and inefficient, whereas just 21 percent said the federal government often does a better job than people give it credit for. (See Goodsell, 1994, for a more positive interpretation of past trust in government data.)

In addition, the public may have become *clientelized* to the point that it cannot bear the thought of change in cherished programs. It is a point well made by another Humphrey Institute colleague, Harry Boyte, and his coauthor, Nancy Kari, who argue that Americans have forgotten how to do the "public work" that builds skills and capacity for self-governance, which these authors call "civic muscle." "In place of government *of* the people and *by* the people, today we focus on government *for* the people whose primary responsibility is to provide services. From a nation of free citizens, we have become a nation of individualists and consumers for whom liberty means the right to be left alone and the right to choose among brands of toothpaste" (1996, p. 16). Americans have been taught to rely on others to do the hard work of solving common problems, and this in turn creates a vision of the citizen as mere client, target, or customer, not coproducer or partner. (See McKnight, 1995, for an assessment of the problem.)

This lost capacity to do public work involves more than the loss of public confidence. Many of the key institutions of a civil society have also eroded over the decades. Nonprofits and government organizations have slowly lost their connections to each other and to the broader public, working within their increasingly narrow fields on increasingly narrow problems, with little incentive to raise their heads to see possible intersections with other organizations. Part of the problem is the rise of categorical public and foundation funding over the years. Such funding encourages every organization to imagine a property right to its set of community problems and its distinct piece of the client. In turn, this specialization leads to competition for increasingly scarce dollars. Organizations have great incentives to focus on their piece of the client as the only piece worth funding. It is a problem that must be addressed in the funding communities, whether on Capitol Hill, in state houses and city halls, or at foundation headquarters. To the extent that funders divide themselves along categorical lines, grantees will naturally follow. Cooperation and barrier-lowering may therefore begin with the dollar.

Funders also need to confront their own impatience for results. Despite its reputation for cutting losses quickly, the private sector is much more patient for change than the public sector. Building an innovating firm is a long-term effort, not a one-year fad. In the public sector, of course, everything needs to be done on a two- or four-year cycle that overlaps with the next election campaign. No president, governor, or mayor wants to start a reform effort that lasts into the next administration. We want reinvention yesterday.

Money and patience are not the only scarce resources in society today, however. America also appears to be facing a deficit in civic trust. Asked in 1964 whether most people can be trusted to do the right thing or whether you just can't be too careful with others, almost 60 percent of survey respondents chose the more trusting answer. By 1994, the percentages had completely reversed, with most respondents expressing mistrust (Light, 1997, pp. 127–130).

The decline in willingness to trust others reflects what political scientist Robert Putnam calls a depletion of America's "social capital" (1995). Not everyone agrees with Putnam's description of the problem (see, for example, Lehman, 1996; Pollitt, 1996), but there is an emerging consensus that communities have lost significant capacity to respond to calls for engagement. This loss may, in turn, weaken public support for innovations that challenge the prevailing wisdom that citizens are best viewed as clients, targets, and customers, instead of partners, coproducers, or stakeholders.

Structural Barriers

If many environmental barriers facing nonprofit and government organizations are created by an increasingly unforgiving world, the most common bureaucratic barriers to innovation reflect decades of accidental thickening in structure. Today's bureaucracies are hardly inviting places for innovative acts. We know, for instance, that many of our government agencies and a growing number of nonprofits have become towering monuments to supervision and control.

In Washington, D.C., for example, the shape of government has slowly changed over the past half-century. In the 1950s, the federal hierarchy was triangular in shape, with relatively few executives at the top, relatively few managers in the middle, and the bulk of the workforce at the bottom, delivering services. By the 1990s, the federal hierarchy was becoming pentagonal in shape, with a larger number of executives at the top, a significant bulge of managers in the middle, and fewer employees at the bottom. If current trends continue, the federal hierarchy of the 2020s will be circular in shape, with most federal services being delivered by state and local governments, private contractors, and nonprofits, each of whom will also be thickening.

This thickening of government, as I label it, is hardly the only structural obstacle facing innovation, of course. Innovating organizations must also confront simple demographics. As organizations age, they may become less flexible and more reluctant to take the risks necessary to innovate (Pfeffer, 1981). The struggle to stay alive can supplant the need to hold an edge. Moreover, they may use promotions in lieu of dollars to reward increasingly senior employees, thereby creating even more thickening. Facing fewer and fewer opportunities to hire new blood, they may become less welcoming of diversity. If a job candidate is not *like us*—meaning, with a similar educational and job history—he or she is out of the running (see Light, 1995). The focus is not on diversity at all but on hiring individuals who will not upset the organization's prevailing wisdom.

Even as these organizations confront the problems of inertia, they are often swept up in staggering internal turbulence. Some are the victims of constant reorganization. When in doubt about how to improve performance, many organizations turn to the easy option: reshuffling the organization chart month to month. Others resort to the latest off-the-shelf innovation—for example, new computer systems, performance appraisal packages, and self-assessment tools. (Elmore, 1991, notes that schools in particular are awash in innovations.)

Not all the turbulence is self-inflicted, however. Nonprofit and government organizations are also buffeted by changing philosophies of reform in Washington and state capitals. One year, it is more hierarchy and the rules that go with it; the next, it is more sunshine in government; the next, it is a war on fraud, waste, and abuse. A good case can be made that nonprofits and government have suffered not from too little management reform but from too much (see Light, 1997).

This turbulence often creates internal barriers to the very collaboration that might actually improve performance and innovativeness. Rare is the management reform, for example, that does not involve a *czar* of some kind—whether of equal opportunity, total quality, learning, even innovation—as if some new officer will finally make reform stick. All too often, we reinvent government by inventing new offices.

Structural barriers are also reinforced by the general professionalization of society. Training officers have their own associations, as do evaluators, volunteer coordinators, personnel specialists, procurement officers, inspectors general, social workers, chemical treatment specialists, school teachers, professors, family therapists, and so on throughout the organization. All journey once or twice a year to national conferences and return empowered to defend the prevailing wisdom against their less enlightened peers.

Unfortunately, nonprofit and government organizations have few of the essential resources for breaking down the internal fiefdoms. Downsizing has weakened the ability of organizations to redeploy staff or liberate time, and discretionary money is exceedingly hard to come by. As a result, innovation is often forced to fund itself; it is a *tub on its own bottom*, which must rise or fall without help. Facing increasing external turbulence and shocks, these tubs often sink.

Leadership Barriers

America's love affair with the single act of innovation is one of the greatest barriers confronting innovating organizations. "The myth of the triumphant individual is deeply ingrained in the American psyche," write Warren Bennis and Patricia Ward Biederman in a call for greater collaboration. "Whether it is midnight rider Paul Revere or basketball's Michael Jordan in the 1990s, we are a nation enamored of heroes—rugged self-starters who meet challenges and overcome adversity" (1997, p. 1). The same may be said of scholars of nonprofit and government innovation.

The problem is not that the nation's heroic innovators are misguided or self-absorbed; they are often truly visionary leaders who are deeply committed to mission. Many have reluctantly concluded that heroic innovation is the only path to serving the people about whom they care. They most certainly make enormous personal sacrifices, often working themselves to exhaustion in their cause.

However, the focus on heroic innovation too often distracts nonprofit and government organizations, and their political sponsors, from the longer-term effort of pursuing more fundamental reform. We get caught up in the momentary success of a particular program and its leader, only to find that the innovation is quickly swept away when the leader makes his or her exit.

These untimely deaths are not forgotten inside the organization. Their tombstones serve as constant reminders of the ultimate price of heroic innovation. More important, by celebrating innovation as an extraordinary act, we lose the enormous contributions of those who are less willing to throw themselves on the swords of organizational resistance. As management professor Alan Wilkins and his colleagues write in an article aptly titled "Please Don't Make Me a Hero" (Wilkins, Perry, and Checketts, 1990), hero worship has a number of potentially destructive side effects, not the least of which is an exaggerated sense of what it takes to succeed.

Again, this is not to disparage extraordinary acts of organizational courage. Indeed, challenging the prevailing wisdom is almost by definition a heroic act. But it is worth asking how organizations should use their heroes. In nonprofit and government organizations, nothing could be more heroic than creating the conditions for others to succeed. The definition of a heroic act must therefore be modified so that it can include, for example, the work of installing a new pay system or building a better board. In many of today's organizations, such efforts constitute the true heroism. They will not win awards, but they will yield mission success.

Heroes capable of such achievements need a different temperament, of course. They must be willing to share power and consider new ideas. They must enjoy empowering others. Alas, this is hardly the prevailing job description for most public executives. The top levels of government are filled with individuals who want to make their mark en route to lucrative private practice. Their self-interest does not allow for sharing credit. Nonprofit executives may have greater staying power, but they, too, live in a society that often ranks individual greatness above teamwork.

Ironically, the drive for individual glory may weaken the organization's ability to say no as funding opportunities arise from the outside. The result can be *projectitis*, in which leaders spread their bets across a host of initiatives. By not investing deeply in any one thing, the organization can slowly lose direction, becoming ripe for collapse when the first innovation fails. By that point, of course, the heroic leader will likely be gone or worn out.

Heroic innovators may also become consumed with keeping secrets. Leaders who are driven by self-interest will not only have difficulty articulating a broad vision for the organization in the first place but will be reluctant to share information with those who most need it to innovate. Because there is little information that can be kept secret in most organizations, be they public or private, the decision to withhold takes on great significance and is usually interpreted as an expression of distrust. When coupled with the lack of ongoing conversation about the organization's mission, the distrust sends a strong signal that ideas not invented here (meaning in the leader's suite) are unwelcome.

These problems with heroic innovation are compounded by a general lack of knowledge about how innovation might occur any other way. Having read countless stories and cases about how to create innovation against the odds, many of today's public leaders know little about how to innovate more naturally. Part of the blame rests on our schools of public affairs and administration, where students can learn just about everything there is to know about personnel, budgeting, planning, the policy-making process, cost-benefit analysis, and organizational behavior but almost nothing about managing change. It is the course most needed in today's schools of public policy and management, yet the one least likely to be taught.

The general lack of coursework on managing change is not because there is no research on the topic. Rather, it may reflect a general distaste for drawing lessons from the private-sector literature and a broad conclusion that nonprofit and government organizations are predestined to be inhospitable to innovation.

Moreover, as long as innovation remains an act of groping along, as Robert Behn (1988) and Olivia Golden (1990) both describe it, it is far more important to teach students how to grope than how to build innovating organizations in the first place. This book draws a different conclusion. Not only is it possible to build organizations that innovate naturally, groping along does not have to take place in the darkness. Bringing light into moribund organizations is very much a teachable skill, and one that schools of public policy and management should teach.

Management System Barriers

As both the cartilage and nervous system of an innovating organization, good management systems are essential to all aspects of success, from sensing changes in the environment to providing the extra resources needed for good ideas. A good strategic planning system can perform the former function, a creative budget system the latter.

Yet ask a nonprofit or government employee what is wrong with his or her organization and the odds are that the answer will be red tape, excessive control, and needless delays. In far too many agencies, mission has come to serve management systems, not vice versa. As a result, rigorous management has become synonymous with red tape and delay, a perception that is one of the greatest barriers to building an innovating organization. In fact, rigorous management is essential to innovation.

Start with mission management. Many organizations work for years to craft the perfect mission statement only to miss the mission itself. Employees spend hours in mind-numbing meetings haggling over single words without ever asking why their organization exists, whom it serves, and how anyone will know if it actually succeeds. Mission, however, is more a state of mind and an ongoing question than a precise set of words that can be enshrined on a coffee room wall.

Nonprofit and government organizations often do no better with pay and personnel. Even more frustrating than all the rules and regulations, the endless delays, and the mythic battles over position descriptions are the false promises of merit pay. For decades, merit pay has been the great hope of organizational reformers. The theory is simple. Promise employees a pay increase for actual performance, and performance should improve.

There are only three problems with the dream. First, it is often difficult to describe what an agency (or more appropriately, the legislature) wants in enough detail to create a fair pay system. Second, even if an agency could describe what it wanted, most supervisors do not have the skill to make the kinds of distinctions between levels of performance demanded by even the simplest merit pay plan. Third, even if an agency could resolve both these problems, there is often no money to distribute. Money cannot be a motivator if the amount available is nil. Yet many nonprofit and government organizations stick with their performance appraisal systems despite the negative impact on employee morale. (See Larkey and Caulkins, 1992, for a discussion of the 80/20 rule, which states that 80 percent of employees believe that they are in the top 20 percent of performers. Most performance reviews involve efforts to disabuse at least three-quarters of employees of their self-assessment. Minnesotans are not the only ones who think they are all above average.)

The tendency to ignore past experience with pay is part of an overall problem with learning systems. In a nutshell, many nonprofit and government organizations create learning systems that can only reinforce the prevailing wisdom. Consider staff training and development as an example. The list of acceptable courses is often restricted to subjects directly relevant to a given staff position: secretaries can take only proofreading, or accountants only spreadsheets. Little discretion is given to employees to determine what their own learning needs might be. This not only denies individuals an opportunity for the development of new perspectives but also reinforces internal boundaries.

The failure to learn can also weaken the ability to generate new ideas, whether from inside or outside the organization. Many nonprofit and government organizations simply do not know how to ask for ideas, whether because they have always taken their cues from on high (meaning from funders, boards, political executives, or legislatures) or because they are so utterly convinced of the rightness of their cause that no new ideas are welcome. Much as these organizations struggle to find new ideas outside the traditional channel, they lack the motivation to listen. Anyone can install a suggestion box. The real challenge is to get someone to read the proposals.

Given the importance of money in organizational life, the budget system is a central source of both help and hindrance for innovation. Not only is money scarce in most nonprofit and government organizations, it is often divided into such tight categories that even the occasional windfall cannot benefit the good ideas. The problem is exacerbated by the spend-it-or-lose-it mentality in many organizations. Here, the legislature or board must take the first step in encouraging flexibility.

Unfortunately, the reason organizations have such tight internal systems is that they are addicted to compliance-based accountability. Money must be spent in categories, training courses must be restricted, ideas must rise on their own, and employees must go through the annual ritual of performance appraisal in large measure because legislatures and boards have so little else to rely on in holding their organizations accountable. The lack of good performance measures for the organization as a whole means that accountability can only be assured through otherwise needless rules and supervision. As with idea generation, some organizations simply do not know how to measure outcomes; others live in fear of the possibility that they are just not generating impacts; and still others are so convinced of their rightness that measurement is viewed as a waste of time. Yet all will complain mightily about the rules and regulations that frustrate their work.

Debunking Myths

Barriers do more than just make single acts of innovation difficult. They often create defensive routines, as Argyris calls them (1993), or myths, that undermine the slightest willingness to imagine a new idea in the first place. There is no doubt, for example, that antiquated management systems are a serious barrier to innovation in many nonprofit and government organizations. At the same time, the fear of dealing with those systems can be greatly exaggerated.

Thus, even as organizations begin to lower the barriers to innovation, they must confront the myths that so often undermine the will to imagine in the first place. After all, the absence of barriers does not automatically create the presence of innovation. Asked about the mental barriers to innovation, the Surviving Innovation organizations talked about ten different myths that prevented them from taking the first steps toward becoming innovative. Each myth will be considered and debunked below.

1.   Innovating Is the Gift of the Few

Debunking this myth is the Rubicon for the innovating organization. If innovation is the work of heroes and mad scientists, if creativity and new ideas are unevenly concentrated in the special few, organizations hardly need worry about removing the barriers to collaboration or creating stovepipes that might let ideas rise. Quite the contrary. All they have to do is pick the winners and give them incentives to produce. Innovation will then emerge from even the most moribund of organizations.

If, however, innovation is the work of ordinary people who are extraordinarily committed to mission, if creativity and new ideas are more evenly distributed throughout the organization and its audience, organizations must take an entirely different route. Assuming that innovation can come from anywhere and anyone has profound implications for how organizations must operate. It means scanning the environment for good ideas and staying in close touch with the audience. It also means lowering the barriers to internal collaboration and sending constant invitations down into the organization. (See Woodman, Sawyer, and Griffin, 1993, for a discussion of the difficulties in predicting creativity on the basis of individual, group, and organizational characteristics. Consider the authors' conclusion at page 316: "After decades of theory development and empirical research, researchers still know surprisingly little about how the creative process works, especially within the context of complex social systems such as formal organizations.")

Obviously, it is easy enough to create a star system in which good ideas come mostly from people like us—that is, the senior leaders of the organization or people with the same college degrees. People like us are easy to spot and easier still to work with. Perhaps that is why a nonprofit or government organization would adopt the myth of the chosen few in the first place. It is the cheapest way to innovate.

The only problem with such star systems is that people like us may not have the good ideas. Unless organizations are absolutely convinced that they know the one or two people most likely to imagine, it is far better to spread the bets across the widest range of possibilities. That is just what the Surviving Innovation organization did. Almost all of them harvested ideas up and down the organization regardless of who had the idea. That meant they had to open themselves to the notion that a good idea could come from anyone—from the bus driver at the Dowling Environmental School, to the janitor at the Chance to Grow/New Visions School, to the patron at the Heart of the Beast Puppet and Mask Theater.

2. Innovating Is the Product of Perfection

It is no surprise that readers are so often discouraged after reading the latest book about innovation. Authors create images of organizations that are bigger than life, write of mythic leaders who surmount incredible obstacles, describe ideas so brilliant that only Einstein could dare dream of similar success, and tell readers that they must be willing to sacrifice all semblance of a normal life to compete.

If there is any one lesson from this book that should go on a bumper sticker, it is that nobody is perfect in innovation. Human beings almost never do anything right the first time. It is a lesson emphasized in virtually every contemporary article on innovation in government, whether in Behn's description of managing by "groping along" (1988) or Levin and Sanger's analysis of innovation as a case of "using old stuff in new ways" (1992). "Such programs are imperfect combinations of bits and pieces," write Levin and Sanger. "Their character—that which makes them innovative—very often evolves over time through trial and error. The source of innovation is often old stuff—old stuff being used in new ways. Indeed, often the innovation itself is simply the novel combination of familiar elements" (p. 89). That hardly rings of perfection.

It is also a lesson that emerges from the Surviving Innovation cases. As noted in the preface to this book, I saw every organizational flaw known to management science in the twenty-six organizations selected for this project: staggering leadership turnover, personality conflicts, breakdowns in internal discipline, errors in timing, just plain bad decisions, and even the occasional embezzlement. As also noted, I watched as one of the organizations, the Phoenix Group, laid the basis for its eventual destruction. That hardly rings of perfection, either.

And yet I came to admire these organizations as I have rarely admired others. They surmounted their own human frailties through a deep and abiding commitment to mission. They built an innovating spirit by focusing on their assets, not by worrying about their liabilities. Where they had flawed personnel systems, they had great internal financial controls; where they had no money for external evaluation, they created internal devil's advocates. They almost never let the perfect be the enemy of the good. As we shall see in the last chapter of this book, they had a profound faith in the rightness of their work—a faith that allowed them to forgive the small mistakes essential to innovation and persevere in spite of strong opposition.

3. Innovating Is Best Done Under Extreme Pressure

The first commandment for killing innovation is "Do It By 3:00 or Else." Yet public leaders continue to pressure their organizations to do just that. Facing a budget shortfall? Innovate or else. Need a foundation grant to keep the organization afloat? Innovate or else. Losing audience? Innovate or else. Losing focus on the mission? Innovate or else. Innovating has become the prescription for all that ails organizations. It is supposed to give life, focus energies, and solve even the most staggering budget crisis. Would that it were so.

The temptation to link innovation with survival is understandable. If innovation is the product of heroism, what better way to create innovation than to apply extreme pressure? If innovation is triggered by shocks to the system (as Van de Ven, Angle, and Poole, 1989, argue), what better way to produce more innovation than to apply extreme shocks? The problem is that human beings do not always do their best work when facing a firing squad. Extreme pressure can freeze an organization, terrify a workforce, and result in anything but innovation.

The trick is to apply shocks to the system in a way that keeps the organization alert but not terrified. Van de Ven and his colleagues suggest, for example, that organizations create mechanisms for "redirecting and jostling the attention of organizational members so that subtle changes and needs will be noticed" before they reach the extreme shock level (Van de Ven, Angle, and Poole, 1989, p. 669). One way to do so is to place "people in direct personal confrontations with sources of problems and opportunities" as a way to "reach the threshold of concern and appreciation required to motivate most people to act" (p. 670). Arrange for zoologists to greet visitors to the zoo; have set designers and costumers meet the audience after the play; invite students to participate in setting the elementary school agenda.

4.   Innovating Is Best Done Alone

This is the myth of the mad scientist: one can innovate only when isolated from all distractions. Create a separate unit—a *skunk works*, as the military used to call it—where the chosen few concoct their secret potions free of ordinary contact. Give Dr. Frankenstein a castle and a few billion volts of electricity, and *voilà*.

There are times when the strategy works in the public sector, particularly in the development of new technologies of one kind or another. Early on in the Surviving Innovation Project, for example, I met with a handful of snowplow drivers in Dakota County, Minnesota, to ask how they had developed the idea of mounting bombsights on plow blades to help the drivers steer during blizzards. They explained that it had been largely the product of a single driver fooling around in his garage after hours. Give a snowplow jockey a garage and a welding torch, and *voilà*.

As we shall see shortly, most organizations do not produce innovation through solitary confinement. To the contrary, most of the innovating described in this book came from collaboration, whether with others in the environment or inside the organization. Indeed, some of the most admirable innovations in the Surviving Innovation sample involved unique collaborations, most notably the creation of the Fond du Lac Community College as a joint initiative of the Fond du Lac Band of Lake Superior Chippewa and the Minnesota State Community College System. Although there are plenty of mad scientists of various kinds in the public sector (some might argue that anyone who goes into the public sector these days is, by definition, mad), their work can only be strengthened by contact with others.

5.   Strong Adversaries Make for Strong Innovations

Innovation produces more than its share of hardball politics and outright opposition. Challenge the prevailing wisdom, and the prevailing wisdom will likely challenge back. That is how the prevailing wisdom prevails. That is also why innovating takes courage.

On the principle that whatever does not kill us only makes us stronger, some organizations go a step further. Even as they pledge allegiance to innovation, they adopt a skepticism bordering on ridicule, expose new ideas to withering critique, deny seed support even when they have it, and second-guess every step of the process. These organizations believe innovation made easy is innovation made poorly. Not only is opposition a way to winnow the good from the bad, but it makes a good idea better, as if too much praise would turn an idea soft and weaken the organization's ability to say no. In short, they test each idea's ultimate worth by challenging its survival. In this Darwinian struggle, good ideas can be forged only on the anvil of opposition.

There is nothing wrong with challenging an idea as it moves forward through the innovation process. Innovating organizations should ask hard questions and demand rigorous analysis. But it is one thing to create healthy debate and quite another to subject an idea to constant harassment in the hope that it will somehow emerge stronger. In the effort to prevent the big mistake that rightly worries a legislature or board, organizations may discourage the small mistakes that are so essential to innovation.

Thus an essential element of innovation management is knowing when to encourage and when to discourage, how to say no and why to say yes. Some ideas can stand on their own from the very beginning, whereas others need extra nurturing throughout. At least in the organizations I have come to admire, the test of a good idea is whether it advances the organization's mission, not whether it is able to withstand manufactured hostility. There is plenty of hostility to be found without creating an extra measure.

6. Innovating Always Means Saying Yes

The more words like *nurturing, support,* and *encouragement* are used to describe innovating organizations, the more some will rightly ask whether such organizations have the guts to say no. The same goes for words like *trust, compassion,* and *loyalty,* which are often seen as incompatible with the toughness needed to survive. In this portrait, the innovating organization becomes little more than a giant hug machine in which no one gets hurt.

Like all myths, the portrait has some elements of truth. Innovating organizations can suffer a paralysis of consensus in which the search for common ground prevents quick decisions. They can also have problems letting go, clinging to a faltering idea long after it should have been cut loose. And they can get confused about who has the power to decide, frustrated by overly broad promises of participation in decisions that only the leadership or board can make.

Nevertheless, just because an organization gives each new idea a greater chance of success does not mean it can never say no. An innovating organization is not likely to succeed unless it can pick winners. In this regard, it is no different from any noninnovating organization.

What makes its decisions different, perhaps, is that it winnows ideas *purposefully.* To the extent possible, it lets ideas fall on their own merit, not because of needless bureaucracy or a lack of seed support. It must be brutally honest with itself about the quality of ideas and exceedingly quick to kill an idea that does not advance its mission, exceeds its basic capacity, cannot be funded, or simply cannot work. For a small nonprofit, the failure to act in this way can result in its own demise; for a large government agency, the failure can result in an I-Team report or a "Fleecing of America" segment on the local news.

The challenge for the innovating organization, therefore, is to distinguish between compassion and loyalty to its employees on the one hand and toughness toward the ideas they produce on the other. Innovating organizations encounter their greatest problems when they confuse the two.

7.   Innovating Is a Choice Between Science and Art

This is not the book to summarize one hundred years of organizational scholarship. (See Morgan, 1986, and Perrow, 1979, for articulate introductions to the field.) Suffice it to suggest that the study of organizational behavior has long been divided between the sciences and humanities, engineering and the arts, quantitative and qualitative, head and heart.

The notion that organizations can be fine-tuned like giant machines can be traced back to Frederick the Great, who converted the nineteenth-century Prussian army from a loose collection of criminals and mercenaries into a tightly disciplined force. But it was a second Frederick the Great, Frederick Taylor, who gave scientific management its core principles. Using a stopwatch to monitor simple jobs such as hauling coal, Taylor developed a set of principles by which any organization could supposedly increase productivity dramatically. The basic imperative was to define each job precisely and tell workers exactly what to do. According to this view, if an organization wants innovation, all it has to do is say so in unmistakable terms. Innovation is merely one aspect of science.

Scientific management worked particularly well in an era of labor surpluses and unskilled jobs. Workers could be treated like cogs in a machine. If they did not fit, they could be replaced. As the labor surpluses of the early 1900s gave way to the information revolution and global competition of today, the pressure to imagine organizational life in more humane terms increased. A new generation of experts began arguing for job enrichment and worker participation. Organizations were not machines, but living entities, with brains, political systems, and cultures (see Morgan, 1986). If an organization wants innovation, what it must do is treat each worker as an irreplaceable asset to be motivated and involved (see Kanter, 1983). Innovation is an art.

This book embraces both views. Although organizational design is essential for building an innovating organization, it is designing organizations for creativity and imagination that holds the potential for innovation. Although rigorous management is essential for minimizing the risks of making mistakes, it is making mistakes that produces the innovative ideas.

This does not mean that innovating organizations can operate any which way, however. There is a science alongside the art.

Organizations may have different ways of spending money, but they must all audit their books; they may have different job descriptions, but they must obey the prevailing labor law. They may not follow every principle of scientific management—particularly principles that demand tight hierarchies and constant supervision—but they are very disciplined about what they do, how much they spend, and how they measure impacts and develop ideas. For them, innovating is both an art and a science.

8.   Good Management Is Hostile to Good Innovation

This myth is often tied to notions of innovation as a pure art. It is one of the most powerful and damaging myths in the public sector, for it belittles the value of management in protecting, nurturing, and accelerating good ideas, and denies those involved in the more mundane tasks of organizational maintenance their due credit for innovativeness. It is the ultimate put-down.

To be fair, traditional control systems have earned the distrust and disparagement. As noted earlier, pay, personnel, budget, evaluation, and accountability systems have often been used as weapons against innovation, and managers of these systems have relished their role as naysayers and cynics.

It is no wonder, for example, that the top priority of Vice President Gore's first report on reinventing government was about cutting red tape. Many of the civil servants involved in the effort rated internal control systems as obstacle number one in doing their jobs. According to Gore, roughly 700,000 federal employees were involved in some form of management control, whether running the government's pay, personnel, accounting, budget, and oversight systems or supervising employees in headquarters or the field (1993, p. 14). That is one out of every three federal employees. No wonder the federal government is becoming circular in shape. More and more staff are cross-checking, overseeing, second-guessing, whereas fewer and fewer are actually delivering services. The front lines of the federal government are increasingly to be found in the states, private companies, and nonprofits.

Such staff-heavy management systems do not serve innovation, which requires forms of management that add value to the process at key points. Good management sees the pay system as a means of reinforcing mission, the personnel system as a tool for recruiting the best and the brightest, the budget system as crucial to both creating seed support and protecting the organization as a whole from hemorrhaging, evaluation as an aid to fine-tuning, and accountability as a way to give the organization freedom in return for impacts.

9. Innovating Organizations Are Good at Keeping Secrets

Private firms have ample reason to keep secrets both inside and outside the organization, particularly because profit is at stake. They worry about a host of threats to intellectual property, including industrial spying and the loss of prized inventors to competing firms, and they move quickly to protect promising ideas with patents and trademarks.

Nonprofit and government organizations rarely have such proprietary interests. To the contrary, they often have much to gain from sharing ideas. Sharing information is the very essence of the interagency collaboration that is so valued today. As Elizabeth Hubbard, my colleague at The Pew Charitable Trusts, argues, "The idea of working together through partnerships is talked about so frequently that the word 'partner' has been adopted as a verb, as in 'we'll partner with other agencies'" (1995, p.1).

Partnering of any kind involves at least some shared information. Whether a partnership involves full-blown *collaborating* (which Hubbard defines as a form of collective problem solving that blurs the lines between agencies), *cooperating* (which involves common, but separate, action to meet a mutual goal), or *coordinating* (a more limited sharing of resources to assist other agencies), information is a key resource, organizations may have to choose between keeping secrets and keeping partners.

Unfortunately, *trying* to keep secrets is habitual among organizations today. The emphasis is on the word trying because practically every secret eventually leaks. On the outside, someone eventually learns just about everything. Legislators and board members ask questions, funders review proposals, and grantees talk to each other. The Government in the Sunshine Act, Freedom of Information Act, Federal Advisory Committee Act, and Administrative Procedure Act all apply, either directly or through parallel state statutes, to virtually every corner of the public sector. Closed-door meetings are not only bad politics, but almost always plainly illegal.

On the inside, almost nothing can be kept secret. Employees talk in the hallways (and not just about innovation), memos fall into the "wrong" hands, aggrieved employees gossip. The notion, for example, that nonprofit and government organizations can keep secrets about individual pay is debunked every year when employees hit the Internet in search of public records or turn to the *Chronicle of Philanthropy* for the new Internal Revenue Service reports on nonprofits and foundations. By their nature, nonprofit and government organizations are leaky.

Organizations will inevitably defend secrets as essential to employee morale, of course. "At least we didn't tell them," they will say of the employees who find out what others get paid. But in keeping secrets, these organizations also send the signal that their employees cannot be trusted. I do not mean to argue that organizations should post individual pay on the bulletin board, but they ought to assume that every employee will eventually know what his or her colleagues earn. Therefore, they should be clear on the criteria by which employees are evaluated and rewarded. If they cannot defend their pay-setting system, they should be honest enough to junk it and start over. It would be far better, for example, to give every employee the same increase each year than to keep secrets as a way of concealing a flawed system.

10.   Innovating Is the Path to Organizational Bliss

Sad to say, innovating is tough work even under the best of conditions. We can make it easier and more natural, but we cannot make it less stressful. Those who suggest that innovation will cure all that ails the organization are just plain wrong. It might increase public confidence somewhere down the road, assuming enough nonprofit and government organizations get moving, and it might solve more public problems. It might raise an organization's fundraising pro-file—at least until the next "hot" shop comes along—and create joy in the hallways from time to time. But it will not make life less stressful.

If innovation is an original, disruptive act, expect innovating organizations to be original, disruptive places to work. Gather a team of strong-willed, extraordinarily committed individuals, expose them to the environment, give them the freedom to imag-ine, loosen the internal systems that bind them, offer encourage-ment and occasional seed support, and expect conflict and stress. It is a natural—indeed, healthy—consequence of creating the inno-vating organization.

Conclusion

Obstacles and myths do not disappear by magic. They must be low-ered and debunked one by one. At least for the twenty-six organi-zations discussed in this book, the first step was not complicated. They focused on the most available target and fixed it with the best available tool. But whether they started big or small—and most started small—they all started.

At the same time, these organizations also began innovating. As ideas bubbled up, they picked one and pursued it. The goal was not to create *the* great innovation on the very first try. Rather, the hope was to show that a single act of innovation was possible. Barriers fell as the organization moved forward; myths faded as it offered contrary proofs. An innovating organization does not suddenly appear like some apparition from the mist; it is built over time and is never quite finished. Thus organizations create a bias for innova-tion in part by producing innovation.

The question is which comes first: lower barriers and new truths or innovation? The answer is that the two go hand-in-hand. Just as the absence of barriers and myths does not create the encouragement needed to innovate, so single acts of innovation cannot create an innovating organization on their own. Rather, the two reinforce each other. Lower barriers and new truths create a more fertile climate for acts of innovation; successful acts of innovation confirm the value of lowering barriers and developing new truths.

When innovation is the result of individual battles against the odds, it is unlikely to recur. It is what it is—a heroic act of defiance that few will likely emulate. By contrast, when innovation follows a lowering of barriers, it is more likely to multiply. It is an expression of possibilities for those among us who are unwilling to sacrifice themselves for a single act of innovation. It also puts the lie to the myth of innovation as the special gift of the chosen few, which may be the most important myth to fall early in the ecological cleanup.

The first steps toward building an innovating organization must take place as part of a continuing concern with mission. An innovating organization begins its journey with honest questions about why it exists, whom it serves, and how it will know if it is successful. Otherwise, how can it know which of the new ideas are worth supporting and which of the e-mails deserve immediate action? Mission is the centerpiece of everything an innovating organization does. It tells the organization how it fits into its environment and why it would want to innovate in the first place. In the following chapter, we will take mission as the starting point for an examination of the role of environment in an innovating organization.

3

Harnessing the Environment
as a Force for Change

The mission of Fond du Lac Community College is visible from every sight line on its Cloquet, Minnesota, campus. Nestled in a clearing on what was once a corporate tree farm, the campus radiates a union of cultures. That there is even a campus at all is something of a miracle.

For it to exist at all, there had to be a charter, which was created through a first-of-its-kind partnership between the Fond du Lac Band of Lake Superior Chippewa and the Minnesota State Community College System. Together, the two entities joined to establish the first tribal and state community college in the nation.

Next, there had to be a campus, which was created through another partnership with the environment. The Potlach Corporation donated the thirty-eight acres of land, the city of Cloquet paid for the sewer and water improvements, the Minnesota legislature funded the bricks and mortar, the U.S. Bureau of Indian Affairs approved the tribal college curriculum and provided needed start-up funding, and the Minnesota State Community College System accredited the degree.

The design for the campus did not start with blueprints but with an inventory of symbols from Native American and non-Native cultures. Drawing on the non-Native culture, the main building is nestled in a clearing among the regular rows of a fifty-year-old tree farm. Students walk to the clearing on walkways laid out in the shape of a cross, symbolizing the Christian heritage of the area's non-Native population.

Drawing upon the Native American culture, the campus is circled by a ring road symbolizing the sacred circle of balance, continuity, and oneness. Plantings at one end of the circle create a bear paw, the Native symbol of strength, and the main building is shaped in the form of a thunderbird, the symbol of energy and power. The outside walls of the building are painted in red, black, white, and yellow, the four colors of the Fond du Lac Reservation, while floor tiles are colored green to represent the earth.

Inside, red pine timbers harvested from the tree farm hold up the glass ceiling in the auditorium, while the drum-shaped archive room echoes the Native American symbol for mother earth. Skylights and windows abound, giving students a view of the sky and the earth at every turn. Wherever one stands on the grounds, the building integrates the two cultures—the tight, ordered grid of the tree farm surrounds the thunderbird, the bright blue of the sky tempers the green tiles that lead to class.

Fond du Lac Community College illustrates two simple points about the role of mission in an innovating organization. First, mission is much more than a set of words written on paper; it is an expression of how an organization relates to the world it serves.

Second, mission is a statement of where the organization wants to go. It is simultaneously about whom the organization serves and what it wants to create. "At its simplest level," writes Peter Senge, "a shared vision is the answer to the question, 'What do we want to create?' Just as personal visions are pictures or images people carry in their heads and hearts, so too are shared visions pictures that people throughout an organization carry. They create a sense of commonality that permeates the organization and gives coherence to diverse activities" (1990, p. 206).

Thus the Fond du Lac Reservation did not just put up a dramatic building. It also created a place that reminds all who enter of the core mission. Although learning is certainly more comfortable than when students were squeezed into five classrooms in an elementary school building, Fond du Lac remains motivated by the union of two cultures, not the maintenance of award-winning buildings. Mission was the centerpiece of change at the beginning and remains so today.

This chapter will examine other lessons for creating the preferred environment of an innovating organization. Some of the preferences involve efforts to lower barriers and debunk myths, others reflect an attempt to harness the external environment for innovation. But in all ten preferences summarized here, the Surviving Innovation organizations showed a commitment to making the external environment a partner in innovativeness.

Facing the Outside World

The Surviving Innovation organizations shared one central characteristic in dealing with their environments: simply stated, they faced into the outside world. They did so by adopting ten practices that helped them achieve a preferred environment:

1. Center on mission.
2. Operate "just beyond the possible."
3. Embrace the volatility.
4. Use the market as an ally.
5. Beware the source of funds.
6. Lower the barriers to external collaboration.
7. Harvest external support.
8. Prepare for hardball.
9. Pay attention to outcomes.
10. Change the prevailing winds.

Center on Mission

There is complete and absolute agreement among the twenty-six organizations on the starting point for the journey to greater innovativeness: ask hard questions and honest answers about why the organization exists, whom its serves, and how it will know if it is succeeding. What is required is a basic conversation about missions—personal as well as organizational.

The question "Why am I here?" is just as important in building an innovating organization as "Why are we here?" An innovating organization can endure many things, including a fair amount of imperfection, but it cannot long endure complacency. Early conversations about personal commitment to mission are both reasonable and necessary for creating a shared understanding that can animate the organization's work.

There is no one right way of developing a mission. Some of the Surviving Innovation organizations used a strategic planning process to get moving; others used cost-benefit analysis. But all seemed to agree on the following lessons about mission.

First, a mission is never a finished thing. It is something to be worked on over time, to struggle with as the world changes. Far too many organizations treat their mission as a kind of sacred tablet, handed down from generation to generation without question.

The evolutionary character of mission can create a certain discomfort both inside the organization and outside, of course. The four directors of Theatre de la Jeune Lune, an ensemble performing theater company now operating out of a renovated warehouse in downtown Minneapolis, know they want to keep the edge, but they also know that the edge will change in response to constant conversation among the four. It is a conversation that often takes place in the community kitchen that doubles as a conference room. Having developed a fondness for fine cuisine while attending theater school in France, the four do some of their best "cooking" while cooking. The very name Theatre de la Jeune Lune, meaning

Theater of the New Moon, speaks to the company's mission-driven innovativeness. "While embracing the 'old moon' of traditional theatrical styles," the theater's mission statement promises, "Jeune Lune seeks to create an entirely new theatre: highly spirited, physical, and visually spectacular."

The reviews suggest that the mission statement is being fulfilled. In 1993, for example, the company was invited to perform its award-winning play *Children of Paradise: Shooting the Dream* at the Yale Repertory Theater, the first-ever invitation to an outside group by that theater. This was a remarkable turnaround for a theater that had faced financial ruin only eight years before. Instead of shutting down at that time, the artistic team had written and produced one of the most successful plays in Minneapolis theater history. With no money for sets or costumes, *The Green Bird* mixed and matched elements from a host of past productions, creating a true act of survival innovation.

Second, the mission does not need to be written down to be relevant. Some of the organizations made their missions visible in other ways. In the Heart of the Beast Puppet and Mask Theater, which occupies a former pornographic movie theater in a poor neighborhood in Minneapolis, has its mission spray-painted on the outside wall: "In the Heart of the Beast is committed to performing professional puppet and mask theater for the entertainment and enrichment of audiences of all ages and cultures, creating a sense of community among performers and audience, and building a vital and healthy culture through art, festivity, and play."

But to truly see the Heart of the Beast mission, one need only attend the annual May Day parade and festival at Minneapolis's Powderhorn Park. It is a riotous celebration of community, populated by twenty-foot-tall puppets, clowns, magicians, and what seems like every food known to humankind. The puppets are built and operated by hundreds of volunteers, symbolizing the theater's commitment to using art as an instrument for renewing the social, political, and economic infrastructure of a once-forgotten community.

Attendance at the festival has grown steadily, up from just five hundred at the first May Day in 1975 to fifty thousand in 1997.

Third, whether written down or not, mission is active, not passive. It drives what the organization wants to do and where it wants to go. One reason the Minnesota Zoo feels like anything but a state agency is that it has a clear and active mission. According to posters that can be found across the five-hundred-acre site, the zoo exists to "strengthen the bond between people and the living earth." That mission gets translated into action through seven objectives:

CREATE *a magical experience*.

THRIVE *as a special place for children*.

KNOW *our customers*.

MANAGE *visitor moments of truth*.

LINK *revenues to results*.

BUILD *a premier service organization*.

INVEST *to keep the existing Zoo great*.

Note that every item on the seven-point list is an action verb. Managing moments of truth means taking care of the little things that can make or break a visitor's experience, from ensuring that the hamburgers are hot and the bathrooms clean to educating each visitor on the need to protect endangered species. "We know shit happens," one officer said to me. "The challenge is to clean it up in a hurry."

The question for the zoo, indeed any organization, is whom it serves. The animals housed in its exhibits or the animals still free? The children with dollars to spend or the poor children who live too far away to attend? The dolphins or the timber wolves? The coral reef or the birds? The answer, of course, is "all of the above." Unlike private firms, which usually have a choice in the markets they serve, nonprofit and government agencies are often required to serve everyone.

It is in the constant struggle to serve these different and often competing audiences that the zoo finds both conflict (some of the zoologists would just as soon keep their exhibits closed lest pesky visitors disturb the animals) and strength. And it is in its willingness to ask about mission that the zoo confronts its relationship to the outside world. When asked if he would sell fur coats on the Northern Trail, which has the tiger and timber wolf exhibits, the director of enterprise programs answered, "What kind of fur?" The effort to find dollars to keep the zoo's "living ark" afloat meant working with the environment to generate funding. If that meant caps, scarves, and coats woven from yak fur, the attitude was "So be it."

Operate Just Beyond the Possible

Central to an innovating organization's relationship with its environment is knowing just how far to challenge the prevailing wisdom. As we shall see later, those who challenge the prevailing wisdom often find the prevailing wisdom challenges back. One key in innovating, therefore, is to push far enough to change the prevailing wisdom without pushing so hard that a given innovative act provokes such hostility that the environment will not yield.

Innovating organizations play two roles in society. First, they criticize the prevailing wisdom. Brain-injured children are warehoused in the public schools, says the Chance to Grow/New Visions School. Child support orders are useless when the parent involved is unemployable, says Anoka County. The needs of artists for housing and studio space are ignored by the housing development community, says Artspace. Abusive spouses and partners are ignored by the treatment system, says the Domestic Abuse Project.

Second, innovating organizations create an alternative vision that energizes others. In a sense, they act as prophets, questioning the status quo and also offering an alternative vision as a draw to action. Brain-injured children can learn; housing can be built for dual use by artists; unemployed parents can be trained for work and taught to be better parents; abusers can be treated. (See Brueggemann,

1978, for a discussion of how the prophetic imagination in ministry acts in much the same way.)

An innovating organization need not have a vision so great in scope and risk that it is utterly beyond reach. Most of the Surviving Innovation organizations profiled here operated in a zone *just beyond the possible*. They created a vision that was far enough out of reach to be compelling, yet not so far out of reach as to be daunting.

For the Dowling Urban Environmental Learning Center, just beyond the possible meant creating a new kind of public school within a building once occupied by the Dowling School for Crippled Children. The new Dowling imagined itself as a magnet school that would simultaneously draw elementary-age students from across the city and still serve its traditional constituency of special children. Not only would these children learn from each other, but the school itself would be built on a participatory model. Every student, no matter what his or her grade, would have a voice in shaping decisions about the school, whether on banning Styrofoam dishes in the cafeteria or selecting software for the computer labs. Even the bus drivers would have a voice on the site council. It was not the typical public school, but neither was it so wildly unfamiliar that parents would petition to leave.

For Advocating Change Together (ACT), just beyond the possible meant a new vision of people. ACT existed to train the developmentally disabled, once shuttered away in institutions, to be advocates for their own rights. They would not only be trained in lobbying and rule making, they would run the organization, staff the board, develop the mission, and train other trainers. ACT would become a member-controlled organization based on the notion that people with developmental disabilities are their own best advocates. Gloria Steinbring, one of the founders of ACT, wrote in an ACT newsletter, "For me, *normal* means people with developmental disabilities, and it means people who don't have disabilities. *Normal* means that you should act like an adult. This is normal to me."

There would be no confusion about innovation being the gift of the special few. At ACT, every person would have a gift to give. Hardly the traditional vision of the developmentally disabled as passive recipients of government's good work, but not so radical that legislators would never make an appointment.

For the Walker Art Center, just beyond the possible meant not just art that would hang on the wall but many artistic disciplines in the widest range of settings. A sculpture garden would feature a footbridge by Siah Armajani across busy Lyndale Avenue and the "Spoonbridge and Cherry" fountain by Claes Oldenburg and Coosje van Bruggen. A film and video series would include directors from Ingmar Bergman to Bruce Nauman. And a performing artists series would range from new classical music by the Kronos Quartet to Reza Abdoh's *The Law of Remains*. In becoming a "safe place for unsafe ideas," the Walker would attempt to lead Twin Cities audiences toward a more inclusive definition of art "for art's sake" without causing a backlash. Hardly the normal art museum, but not so radical that the community would never come.

Embrace the Volatility

All of the organizations in the Surviving Innovation sample faced turbulence or shocks. Despite its reputation for progressive government and foundation activism, Minnesota feels the same pressures as any other state. The state government has been under siege even as the devolution revolution accelerates, as counties and cities continue to endure taxpayer rebellions. As for foundation support, Minnesota is not just the land of ten thousand lakes; it is also the land of ten thousand nonprofits, each one competing against the others for increasingly scarce dollars as the state's once-active corporate philanthropies fade from prominence through mergers and acquisitions.

This volatility forces a simple choice on organizations. Option one is to hunker down in the hope of riding out the latest funding crisis, begging members to remember the good old days even as the paint begins to peel. Under this option, an organization can also tighten the rules against launching new programs, thereby instilling a near-hysteria among its staff, who will spend most of their free time calculating the bumping sequence for future downsizings.

Option two is to harness the volatility to the organization's advantage, using crisis as a wake-up call and riding the turbulence to new ideas and public support. They can loosen the internal barriers to ideas and open themselves to risk. They may come to the same sad end as their more complacent peers, but they will have done so while remaining in charge of their own destiny.

The Surviving Innovation organizations chose this latter option. All would have preferred a friendlier, more predictable world, but they came to see the volatility as a source of energy for innovativeness. The lesson is fundamentally one of organizational attitude. One either fights the volatility or embraces it.

It is important to note that nonprofit and government organizations often harness very different environmental pressures to create momentum toward innovativeness. As Chapter Eight will show in more detail, the eight government agencies in the sample were much more likely than the nonprofits to use shocks in the environment as a wake-up call, whereas the nonprofits were much more likely to draw on the nearly constant turbulence as pressure for innovativeness. Part of the difference, of course, is that government agencies face less turbulence—budgets tend to go up and down by small increments, staff turnover is light, and institutional immortality is virtually guaranteed. The challenge for most government organizations, therefore, is to wake up to the shocks in time; the challenge for most nonprofits is to not become inured to the unrelenting turbulence.

The Minnesota Extension Service (MES) and the Cyrus Math/Science/Technology Elementary School are both examples of government innovation forged by shocks.

Created in 1909 as an outreach arm of the University of Minnesota, the extension service entered the 1980s with a traditional agricultural and home economics focus. Its staff of seven hundred was neatly divided into eighty-seven county offices, which were in turn divided by simple program categories. Extension agents were always at the ready for pretty much any question a citizen might have about the latest crop disease or baking challenge, but they almost never sought out a problem on their own. Federal, state, and county governments paid their fair share, adding a tiny increment each year.

Then the farm crisis hit, followed by sharp budget cuts at all levels of government, including a 50 percent cut in the federal appropriations. The question was whether MES would merely hang on for dear life, holding to traditional job titles and county boundaries, or change. It elected to harness the crisis and take control of its future. Facing further staff cuts and a new agenda of rural economic and social problems, MES began a five-year restructuring effort in 1989 designed to create clusters of innovation across counties. Extension *agents* became extension *educators*; new programs were launched on a range of topics, from teenage pregnancy to rural racism oppressing migrant farm workers; counties began to share staff.

Cyrus Math/Tech was forged in a similar crisis, this time of the state legislature's making. Already facing dwindling enrollment in its high school and elementary school, Cyrus (population five hundred) faced further cuts under the provisions of a new public choice initiative that gave parents much greater freedom to move their children from one school to another. With two larger school districts on either side (Morris with eleven hundred students and Glenwood with two thousand), Cyrus was sure to lose one or both of its schools through attrition. Down to just eighty students in its elementary program in 1988, Cyrus would have to consolidate with Morris or Glenwood or create a miracle.

It chose the miracle, closing its high school and creating a magnet school on the prairie in northwest Minnesota. Starting with an innovation investment fund raised by selling its high school memorabilia, Cyrus fired its principal (too expensive); created a self-managed team of eight teachers; put computers, satellite television, and Internet hook-ups in every room; designed a new curriculum heavy in math, science, and technology; and gave students access to a twenty-acre environmental laboratory. Because each new student from outside the district came with dollars from that district, Cyrus would control its future, shocked into alertness by a crisis that no one wanted but that generated public value nonetheless. By 1993, the school had pushed its enrollment to 116, half of whom came from outside the district. It was also named as one of America's fifty-one best public elementary schools by *Redbook*.

Unlike these two government organizations, which were startled into action by specific shocks, many nonprofits live with constant turmoil. In many respects, their challenge is to occasionally pull out of the white water and reflect on ways to change course.

Turbulence was nothing new for St. Joseph's Home for Children, a crisis shelter and treatment center that was originally created in 1886 as an orphanage. Workloads had been going up for the better part of three decades, while budgets were under constant pressure. The children under its care had changed, too. They got older and more troubled. Along the way, St. Joe's became the county's trauma center for family crisis. "One of the biggest things we do here is divert kids so they aren't constantly thinking about what it will be like when they go home," one St. Joe's intake counselor explained. "Kids come in here stripped of everything—they have no possessions, no toys, no one they can talk to on the phone because of police orders. We start to rebuild."

Even with declining support from the county government (its prime funder) and uncertain support from Catholic Charities (its parent), St. Joe's probably could have ridden the turbulence, plugging one small leak after the other until the home finally collapsed in some distant budget crisis. It would have been death by a thousand paper cuts. But St. Joe's chose instead to use the turbulence as a stimulus to innovation, inventing new programs to address problems before they reached the crisis stage. One such program, Effective Parenting and Family Stability, provides crisis intervention to prevent out-of-home placement. A second, Family Outreach, offers intensive prevention services of other kinds for at-risk families.

Use the Market as an Ally

The market is one of the most powerful tools for igniting and sustaining innovativeness in nonprofit and government organizations. Although the market is traditionally viewed as a *hidden hand* that exerts its pressure from the outside, the Surviving Innovation organizations actively courted market pressure as a force for change. For them, managing the market was very much a skill to be learned. From Cyrus Math/Tech, which capitalized on the market for high-tech schooling, to Heart of the Beast, which actually lowered its ticket prices to raise its revenues, to the Minnesota Zoo, which competes for the entertainment dollar against amusement parks and major league baseball, the majority of the Surviving Innovation cases saw the market as something to be channeled and exploited.

Just because nonprofit and government organizations cannot make a profit does not mean that they cannot make money. Moreover, the fact that the money goes for children or wildlife preservation may increase its power as a motivating force for innovativeness. More than any private firm, these organizations can see the impact of each dollar past the break-even point. It is the very best dollar an organization can get.

That dollar buys extra supplies at a public choice school, supports new work at a nonprofit theater, and helps build new exhibits at the zoo. And in several of the Surviving Innovation cases, it can also be reinvested in an innovation fund to provide seed support for future new ideas. Zoo "profits" have been plowed back into everything from a new IMAX wide-screen theater (which was funded through a unique collaboration with a for-profit firm that built the theater on zoo grounds in return for a split of the ticket proceeds) to exotic plants for the exhibits. The notion is to keep the visitor an entire day, if not just for the magic, then at least for another hot dog (and the attendant revenues).

For many of these organizations, the market is not just something to be called on for occasional reality checks; it is a constant lever for change. At the American Indian Business Development Corporation (AIBDC), for example, the market is a reason for being. Established to serve an economically depressed neighborhood in Minneapolis, AIBDC opened a 56,000-square-foot business incubator in 1989, using the market as an essential partner in its effort to strengthen economic capacity in the Native American community.

AIBDC saw no shame in making money—that was the whole point of the enterprise. "No project will ever allow the AIBDC to become self-supporting as a nonprofit," wrote the director, Brenda St. Germaine, in a description of the corporation. "However, our work here does more than replace blight. We visually change the community, we offer new employment opportunities, we bring in new businesses, we promote other projects in the area, we bring in federal, state, and city dollars, and we offer hope for change."

Although AIBDC reserves some of its incubator space for Native American ventures, it has to break even across the full range of its tenants. If Coyote Chile cannot find a niche in the salsa market and Banner Creations cannot sell banners and balloons, they must leave. The pressure to cover costs makes AIBDC remarkably alert to both the upside and downside of each decision. It cannot be so conservative that the market yawns, yet cannot be so far ahead of the curve that the market balks. It must operate in the zone just beyond the possible.

Making money is more than just a staple of survival, however. It is also a path to greater independence. Making a little bit of money here and there can provide the sweetest kind of funding possible: the discretionary dollar. Money made by one's own hand is money that can be invested just about anywhere—in a new computer, in a staff retreat, in building repairs, in a fundraising campaign. The market thus helps lower the barriers to innovation created by categorical funding lines and what seem to be shorter and shorter foundation grants. Sell some pamphlets, offer some fee-for-service training programs, provide some technical assistance— in short, figure out what the organization makes that others might buy, and sell it.

At the Project for Pride in Living (PPL), the big revenue producer is the Surplus Home and Office Products (SHOP) store. Located in a North Minneapolis warehouse far from PPL's main site, SHOP has been selling home and office supplies donated by local contractors and businesses since 1988. Looking for an office desk or a toilet, a pre-Pentium computer or a door, a welding torch or a couch? SHOP likely has it at a deep discount. Everything is just a bit past prime, and the stock varies week to week, but SHOP still makes money. (My $5 chemical beaker serves to demonstrate that SHOP can sell just about anything to anyone.) The profits cross-subsidize other PPL ventures such as Project Self-Sufficiency, a life skills program for PPL's housing residents. SHOP also trains a small number of unskilled employees for future placement. It is a classic twofer.

Facing into the market does not always mean making money, however. For Luther Theological Seminary, it meant making education more responsive to the needs of its students. There is no question that a rapidly changing "market" of parishioners prompted the soul-searching that helped Luther become an innovating organization. (Even seminaries can be innovating!)

Luther's journey began with the 1982 merger of three Lutheran bodies that created the Evangelical Lutheran Church of America (ELCA). By itself, the merger would have created an enormous shock to the seminary—Luther joined seven other seminaries competing for scarce dollars in the new church. But the shock also happened to occur in the midst of enormous turbulence. A new statement on human sexuality had split the seminary faculty, rural congregations were dying at an alarming pace, urban parishes were failing, and the pastorate was increasingly unable to answer a host of new challenges, from diversity to poverty. "If congregations die," as one Luther faculty member explained, "I don't have a job and my students are out of work. But more importantly, none of us has a flock."

Luther could have toughed it all out, of course. Whatever the new competition, it instantly became the ELCA flagship seminary and has shown impressive resilience in raising endowment money in a lean period. But it chose to listen more closely to its market, launching a strategic plan that would convert the seminary from a bastion of traditional teaching and outreach to a leader in defining theological education for the real world. It took a hard look at its students and saw a mismatch with the increasingly diverse communities of the future. It took an honest look at its curriculum and saw a professorate too often absorbed in theory to the exclusion of practice. It took a tough look at its own bureaucracy and saw a structure that reinforced a lack of concern for faith and character issues among the pastorate. "The church needs to speak to its members as they live in society," one faculty member argued in supporting the effort to find common ground on human sexuality. That also meant listening to those members as they speak. There was no Surviving Innovation organization more rigorous in making this effort.

Government organizations may not have such an obvious market, however. Speaking from its own experience, the Minnesota Zoo might say, "Then create one." As one of only two state-run zoos in the nation, it had long depended on the legislature for annual operating appropriation. Whether visitors came or not, the zoo received its budget. In 1992, the zoo petitioned the legislature to make each visitor matter by using the gate receipts as the core of the zoo operating budget. The zoo thereby created a market where none had previously existed. Every employee, from top to bottom, now has an incentive to take responsibility for "visitor moments of truth," as the legislature is not likely to go back to annual appropriations in this era of tight budgets. To remind the organization of the market, the zoo announces each day's attendance on a hotline recording. Employees can find out instantly whether the zoo is up or down in the competition for entertainment dollars against heavyweights like the Mall of America's Camp Snoopy, America's first and largest indoor amusement park.

Beware the Source of Funds

Although most innovating organizations are extraordinarily effective at raising funds, they are often highly selective about what kinds of funds they will take. All dollars do not spend the same. They can create costly obligations, often in the form of new accounting systems or frequent reporting requirements. They can compromise organizational integrity, particularly when they allow a funder to cleanse itself by giving funds to a pristine cause. Finally, they can carry hidden "interest rates," creating lasting dependencies and deflecting the organization from its primary mission. It is often difficult, if not impossible, for an organization to say no when a huge grant comes knocking at its door. But at the very least, it is important to ask a few hard questions before letting the dollars in for a stay.

Consider the government dollar as an example. Taking a government grant or contract may be tempting for the bottom line, but it inevitably changes the character of the organization. Accounting rules vary by level of government, as do rules for allocating indirect, or administrative, costs. Organizations may soon find that they are keeping two or three sets of books—one for the feds, another for the county, and still another for the foundations. And, as more than one of the Surviving Innovation organizations testified, government money can create a dependency that is difficult to break.

That is one reason why the Phoenix Group decided never to take money from the Minneapolis Neighborhood Revitalization Project, a multimillion-dollar city and state effort to pump new monies into economic revitalization. Created in 1991 to combat poverty in one of the city's poorest neighborhoods, the Phoenix Group felt that government money would force the organization to accept the prevailing wisdom of economic development. "They got us into this mess," said one of the founders. "How is it that their money and the rules that go with it will make us better? Our job is not to make little pieces of paper happy."

Foundation funding is infinitely easier to absorb but may carry its strings, too. The Surviving Innovation cases certainly knew how to package and repackage ideas to fit the latest philanthropic fancy. "We spend so much time inventing new ways of explaining what we do to funders," said one theater director. "We are what we do, not always what we say, but that sometimes isn't enough for our funders." At the same time, however, there was no question that foundation funding sometimes became the tail that wags the dog.

Several Surviving Innovation organizations confronted these issues with strict rules governing the source of funds. The Land Stewardship Project (LSP) is a case in point. Founded in 1982, LSP had firm rules regarding foundation funding. Dedicated to sustainable agriculture and preservation of the family farm, the organization would not take dollars from agribusiness, chemical companies, or the tobacco industry, all of whom had some interest in capturing the sustainable agriculture movement. In addition, LSP invested its pension funds carefully, putting its retirement dollars at risk in socially responsible investments. "You are known by the company you keep," said one officer. "That includes the money you take, too."

Several others, including the Minnesota Extension Service, created internal review systems for vetting grant requests. "When you're a hot organization, foundations want you to take on the world," said one of the Surviving Innovation executives. "You might have made your reputation by being very focused about your work, but they may still want you to broaden out and take on their issue. Once you get on that treadmill, it's hard to get off. You get attached to the people you hire and the dollars they bring in." Most of the Surviving Innovation organizations had been on the treadmill at some point in time, and many could remember at least one grant or contract they wished they had never taken. What distinguished them perhaps from other nonprofit and government organizations in Minnesota is that they were remarkably candid about these decisions. They asked hard questions about what each grant meant and rarely misled themselves about the answers. If and when they needed to take a slight detour to stay alive, they acknowledged the reality and moved on. It is easier to get off the treadmill when an organization knows it has gotten on.

Chicanos Latinos Unidos En Servicio (CLUES) stayed off the treadmill in part by refusing to spend leftover grant money. As a leading social service provider in the Hispanic communities of West St. Paul, CLUES could have won easy approval of almost any reasonable request to keep the small amounts of funding that are sometimes left over at the end of a project. Instead, CLUES steadfastly insisted on giving that money back, a practice that began in the mid-1980s when it tried to return $25,000 to a local foundation after completing the promised project under budget. The problem, or so the story goes, was that the foundation involved did not want the money back. Most foundations are good at giving money but unaccustomed to getting it back, perhaps because such opportunities arise so rarely. Nevertheless, CLUES insisted, creating a reputation as a focused organization that has aided its growth ever since and has discouraged foundations that might have otherwise tried to turn its head.

All of this is not to argue that nonprofit and government organizations should "just say no" to outside money. Rather, the Surviving Innovation organizations adopted two simple strategies for minimizing the dependencies created by individual grants and contracts.

First, they diversified. The Surviving Innovation organizations worked hard not to become the darling of any one foundation. They spread their funding sources so that any one turndown would not create financial disaster. However tempting it may be to become the wholly owned subsidiary of a foundation angel, a diverse funding base (with, say, no more than 20 percent from any one foundation) provides a precious independence.

Second, they practiced saying no. It is always easy to invent a reason to say yes to a given grant. "We have to grow to survive." "We need to establish a track record with this funder." "We can handle the pressure." It is much, much tougher to say no. The organizations I came to admire were hardly perfect on this score—it is difficult not to open the door to a $100,000 grant—but most of them certainly knew when they were crossing over to dependency. They struggled with the consequences of particular grants. And sometimes that was the best they could reasonably do.

Lower the Barriers to External Collaboration

There are few hotter concepts in nonprofit and government life than collaboration. Call it public-private partnership. Call it a shared power world (Bryson and Crosby, 1992). Call it clustering or cross-sectoral participation. Call it public work (Boyte and Kari, 1996). Even call it "achieving inter-organizational effectiveness through meta-strategy" (Huxham and Macdonald, 1992). But it all means working together toward common ends.

The first step toward collaborating is to define the term a bit more precisely. My colleague Elizabeth Hubbard has done just that, separating the word *partnership* into three C's: cooperating (using resources to assist other agencies), coordinating (organizing or combining resources to more effectively reach a mutual goal), and collaborating (collectively applying resources toward problems that lack clear ownership) (Hubbard, 1995).

The three types of partnership vary in terms of the degree of power sharing (cooperating involves less; collaborating much more) and the levels of resource involvement (sharing information is relatively cheap; sharing resources is more expensive). As Table 3.1 shows, there are, in all, nine forms of partnership. The bottom left cell ("sharing information") indicates the least costly form of partnership, whereas the top right cell ("sharing program responsibilities") indicates the most costly.

Table 3.1. Defining Partnerships

COOPERATING	COORDINATING	COLLABORATING
using resources to assist other agencies	organizing or combining resources to more effectively reach a mutual goal	collectively applying resources toward problems that lack clear ownership
Contributing Resources	*Reconciling Activities*	*Sharing Program Responsibilities*
Agencies contribute resources to another agency's project or effort: contribution is clearly defined and usually material.	Agencies adjust or combine existing programs in order to deliver services more effectively: usually entails on-going relationships among partners.	Agencies come together as a new entity to provide services or to manage a resource.
Primary goal: to help a worthy endeavor	Primary goal: to improve programs	Primary goal: to meet a need that can only be addressed by working together
Promoting Others	*Sharing Resources*	*Creating New Systems or Programs*
Agencies willingly share information about the work or services of others.	Agencies that use the same good or service agree to share in its cost; often defined by contract.	Agencies work to create and implement a new model to deliver services or address a public problem.
Primary goal: to meet the needs of a shared constituency	Primary goal: to save money	Primary goal: to develop a new means of responding to public problems
Sharing Information	*Producing Joint Projects*	*Collective Planning*
Agencies share information on a formal or informal basis.	Agencies depend on each other for producing a specific product or event; generally involves short-term commitments.	Agencies develop a collective vision (and/or study) for the management of a resource or the alleviation of a social problem.
Primary goal: to improve agency performance by staying informed	Primary goal: to produce an outcome that no single agency could achieve on its own	Primary goal: to promote a collective vision and coordinated actions

Source: Modified from Hubbard, 1995.

All of the Surviving Innovation organizations engaged in one or more of the partnering activities, whether sharing information to eliminate duplication, sharing resources to reduce costs, or coming together for collective planning. The data are unequivocal: innovation is not a solitary act.

Some of the partnering was driven by events beyond the organizations' control. That was certainly the case when Luther Theological Seminary gave Lutheran Social Services the land for a new building on its campus. It was a space shortage at its Minneapolis headquarters, not some elegant strategic plan, that led the huge social service agency to start searching for a new home in St. Paul, five miles away. Although the two organizations had once been close, their boards were separate and their fundraising operations quite competitive. "There are only so many Lutherans with deep pockets," said one Lutheran Social Services official.

Nevertheless, God works in mysterious ways. As government contracts came to cover nearly two-thirds of Lutheran Social Services funding, some inside the organization began to ask whether it had lost its links to the faith. The question came just about the same moment that the seminary was wondering how to give its students more contact with the real world. The move to the Luther campus helped answer both questions. Lutheran Social Services got a seventy-five-year lease and a visible reminder of its mission, and the seminary got an opportunity to bridge the theory-practice divide, making the partnership an example of the *contributing resources* described in Table 3.1. It was also one of those unique collaborations that make so much sense but are so difficult to achieve.

Other partnering was driven by the desire to eliminate duplication. That was the case when Anoka County began planning a new human services facility. By designing a one-stop-shopping Human Services Center with space for twenty-four service providers, including United Way agencies, nonprofits, school programs, and county and state agencies, Anoka weighted the odds in favor of better service. Even the floor plans focus on the client. Job training programs all are on one floor, family services on another, income assistance on another. This was more than *colocation*, which was all the rage in the human services field at the time; it was a way to stimulate conversations about how to serve the public better, making it an example of the *reconciling activities* and, assuming success, *collective planning* described in Table 3.1. A similar collaboration led to the county's Parents' Fair Share program, which won a 1995 Ford Foundation Innovation Award.

Finally, some Surviving Innovation organizations' collaborations were driven by a pure survival instinct. WomenVenture is a classic example. Created in 1989 through a merger of two struggling organizations—CHART, a career counseling agency, and WEDCO, an economic development agency—the new organization became a sum greater than its two original parts. It was able simultaneously to sustain past innovations by both organizations and to provide encouragement for new ideas. Thus it kept WEDCO's micro-loan program for small business start-ups, which was one of the first of its kind in the nation, and also launched Project Blueprint, which provides job training for low-income women through a collaboration with the building trade unions.

Whatever the reason for collaboration, a surprisingly high number of the Surviving Innovation organizations also engage in the most costly form of partnership, *sharing program responsibilities*, meeting needs that can be addressed only by working together. My favorite example is from the Minnesota Zoo, which launched an environmental high school in 1994 in collaboration with the Apple Valley school system. Built on the zoo grounds, the high school is a fully accredited part of the Apple Valley system, drawing students to a unique blend of traditional high school curricula and exposure to environmental issues. "This was really cool because three units of government had to cooperate," explained the zoo's director, Kathryn Roberts. "The state gave the land, the school system built the building, and the City of Apple Valley provided the bonding authority."

The collaboration was immediately successful. All four hundred student spaces were filled in the very first year. Zoo staff designed the environmental education curriculum and teach the special topics courses (marine biology, horticulture, zoo keeping). Students do their practicums at the zoo and provide extra staff muscle along the way, whether for milking the cows in the children's zoo, mucking out the bear pens, or planting some of the thousands of shrubs around the new marine science building. The collaboration is not painless—for example, students sometimes speed through the zoo parking lot—but the benefits of the collaboration are obvious and right on mission.

All of the Surviving Innovation organizations learned to collaborate by doing. They started at the bottom left of Table 3.1 and moved up. It is not hard to do. Pick up the phone, share some information, host a meeting, get out and about, do what partners do. Innovation is not a solitary act; someone has to make the first call.

Harvest External Support

Innovating organizations do not wait for divine providence to shine on them. They actively seek support from the outside world, cultivating funding sources, volunteer energy, and political support. They also try to live in a state of grace, as the Land Stewardship Project describes it, where they are able to take advantage of divine intervention when it occurs.

In their effort to cultivate support, all of the Surviving Innovation organizations had fundraising operations of one kind or another. For one or two, fundraising rarely involved more than an annual bake sale or charity auction. At Cyrus Math/Tech, the annual bake sale involved 1,800 dozen cookies, at $2 a dozen. For an organization that scrimped on almost everything but technology—no health insurance for the teachers, no textbooks unless absolutely necessary, double and triple recyclings of computer paper—the $3,600 meant motherboards, new computer chips, and a field trip to a Minnesota Twins baseball game. "We were using baseball statistics to teach our sixth-graders math," said one teacher. "What better way to reward students?"

For many, however, fundraising involved a more rigorous effort. Luther Theological Seminary was remarkably skilled at finding the dollars for its reform effort. The Lilly Endowment provided a large grant in support of curriculum development, and an alum provided the needed dollars for the Integrated Quarter, a unique course experience designed to immerse students in the real world. Fundraising was hardly restricted just to the nonprofits, however. The Minnesota Office of Waste Management (OWM), which had existed under one name or another since 1981, was able to win grant after grant from the U.S. Environmental Protection Agency in its pollution prevention campaign.

At least one state agency, the Minnesota Zoo, even had a development office, again behaving more like a nonprofit than a government organization. The state civil service system had no personnel classification for "fundraiser," so the zoo hired its fundraisers under a general classification. Other Surviving Innovation organizations had part-time grant writers and hired fundraising help on a fee-for-service basis. To my knowledge, none of the organizations used any contingency services, which take a percentage of each dollar raised. Although such firms can generate impressive results, they often do so by blurring the mission. Keeping the fundraising operation close to the heart improves the chance that the organization can say no when an inappropriate opportunity knocks.

Moreover, the most skilled fundraisers I met were almost always at the top of the organization. For me at least, the best case for funding is made by the person who is ultimately accountable for the dollar. However, the case is usually enhanced when the organization's executive pairs up with project staff to make the call. My sense is that foundations are increasingly reluctant to make *confidence* or *good faith* grants based on the reputation of the organization or its leader. Many of my colleagues want to see the person(s) responsible for delivering results. Although grants are still made on a personal basis, outcomes-focused proposals are becoming more and more important to the final decision. And as we shall see, a careful description of results is becoming the single most important threshold for funding. If an organization cannot describe how project A will produce result B, the odds of receiving funds are poor at best.

Project for Pride in Living was among the best of the Surviving Innovation organizations at old-style fundraising. And no one was better at one-on-one personalized fundraising than Joe Selvagio, the former Catholic priest who founded the organization in 1972. "No one else here could go to breakfast and come back with a check for $100,000," one staffer explained. "But that's Joe. He won't take no for an answer." PPL launched a $4.5 million endowment campaign in 1993 precisely to capitalize on these skills.

PPL was also becoming more effective at new-style focused fundraising, partly in anticipation of Selvagio's inevitable retirement and partly under pressure from the funding community, most notably the McKnight Foundation, which had launched a $10.5 million Families in Poverty initiative in 1988. This initiative supported a number of projects in the Surviving Innovation sample, including work by Anoka County, Episcopal Community Services, and CLUES, all of which were living in a state of grace at the time of the initiative. McKnight was unapologetic about its outcomes focus and challenged the state's nonprofit and government organizations to compete for funds on that basis.

Harvesting external support involves more than money, however. Almost all of the Surviving Innovation organizations recruited unpaid volunteers. In 1994 alone, St. Joe's estimated that it generated $350,000 worth of volunteer support (3,500 hours at $10 an hour). In addition, a third of the Surviving Innovation organizations had a membership base of some kind, and of that third, 90 percent had made some effort to expand that base over the prior five years. For Dowling, this meant giving volunteers a strong voice in decisions about how the school ran. For Theatre de la Jeune Lune, it meant a host of rewards, including more contact with the artistic team for the Jeune Loonies, who usher audiences and sell tickets. For the Walker Art Center, it meant private tours of popular exhibits. And for Episcopal Community Services, it meant listing every volunteer by name in the annual report.

Prepare for Hardball

Without exception, every organization in the Surviving Innovation sample faced external opposition of one kind or another. When a Cyrus teacher mentioned the benefits of transcendental meditation in her introduction to world religions, several parents organized a phone tree to protest this assault on Christianity. When the Minnesota Zoo decided in 1997 to build its IMAX theater, the Minnesota Science Museum defended its turf as the only other IMAX in town. And when the Domestic Abuse Project (DAP) announced that it would expand its program to cover gay and lesbian abusers, the entire community reacted. Some gays and lesbians were outraged that DAP would shine the light on a hidden problem, and religious conservatives went on the offensive against this further legitimization of an "unholy" lifestyle. Although none of these adversaries succeeded, each organization felt the sting of a hostile environment.

The fact is that true innovation makes the outside world uncomfortable. Foundations may reward it, governors may applaud it, vice presidents of the United States may even call for much more of it, but innovation creates discomfort. That is, in fact, one of its purposes. It criticizes the prevailing wisdom even as it defines a new possibility. Entrenched interests rarely embrace an idea that might unseat them. The more an idea challenges the status quo, the more the status quo will fight back.

None of the Surviving Innovation organizations had more conflict with the status quo than the Chance to Grow/New Visions School. Established in 1983 by the parents of a brain-injured child, Chance to Grow was designed to help children exercise their brains much as they might exercise their bodies. Alongside more traditional classes, students would spend time in the *brain gym* improving their physical coordination. In theory, learning skills would improve with practice.

The founders, Bob and Kathy DeBoer, made no pretense of their basic impatience with the learning establishment. "They said, 'Get used to it' when we asked about our daughter," said Kathy DeBoer. "We just felt we could do better. There are a lot of ideas out there that might work—biofeedback, the healing touch, colored glasses—but not much solid research. We decided to act and experiment at the same time. Time is the enemy of these kids."

The more the DeBoers learned, the more they wanted to help other brain-injured students. And the more they wanted to help, the more the educational establishment pushed back. It was one thing to try the brain gym on their daughter—parents will be parents—but quite another to seek funding from the Minneapolis public schools. Skepticism escalated to outright hostility; curiosity gave way to investigation. Still, Chance to Grow persevered in its effort to win a public school charter. "You have to learn how to count votes," said Bob DeBoer of his strategy for winning school board approval. "You also have to learn to analyze data. You'd better be able to defend what you're doing."

For Chance to Grow, that meant data, data, data. As we shall see, every facet of the Chance to Grow curriculum was evaluated through control-group experiments, which provide the most powerful means of finding out what works and what does not. Although Bob DeBoer described the politics as "negative energy," it is a fact of life for nonprofit and government organizations. "I'm not a politician," he said after winning the charter school vote, "but I do know how to frame issues and mobilize people."

Although new organizations such as Chance to Grow are the most vulnerable to strong opposition, even well-known organizations can create strong adversaries. The Walker Art Center, for example, provoked enormous controversy, both locally and nationally, when it presented HIV-positive performance artist Ron Athey in March 1994. The performance drew in part upon an African tradition in which Athey cut several small patterns into the back of a fellow (HIV negative) performer.

The Walker clearly knew the event would be uncomfortable. Its monthly calendar even included a description of the performance and a disclaimer—"Due to the nature of this material, viewer discretion is advised"—and the event was held in a small off-site theater. The staff exercised extreme diligence to create a safe space for the artist and the audience alike to explore issues surrounding HIV.

Nevertheless, the event caused an explosion of controversy. Here is how the *Minneapolis StarTribune* described the performance in a front-page story three weeks later: "A Walker Art Center member has complained to state health officials about a Walker-sponsored event in which a performer sliced an abstract design into the flesh of another man, mopped up his blood with towels, and sent them winging above the audience on revolving clotheslines" (Abbe, 1994).

Further complicating the controversy, the Walker performance arts seasonal program was funded in part by the National Endowment for the Arts. The newspaper article eventually found its way to Senator Jesse Helms, becoming fodder for his continuing campaign against the NEA. Although the *StarTribune* clearly sensationalized the event, the controversy was inevitable. If it had not been Athey, it would have been someone else. The very mission of the performance arts effort was to test limits. That did not make the controversy less dangerous—the curator of performing arts received death threats in the weeks following the article—but it did provide some reassurance, as the Walker became a cause célèbre in the latest battle over freedom of the arts.

Not all innovation involves political hardball. Some of the hardball involves simple jealousy, which one can encounter almost anywhere. Nevertheless, organizations must be aware that innovation is risky. Courage is essential, a good public relations strategy is always a help, and preparing for the inevitable opposition is highly recommended.

Pay Attention to Outcomes

One of the ways innovating organizations stay in touch with the environment is to focus on outcomes. Instead of looking inward for measures of effectiveness, innovating organizations look outward to see what works and what does not. The bottom line is not how well they spend their time or money, but how time and money, and the activities they purchase, translate into real-world impacts. One way to escape the needless rules that hamstring so many organizations is to move toward performance-based accountability that rewards staff for producing results.

This concern for outcomes is not just good practice for an innovating organization, however. It is becoming standard good practice for all nonprofit and government agencies, as well as the standard device used by funders when they consider grants. In 1995, for example, the United Way of America called on its members to "allocate funds according to their impact on targeted causes and to measure the outcomes of health and human services and allocate funds accordingly." Organizations that cannot speak the new language of outcomes are less likely to win support.

(For those unfamiliar with the jargon, outcomes are the end point of a chain that runs from inputs through activities and outputs. Imagine an antismoking campaign as an example. Inputs are everything consumed by a given program—nicotine patches, smokers, counselor time, funding, and counseling space. Activities are the specific interventions used to achieve a program goal—teaching smokers how to use the patch, providing motivational support. Outputs are the immediate products of those activities—the number of smokers trained, numbers of patches worn. Outcomes are the ultimate benefits desired and achieved—increased number of nonsmokers, better health, lower absenteeism.)

Not only did most of the Surviving Innovation organizations understand the outcome chain, they were exceptionally committed to careful measurement as a source of learning. As noted earlier,

Chance to Grow used tight outcome evaluation as a defense against its critics, while St. Joe's and Episcopal Community Services both made outcomes a centerpiece of their quality assurance systems for residential treatment programs. Both also sought outside accreditation of their programs, which one St. Joe's staffer likened to "calling a bombing run on your own foxhole."

Pound for pound, however, the Domestic Abuse Project was the most rigorous of the Surviving Innovation organizations in focusing on outcomes as the measure of success. Founded in 1979, DAP soon became more than a support service for victims of abuse. It also became a strong force for prevention, whether in taking visible public positions against domestic violence or in treating batterers, most of whom were men.

Whatever the effort, DAP was constantly learning through evaluation. It formed an evaluation and research unit in 1983, working closely with the University of Minnesota's School of Social Work. "Few programs are willing to risk evaluating themselves, and even fewer will take the further risk of disseminating their findings widely," DAP explained in one of its research newsletters. "The unfortunate result is that so much powerful work is being done by so many, but so few know about it." Careful research allowed DAP to shorten its treatment programs over time and eventually generated an unexpected revenue stream from the sale of treatment manuals. DAP's bimonthly *Research Update* also showed an unusual willingness to share information with the environment, and the organization's decision to put one of its first clients on the board demonstrated its readiness to listen and learn from those it served.

Indeed, one of the easiest ways to start paying attention to outcomes is to add clients, customers, audience, or partners to the governing board. Engaging clients in governance is actually a requirement for the Central Community Housing Trust (CCHT), which was founded to develop housing for those displaced by construction of the Minneapolis Convention Center. Under its articles of incorporation, 30 percent of its board has to be composed of residents of CCHT buildings and another 40 percent must be residents of the neighborhoods it serves.

CCHT also expressed concern about impacts through research on *negative* outcomes. Instead of asking why residents stay, CCHT was more interested in why residents left. Although quite unwilling to call its residents customers, CCHT clearly cared about reducing the turnover rates in its buildings. High turnover would mean empty apartments, which in turn would mean less social trust in the buildings, which would mean even higher turnover, which would mean an eventual budget crisis for CCHT.

Change the Prevailing Winds

Many nonprofit and government organizations take the prevailing winds as a given. They encounter resistance and give up, come under fire and surrender. They see the outside world as an immutable force against which they must struggle.

The Surviving Innovation organizations had a very different image. St. Joe's Home for Children and Episcopal Community Services, worked to prevent the very problems that kept them in business; Advocating Change Together, Artspace, the Domestic Abuse Project, Heart of the Beast, Theatre de la Jeune Lune, and Walker Art Center worked to change public attitudes on what constitutes safe or acceptable ideas.

Anoka County even went to the state legislature to win permission to reorganize itself. Against the determined opposition of other counties, Anoka petitioned the legislature to convert its auditor, recorder of deeds, and treasurer posts from elected to appointed status. Once the conversions took place, the county fired two of the three incumbents and merged their offices into a one-stop finance unit that provided infinitely better service to taxpayers and home buyers.

Although the consolidation was not an innovative act per se, the resulting increase in taxpayer satisfaction played no small part in generating political capital for new ideas elsewhere in the organization. Moreover, the merger saved money and staff time that could be redeployed to support promising ideas. Under a no-layoff policy adopted as part of the plan, five clerical employees were transferred to other units in the county.

Finally, for at least one Surviving Innovation organization, changing the environment *was* the core mission. The Minnesota Office of Waste Management had an explicit responsibility to educate its environment on how to prevent pollution, whether by helping local governments create recycling and composting programs or by offering businesses matching grants to encourage waste reduction. This meant changing more than attitudes, however. It also meant creating markets for recyclable materials and compost. It meant loans and financial assistance, the Governor's Award for Excellence in Pollution Prevention, advertising campaigns, and assorted clearinghouses on how to handle everything from fluorescent lights to household batteries.

OWM was convinced—rightly, I think—that it had to become a partner with government, business, and private citizens to get the message across. The remarkable range of innovation it engendered was due largely to the fact that the agency was set apart from the rest of the government. "We might as well be flying the skull and crossbones," one staffer said. "The less we look like government, the more we can succeed."

This image was essential for winning the cooperation of polluters. OWM had an office in an industrial park far from the state office complex and worked hard to convince its external partners that it existed to help, not prosecute. The state legislature had this in mind when it created OWM as an independent agency separate from the Pollution Control Agency (PCA), which carries the heavy hammer of environmental enforcement in the state.

The problem was that PCA did not much like the competition; it wanted to control both the carrot and the stick. OWM had survived numerous battles with PCA over the years, losing the staff of a particular program one year only to win it back the next. (OWM referred to those staffers as "hostages," which is exactly what they were in a bureaucratic sense.) After years of internecine warfare, PCA finally persuaded the governor to order a merger. The skull and crossbones came down in 1994 as the agency became merely another subunit of PCA. To make sure no one missed the point, the larger organization insisted that OWM close its outpost and move into PCA's sterile headquarters. Although most of OWM's programs have survived to date, the merger clearly raised the barriers to innovation, making new ideas more risky and therefore less likely.

Sometimes, of course, it is impossible to change the prevailing winds. Laws are laws. But many of the Surviving Innovation organizations showed great talent at finding seams in the wind. At the Fond du Lac Community College, for example, the unique partnership between the tribal college system and the Minnesota State Community College System created its share of problems. The Bureau of Indian Affairs, which provides core funding for the nation's network of tribal colleges, threatened to pull its dollars if Fond du Lac did not enroll a 100 percent Native American student body, whereas the state of Minnesota threatened to pull its dollars if the college closed its doors to non-Native students.

After months of negotiation, the Fond du Lac staff finessed the pressure: they created the illusion of two colleges under the same roof. There would be separate accounting systems for each college, separate student tracking systems, and separate course catalogues, but everything would actually be the same. All that was required was a different label at the top of the reports. Go to Fond du Lac today and you can still pick up two separate catalogues, the only difference being a slightly different cover. One says, "Fond du Lac Community College: A Union of Cultures"; the other, "Fond du Lac Community College: A Union of Cultures Chartered by the Fond du Lac Band of Lake Superior Chippewa in 1987." Is it a hassle to do the two covers? Yes. Is it worth the sleight of hand to continue the work? Absolutely.

Conclusion

Facing into the outside world is no easy task. Organizations often have foggy missions and strong opponents, reluctant publics and impossible shocks. There are plenty of reasons to batten down the hatches and hope for a brighter day.

Unfortunately, the forecast is not particularly hopeful. Non-profits and governments alike appear stuck in permanent turbulence, with a high probability of shocks. One might say that they are caught in a thirty-year low-pressure zone of decreasing public confidence in social institutions, whether government, nonprofit, or private.

Organizations that want to control the environment rather than letting the environment control them have a relatively simple first task. They must ask themselves why they exist, whom they serve, and how they will know if and when they are succeeding. "Why are we here? To take up space? Spend money? Provide secure employment for our staff? Because we were here yesterday?" These are questions to be asked by the organization as a whole and by every employee—and asked more often than just once every five years. They have no "right" answers, but it is in the asking and answering that innovating organizations orient themselves properly. Like reading a compass on a long journey, asking about purpose is a critical tool for keeping an innovating organization on the right path.

This is not to suggest that innovating organizations never get lost. They may accept a bad grant, lose a legislative battle, or ignore negative outcomes. But mission always serves as the magnet that draws them back to their true course.

A Brief Note on Customers

One way to create a focus on the environment is to call one's clients, audience, residents, or visitors *customers*. Some experts, most notably David Osborne of *Reinventing Government* fame, believe the word has an almost magical quality in creating the illusion of market pressure. True, older Americans cannot get their Social Security checks from anyone but the Social Security Administration, and true, airline passengers cannot get their air traffic control from anyone but the Federal Aviation Administration. But thinking of older Americans and airline passengers as customers can make the agencies more responsive to the outside world. The customer metaphor is at least a useful first step in turning an organization outward.

However, only two of the twenty-six Surviving Innovation organizations featured the word customer prominently in their work. One was the Dowling School, which used the term to describe its students; the other was the Minnesota Zoo, which used the word in conjunction with money-making enterprises such as food and souvenir sales. Two others, the North Branch School District and Minnesota Extension Service, also experimented with the customer metaphor in some of their work but did not adopt the word as the primary description of their audiences.

There are two reasons why the rest of the Surviving Innovation organizations did not use the customer metaphor. First, they did not need to create the illusion of a market by calling their clients, audience, or visitors customers. They knew the market mattered and could call their customers whatever they wanted. Whereas some government organizations use the word to simulate the presence of a market, most of the Surviving Innovation organizations paid attention to the outside world because it truly mattered to their futures—a full house at Heart of the Beast meant a fuller budget, satisfied parents at Chance to Grow meant political support.

Second, many of the Surviving Innovation organizations saw customer as an impoverished term. Customer is not the right word for creating collaboration, for example. Customers are entities to be persuaded, cajoled, even manipulated, but they are not always persons to be consulted or given a role in design. Customers do not flip burgers at McDonald's or design clothes for Macy's. They do not build airplanes at Boeing or write programs for Microsoft. However important customers may be to an organization, they are rarely coproducers, partners, or stakeholders.

For the Surviving Innovation organizations, customer was just not deep enough. They wanted the public's judgment and insight, not just its immediate reactions. They wanted its help in designing more effective programs, not just its short-term enthusiasm. For this reason, the Domestic Abuse Project put a former client on the board, Episcopal Community Services worried about how well fathers did after participating in its parenting skills program, and Theatre de la Jeune Lune stayed in constant touch with its audience. They were seeking not just to satisfy the customer, although they all did conduct ongoing satisfaction surveys, but to win new partners in their mission. They wanted to solve problems, permanently. Although they could have called their abusers, fathers, and theater-goers customers, they all aimed for something deeper. I recommend *partner* as an alternative, though *citizen* is not bad either.

4

Structuring the Organization
to Encourage Creativity

Public administration scholars have long recommended that organizations establish clear lines of authority between the top and bottom. As public administration expert Luther Gulick wrote in his 1937 classic *Papers on the Science of Administration*, "From the earliest times, it has been recognized that nothing but confusion arises under multiple command. 'A man cannot serve two masters. . . .' The rigid adherence to the principle of unity of command may have its absurdities; these are, however, unimportant in comparison with the certainty of confusion, inefficiency, and irresponsibility which arise from the violation of the principle" (Gulick and Urwick, 1937, p. 9). In theory, employees must know who the boss is.

In reality, many of the Surviving Innovation organizations got away with a staggering amount of confusion about reporting chains, unity of command, and spans of control between supervisors and subordinates. Although there are preferred states of being regarding an innovating organization's internal structure, absolute clarity about just who is the boss is not one of the prescriptions.

The Minnesota Extension Service is a case in point. Its 1994 organization chart was more of an oval than a traditional pyramid, and more confusing than clarifying about who reports to whom. The dean of MES sat at the top of the chart, overseeing a confusing empire of district directors and extension program leaders, cluster committees and cluster program leaders, state extension faculty and county extension educators. Elected county boards were also in the chart, as were university deans, the MES administration, and the University of Minnesota president, not to mention the United States Department of Agriculture. As a result, it was never clear just who was responsible to whom. The county extension educators (who used to be called county agents) reported directly to their county extension committees, who reported to the elected county commissioners. But the educators also reported to the MES district directors and the cluster advisory committees invented in the late 1980s to encourage greater cross-county collaboration.

Offensive as the MES chart might be to an organizational purist, it worked. It certainly showed the complexity of the extension educator's job. But much more important, it gave this ninety-year-old agency the cover to innovate. Not knowing exactly who reported to whom was one way for MES to get the breathing room to experiment. Unlike most public agencies, MES had at least three bosses. One part of its budget came from the U.S. Department of Agriculture—some of its older employees were even covered by the federal civil service retirement system. Another part came from the state through the University of Minnesota—all MES employees were on the university payroll. And still another part came from the counties, who also provided office space. If MES was to survive the farm crisis and repeated budget cuts of the mid- to late 1980s, it had to blur the lines of traditional bureaucratic accountability.

Clustering, which involved sharing staff and resources across county lines, would be impossible, for example, if the counties continued to expect absolute loyalty. If the rural-racism expert was in Blue Earth County but the racism was in Pipestone, county loyalties had to bend. MES also had to blur the lines between the federal agriculture program and the extension agenda. If the problem in Dakota County was teenage pregnancy, a staff of agriculture and home economics experts would not be enough. Even using the term extension educator reflected a blurring of the lines. Whereas the term extension agent suggests a tight relationship with government (experts on top), extension educator is more proactive (experts on tap).

Moreover, the blurring allowed MES to imagine itself as something other than a traditional government agency. To some extent, all of the government organizations in the Surviving Innovation sample pretended to be nonprofits or private firms. The Minnesota Office of Waste Management flew the skull and crossbones; the Minnesota Zoo competed against Camp Snoopy; the three schools (Cyrus, Dowling, and the North Branch School District) were intensely focused on their markets; Fond du Lac Community College was unlike any community college in the nation; and MES was impossible to pin down. Even Anoka County looked unlike any other county—its one-stop finance office is a case in point.

They also felt radically different from the typical government agency, in part because they had worked so hard to remove the barriers to innovation. None worshiped the principles of administration that once dictated what a government agency should look like—a tight span of control between supervisors and subordinates, the one true master at the top of the organization (try that phrase out at Luther Theological Seminary and see whom its staff see as the one true master!), and highly specialized offices that are kept separate from the whole. (See Light, 1995, for a discussion of how these principles invariably produce thickening.)

For the Surviving Innovation organizations, internal structure was an instrument for innovation, not an end in itself. Their goal was not to build a towering monument to bureaucracy but to create reporting relationships that worked for the organization's mission. They did not see internal structure as irrelevant—they did worry about who reported to whom (extension educators may have had multiple reporting lines on the written chart, but the unwritten chart was clear: they increasingly reported directly to the public). However, their main focus was not on manipulating structure for innovation but on making sure structure did not weaken the freedom to imagine.

Creating the Freedom to Imagine

I started the Surviving Innovation Project as a *structuralist*—that is, as someone who worries about how organizations are wired together. As a general rule, structuralists see organizations as machines to be fine-tuned. When in doubt about what to do, structuralists almost always recommend reorganization as the path to excellence or innovativeness. And when they cannot reorganize, they almost invariably recommend new procedures of one kind or another. Unfortunately, much of their work produces greater barriers to effectiveness and more pieces of paper to be kept happy.

The Surviving Innovation organizations saw structure in a very different way. It was a natural part of organizational life—the skeleton of the bureaucracy—but far less important to innovativeness than I had allowed myself to believe. It was something to be manipulated, even attacked, but it was also something to be bypassed. Much as these organizations worried about having too many layers of management, for example, they did not spend much of their energy stripping away layers. Confronted with an organizational Maginot Line, they went around it. They did so by adopting ten practices that helped them achieve a preferred structure.

1. Stay thin.

2. Create room to experiment.

3. Push authority downward.

4. Lower the barriers to internal collaboration.

5. Democratize!

6. Prime the organization for innovation.

7. Create a marketplace of ideas.

8. Prepare for stress.

9. Maximize diversity.

10. Age gracefully.

Stay Thin

Most nonprofit and government organizations today have a metabolism that thickens them over time—that is, they grow taller and wider almost automatically, adding new layers of management and new managers to each layer. As they thicken, the basic shape of the hierarchy changes. They tend to move from the traditional pyramid, where more people work at the bottom of the organization, delivering services, than at the middle or the top, toward a pentagon, where more people work at the middle, overseeing and cross-checking others, than at the bottom.

This is not the book to describe the causes of thickening (see Light, 1995, for the details). Suffice it to note that much of the thickening results from the prevailing wisdom about what constitutes good practice. Much of that wisdom rests on the "principles of administration" described by Gulick (Gulick and Urwick, 1937). According to these principles, good government is the natural product of narrow spans of control between supervisors and subordinates (a ratio of six to one is considered about right), tight centralization from the top (everything revolves around the "one true master" of the organization), and clear rules on who does what and when. "Just as the hand of man can span only a limited number of notes on the piano, so the mind and will of man can span but a limited number of immediate managerial contacts," Gulick wrote in describing the need for small spans of control. "As a result the executive of any enterprise can personally direct only a few persons" (p. 7). That single statement alone launched a thousand management layers and still represents the dominant view of many public officials.

(At the Veterans Administration Medical Center in St. Paul, for example, floor nurses have nine layers of formal review. They are reviewed by their immediate nursing supervisor, who is reviewed by the chief nurse, who is reviewed by the chief of staff, who is reviewed by the hospital center director, who is reviewed by the regional director in Ann Arbor, who is reviewed by the associate chief medical director for operations in Washington, who is reviewed by the deputy under secretary for health, who is reviewed by the under secretary for health, who is reviewed by the secretary of Veterans Affairs. That is just nine layers in a 250,000-employee agency. But when one looks at policy ideas going up and down, the number of layers jumps to forty-one, meaning an idea has to survive a great deal of listening to make it to the top.)

By any measure, whether formal or informal, most of the Surviving Innovation organizations were relatively thin. As one might expect, younger, smaller organizations were the thinnest, whereas older, larger organizations were the thickest. Nonprofit and government organizations tend to thicken as they age, just as human beings do. But as a general rule, the Surviving Innovation organizations paid attention to their thickness, worrying about the extra weight that comes with the creation of each new management layer, and watching to make sure the front line was broad enough to do its job.

The easiest way to stay thin, of course, is to have no layers of management at all. That was precisely the case at Cyrus Math/Tech, where teachers formed a self-managed team to run the school. With its tiny staff of teachers and secretaries, Cyrus could easily compose itself as a single-layered organization, delegating specific responsibilities, such as testing new software, to one or two teachers as necessary. The dollars saved by eliminating the full-time principal could go toward making the math/technology magnet more powerful in drawing paying students from other school districts.

The problem with a self-managed team is that some situations call for a single voice. That would have helped Cyrus when parents, using a phone tree, organized the transcendental meditation protest. (Phone trees are particularly powerful organizing devices. Instead of meeting face-to-face, one parent calls two others, who call two others, who call two others, and suddenly the school is under siege.)

In the Cyrus controversy, the self-managed team faced two challenges. First, by virtue of its composition, the team was seen as sympathetic to the teacher involved; there was no way for it to broker a resolution. Second, it had no capacity for managing the public reaction. Although there were specialists in computer software on the team, for example, there was no one who had much training in conflict resolution or public relations. The crisis was resolved when other parents mounted a counteroffensive, taking a strong position as protectors and stakeholders. It was hardly a bad outcome, for it spoke to the tight bond between the school and the children it served.

Cyrus was not the only self-managed team in the Surviving Innovation sample. Theatre de la Jeune Lune also had a self-managed team, composed of its four artistic directors. In turn, the leadership committee was linked to a three-person administrative team created under a 1985 Advancement Grant from the National Endowment for the Arts. "We knew how the theater should run," said one of the four founders, "but not how to run it." In essence, the theater operated with two self-managed teams, reporting and interacting with each other. Although the founders had the final say over artistic direction, the administrative team operated as a fail-safe mechanism on particularly risky productions. If they said no, the production could not go forward.

Another way to stay thin is simply to build around the layers of management, using e-mail or other technologies, or to ignore them altogether. The latter approach is exactly how the Office of Waste Management dealt with its leadership turnover. OWM had seven executive directors in seven years, two of whom left office only to return one or two directors later. Counting that leadership layer, there were just two steps between top and bottom in the staff of forty-three; ignoring the leadership layer, there was just one person who had to say yes. Having frequent turnover is most certainly not a preferred state of being for an innovating organization, but as OWM demonstrated, it is not an impossible barrier to surmount either.

Still another way to remain thin is to stretch the organization over a wider space. Episcopal Community Services did just that by having eight programs and roughly one hundred staff reporting to a single operations director. So much for handling multiple notes of the piano! North Branch School District, a $15 million rural school district forty miles north of St. Paul, thinned itself by creating the state's first year-round high school, allowing a more flexible schedule and a wider curriculum than the traditional nine-month school while stretching a nine-month faculty over an extra quarter. ECS was able to lengthen its span of control by stressing outcomes as a measure of success. There is less need for face-to-face oversight when managers have good and timely information on how programs are working. North Branch achieved this by staying in touch with its community, which clearly wanted year-round schooling.

At the risk of reverting to my old structuralist ways, I must acknowledge that there are times when a little thickening cannot hurt. Sometimes organizations become too far-flung, too decentralized. In a 1991 effort to impose a modicum of control on itself, Anoka County collapsed twenty departments into six divisions, bringing much greater tightness to its hierarchy. Three years later, it reorganized again, this time collapsing the six divisions into five. Of particular importance in this second reorganization was the decision to merge community corrections into the Human Services Division. The decision created a much stronger presumption in favor of crime prevention by giving first offenders access to mental health services, community social services, and job training, which were also part of the new division.

Create Room to Experiment

One way to render an organization's hierarchy less of a barrier to innovation, is to create space to experiment. This might mean creating a special task force that is given a mandate to think outside the box, a separate unit to scan the external environment for promising ideas, or a laboratory of some kind to research and test a particular approach. The goal is *not* to pick a handful of stars and mad scientists who will be freed from all earthly duties. Rather, it is to create an opportunity to pretend, if only for a moment, that anything is possible.

The North Branch School District actually thought of its entire system as a place to experiment and won state approval to do so. With a substantial portfolio of innovation already under way in 1993, including the year-round high school and a laboratory school for at-risk students, North Branch petitioned the Minnesota State Board of Education, which oversees local school districts, for an "umbrella waiver" from all state rules. This was not just a case of a tiny rural school asking for permission to establish a new magnet school. North Branch had four schools, one hundred teachers, and 2,500 students.

The waiver request was hardly noncontroversial. "It's the first time that we're hearing a waiver request of this type and this magnitude," a State Board staffer remarked at the time. "Obviously, we're going into uncharted waters here." Despite the promised liberation, North Branch teachers and the state teachers' union both opposed the waiver. So did advocates for disabled children. "How do you deal with other districts that want to feel special?" one opponent asked. "I would hope that we will be bombarded with requests for innovative ways to approach and improve learning" was the answer.

Although the waiver was more symbolic than essential for innovating, it did give the district formal permission to substitute performance-based accountability for compliance. North Branch had established site councils composed of parents and community leaders to govern its schools several years before the waiver and was in constant touch with the wider community through formal and informal channels. It could assert, for example, that over half of the area's residents felt they could have an impact on school decisions because it had commissioned the independent survey research to find out.

This record of citizen involvement was central to the "spirit of trust" that led to the board's unanimous vote to grant the waiver. "It just doesn't make sense to me to think that standards are going to be dropped down when parents of children themselves are involved," said a senior administrator in response to the waiver opposition. He clearly had the results to prove it, including high levels of parental satisfaction.

North Branch was not the only Surviving Innovation organization that structured itself as an incubator of innovation. With a mission to "get homeless persons permanently off the street and into a productive life," the Phoenix Group was both the youngest of the sample organizations and one of the most visible. Located in the Phillips neighborhood of Minneapolis, its mix of housing, employment, and counseling programs earned local and national visibility, including a *Newsweek* 1995 American Achievement Award.

There was no question that Phoenix filled a void in economically depressed Phillips. In a neighborhood where 7-Elevens and Quick Stops were the only grocery stores, Phoenix opened a supermarket. In a neighborhood without public spaces in which to congregate, Phoenix opened a café. And in an environment dominated by dilapidated housing, Phoenix rebuilt houses and apartment buildings. At the height of its expansion in 1995, Phoenix ran an auto repair shop, a café, an upholstery business, a grocery store, and a housing development operation, employing two to three hundred people, most of whom were recovered or recovering alcohol or chemical abusers. "Any organization chart that could fit us would have to be an aerial photograph," said one of the Phoenix cofounders. Phoenix was evolving so quickly that an organization chart would have been outdated the minute it was drawn up.

Nor was there any question that Phoenix was willing to challenge the prevailing wisdom. "These guys would not operate in the usual manner," its board chair later told the *Twin Cities Reader*, "and that caused problems, and on the other hand they were the fair-haired golden children, too. The philosophy was, 'If you don't have 50 percent opposition, you aren't worth a shit. If everybody loves you, what are we doing?'" Phoenix's resistance to management systems, and the resulting financial catastrophe that led to its demise, were natural by-products of its willingness to flow with the needs of the neighborhood. "It was like being caught up in a whirlwind, you know," one of the cofounders argued in the wake of Phoenix's collapse. "You never had time really to sit back and reflect because stuff was happening so fast and because the need was great. There were many more people coming than we could truly accommodate, yet we had a philosophy of 'Turn no one down,' so it created an enormous workload. There were a whole lot of folks like that—a lot more than anybody dreamed."

The lesson from Phoenix is not to stop innovating. Rather, it is to always remember that single acts of innovation are not enough to ensure either success or survival. Phoenix would have survived had it created both the space to imagine *and* the systems to provide a reality check. Phoenix was never short on mission or leadership. It paid close attention to the outside world and was deeply committed to a high-risk strategy. Where it failed was in ignoring the ordinary good practice that would have kept it afloat as it encountered the natural turbulence of innovation.

In the end, Phoenix fell to the ordinary setbacks that affect every innovating organization. For some organizations, the setbacks are self-inflicted. But in this case, it was an event completely beyond the organization's control: a floor sealant seeped into the grocery store from the adjacent building and contaminated the space. Every food item was ruined. Although Phoenix raised enough money to restock the store, the setback was the first in a line of dominoes that brought down what had been an $800,000 organization. Phoenix had hoped that profits from the grocery store would subsidize its riskier ventures; in fact, the store never broke even.

Phoenix finally collapsed when the Super Valu food chain, which supplied the grocery store, sued for back payments. Apparently, Phoenix had not been paying its bills before the crisis. (The American Indian Business Development Corporation had rented the space to Phoenix and took a loss on its investment, too. Unlike Phoenix, however, the corporation had a financial buffer that protected it against catastrophe.) Lacking a business plan and financial rigorous management, Phoenix never knew what hit it. In retrospect, however, what hit Phoenix was that lack of a decent business plan and good financial management. It was unable to stop the bleeding.

Push Authority Downward

Innovating organizations are particularly good at pushing authority down to the front lines where the organization meets the outside world. If innovation often involves using old stuff in new ways, as Levin and Sanger argue (1994), one way to increase innovativeness is to give frontline employees the authority to start restitching the old stuff on their own. As one North Branch teacher put it, "We like to ask forgiveness after the fact."

In striving to be "the most responsive and farsighted agency in state government," OWM imagined each frontline employee as a kind of entrepreneur. To the extent that those employees could imagine a new project idea or a new way of reaching out to the external audience, they were given the freedom to do so. Expanding the base of ideas was not only good for OWM's overall mission, it also made the organization harder for the Pollution Control Agency to swallow.

The resulting freedom to imagine was particularly important in OWM's effort to develop new markets for recyclables where none had existed before and anyone could make a difference with just one new application. This freedom was also essential for imagining new ways of preventing pollution in the thousands of small businesses around the state. Some of the new ideas were big—finding support for a $70 million facility to convert 120,000 tons of office paper and printing plant overruns into pulp. Others were tiny by comparison—finding a way for the *Grand Rapids Herald Tribune* to recycle its printing ink.

OWM's readiness to share authority was also based on the size of its staff in relation to its mission. "We try to have the lowest level of the organization make as many decisions as possible," one of the senior staff explained. "We are just too thin to do otherwise. Supervision has a cost." When an agency is too big for its mission, there is no penalty for forcing every decision upward. But when an agency is too small for its mission, everyone must count.

Where mission is not quite so pressing, innovating organizations may have to push authority downward by more formal means. The North Branch School District emerges again as an example. Along with waivers of state rules, North Branch also gave its elementary school teachers authority to decide how to allocate the supply budget. If they wanted more pencils, they could buy more pencils; if they wanted more construction paper, they could buy more paper. All they had to do was make the trade-offs needed to keep the budget in balance. Who better to decide than the teachers?

The Dowling School went one step further. Not only did it push authority down to its teachers, it gave authority to its students. Students from first to sixth grade had a formal voice in making school policy. That the principal, Jeff Raison, adopted Total Quality Management and employee empowerment as management strategies was hardly innovative, even for a public school. That he brought students into the process as full participants most certainly was.

Yet there the students were, organized into teams for making software recommendations, mounting protests against the use of Styrofoam cups, and participating in the Positive Action Response system by requesting changes in the way the school operated. These were not junior high or high school students, mind you, but kindergartners and first- to sixth-graders. With "I am the solution" as its motto, Dowling had no choice but to include a host of nontraditional partners in its work—students, bus drivers, cafeteria workers, janitors, and just about anyone else who contributed value to the school's success.

This was much more than just make-work for kids. Asked to help develop a technology plan in 1994, for example, the Dowling Student Roundtable, which was composed of nine students, produced a remarkably prescient report, complete with near-term recommendations ("the first priority is to get two Macintosh LC 520s" to be "placed in each 6th grade classroom"), supporting reasons ("the upper grades need to learn how to use the more sophisticated software that is available mainly on Macintoshes"), long-range recommendations ("every classroom should always have one fully functioning computer setup"), and even a recommendation for the Minneapolis school district ("wire the entire building and each classroom so that each one is connected to a CD-ROM tower that would be located in the media center"). Who better to contribute to such a decision than the students themselves, particularly in an era in which they have the fresh perspective and technical expertise? Would that adult teams did as well.

The key in all of these cases was to pass the freedom downward. It would have made no sense for North Branch to win a waiver from state rules only to invent a new set of its own. Unfortunately, many nonprofit and government organizations do just that, hoarding new-found freedoms at the top. "When organizations gain autonomy from the center," write David Osborne and Peter Plastrik in *Banishing Bureaucracy*, a how-to manual on reinventing government, "it goes to their heads—literally, to the managers at the top of the agency hierarchy. All too often, that's where it stays" (1997, p. 224). As we shall see in the next chapter, breaking the control habit is an essential first step in leading the innovating organization.

Lower the Barriers to Internal Collaboration

An organization would lower the barriers to internal collaboration only if it believed that creativity is randomly distributed throughout its halls. If it believed that creativity is the gift of the special few, it would focus on finding those individuals and giving them the resources to innovate. The rest of the organization would concentrate on ordinary chores and routine duties while the innovators generated the new ideas.

The Surviving Innovation organizations believed otherwise. They saw the potential for good ideas in every corner. This does not mean they thought every last person in their organization was capable of innovation. But it did mean that they were ready to bet that a good idea could come from just about anywhere, including snowplow drivers, first-grade teachers, and theater ushers. By refusing to anoint the special few, they opened themselves to the possibility of innovation from any quarter.

Toward that end, the Surviving Innovation organizations worked to create opportunities for employees to share ideas, exchange information, build friendships, and form partnerships. Although the organizations could never be sure what might come of these interactions, they lowered the boundaries nonetheless. By allowing their employees to bump into each other, they increased the odds that new ideas, or at least old stuff used in new ways, would emerge.

Part of that effort involved creating public space. Although employees can always bump into each other in the hallways, bathrooms, and parking lots, there is some value in creating a common space where employees of different ranks and units can interact without a particular agenda. The point is to develop solid relationships *before* moving on to the stress and conflict of innovating.

For some of the Surviving Innovation organizations, creating public space simply meant capturing a familiar venue—say, a library, coffee room, or lounge. For others, it meant building space where none had existed before. The founders of Theatre de la Jeune Lune made sure their new theater had a kitchen that could serve double duty as a conference room. "That's where we cook and where we cook," one of the artistic directors said.

For still others, it meant buying space outside the organization. That was certainly the case when the Phoenix Group bought the neighborhood café to keep it from closing. The prices were great, the Friday catfish a soul-food delight, and the coffee always hot. "Every neighborhood needs a café," one of the founders argued. "And we needed one where we could meet over a cup of coffee." With Phoenix main offices crammed into a partially renovated two-bedroom house, the staff did some of its most creative thinking over breakfast and lunch at the Phoenix Cafe.

Common space is useless for innovativeness, of course, unless the organization lowers the barriers to using it. At least two of the Surviving Innovation organizations made explicit efforts to do just that.

The Minnesota Extension Service used what it called *clusters*. Grouping Minnesota's eighty-seven county extension offices into eighteen clusters was a restructuring clearly designed to break down the old county loyalties in a time of staff cutbacks. But the effort involved more than just a new map. Extension agents were renamed extension educators in an effort to weaken historical ties to agriculture and home economics; specialty titles tied to specific fields were eliminated for the same reason. Cluster program leaders were appointed as a source of ongoing advocacy for interdisciplinary work, and employee performance appraisal was linked, at least in part, to cluster activities. Although old loyalties to counties and specializations would certainly remain, MES was laying the groundwork for future collaboration. This meant removing the old structure first.

Luther Theological Seminary also worked on tearing down barriers to collaboration, again by emphasizing the need for interdisciplinary work. What I admire most about Luther is that it started with the students (and, by implication, the parishioners those students served), moved next to curricular reform, then went on to changes in the teaching calendar, and ended with fundamental changes in the basic structure of the seminary. In other words, it moved in the direction almost exactly opposite to that of traditional academic reform, which usually starts with the assumption that structure and calendars are unchangeable and often ends by seeing students and the outside world as the problem.

Luther's first priority was to train ministers to serve what it described as a "world of many cultures." Toward that end, it asked hard questions about what its students needed as Christian leaders in God's world. As it developed new expectations of its graduates—

for example, that ministers needed to show "spiritual courage on be-half of evangelical freedom"—and core values for its curriculum—for example, that "the church needs all graduates to be multi-culturally and religiously aware"—it came to the obvious conclu-sion that calendars, department lines, and governance structures had to change.

The school created interdisciplinary *course construction teams* to design new curriculum; grouped its academic departments into three new divisions (bible, history/theology, and leadership); modified the calendar and course sequence to give students more options on scheduling, independent study, internships, and travel; changed the faculty appointment and promotion policy to emphasize common mission; and perhaps most revealing of its commitment, created a new academic leadership team at the top of the seminary to keep the effort alive. New structure flowed from mission, not vice versa.

Whether the Surviving Innovation organizations created col-laboration through formal restructuring or by providing simple com-mon space, a straightforward lesson emerged: *wherever internal collaboration occurred, it produced innovative acts*. Anoka County has a 1995 Ford Foundation Innovation Award to prove it. It was an award that came in large measure from giving employees the chance to imagine together. The project, Parents' Fair Share, involved a unique internal collaboration between three county offices: the county attorney, child support enforcement, and employment and training.

The problem was simple: noncustodial parents, usually fathers, who are unemployed or underemployed often fall behind in court-ordered child support payments. The solution was equally simple: find those parents jobs, and they will honor their child support orders. The barrier was that county attorneys usually get rewarded for prosecuting, child support enforcement offices for enforcing, and job training offices for training, and none get rewarded for working together. In Anoka County, the catalyst for innovation was simple common sense. Staff from the three offices not only had the space to interact in the hallways, cafeteria, and neighborhood café, they had the strong support of the county executive and board. Thus was an award-winning program launched.

Democratize!

Like the communist governments of Eastern and Central Europe, many of the Surviving Innovation organizations experienced an amazing liberation in the late 1980s and early 1990s: they switched from centralized rule to democracy. Of the twenty-six organizations in the sample, seventeen experienced a major leadership transition during the ten years prior to the site visits. Of the seventeen, all but two shifted to a more participatory style. One of the two others, the Office of Waste Management, switched to de facto democracy by operating mostly as a self-managed team. Only Artspace continued with a concentrated hierarchy, in part because of the enormous financial risk involved as it considered a national expansion.

(See Cotton and others, 1988, for a summary of the literature on the link between employee participation and performance; and see Wagner, 1994, for a contrary view. To summarize what is a very broad literature, there is general agreement that participation does improve performance and satisfaction, but much less agreement on just how significant the effects might be and which types of participation make the most difference. "Though *statistically* significant," writes Wagner, "the average effects revealed in this article are so small as to raise questions about *practical* significance" [p. 325].)

It is worth mentioning that, excluding Cyrus and OWM, only three of the shifts involved a change in the gender of the executive. Two went from male to female, one from female to male, and six each from male to male and female to female. Eight of the twenty-six organizations were led by women, fourteen by men, and four by teams of men and women.

Establishing organizational democracy does not mean taking votes on every issue. Rather, it means giving employees a greater voice in making decisions through broad opportunities to participate.

Whether through town-hall forums, internal surveys, formal policy councils, or a modified form of profit sharing (Cyrus teachers shared equally in the school's financial success), organizational democracies give employees a chance to be heard. Some experts call this *employee empowerment*; others label it *employee involvement* or *participation*; still others refer to specific techniques like *quality circles* (now out of fashion) or *self-managed teams* (now in). But the result is generally the same: employees acquire a greater stake in the organization's success.

Organizational democracy is also linked to innovativeness. First, assuming good ideas are to be found just about anywhere, democracy creates more channels to the top. Just as they push authority downward, innovating organizations invite ideas upward. Although they often create specific *idea generators* to do so (a topic in Chapter Six), a general invitation to participate is essential. Second, assuming that innovating organizations are composed of mostly ordinary people who are extraordinarily committed to mission, democracy provides a powerful means for creating a shared sense of commitment.

As for its effect on plain good performance, innovative or not, democracy appears to matter. Asked if America could raise productivity by changing the way it pays its employees, economist Alan Blinder, a member of President Clinton's first-term Council of Economic Advisors, answered as follows: "It appears that changing the way workers are *treated* may boost productivity more than changing the way they are *paid*, although profit sharing or employee stock ownership combined with worker participation may be the best system of all" (1990, pp. 203–204). Although employee stock ownership seems impossible in nonprofits and government, several Surviving Innovation organizations came pretty close. For the Minnesota Zoo, the profit was always in psychic income—for example, in the knowledge that increased gate receipts helped endangered species—but it added up nonetheless.

The fact that so many of the Surviving Innovation organizations had shifted from concentrated rule to democracy also suggests the value of participation for sustaining innovativeness. One example is the Walker Art Center, which moved from a concentrated style under legendary director Martin Friedman to a more democratic approach under Kathy Halbreich.

Arriving in 1991 after serving as curator of contemporary art at Boston's Museum of Fine Arts, Halbreich chose a more participatory approach from her very first day. She started by creating a senior management council to help her make decisions and by consulting with the Walker staff—from curators to gallery guards, fulltimers to volunteers—about the future of the organization and quickly proceeded to the development of a long-range plan and Walker's first-ever mission statement.

The long-range plan clearly committed the institution to democracy. Goal one of the plan was to support artists, goal two was to actively engage audiences, and goal three was to "manage staff creatively and progressively." Achieving this third goal meant attracting *and* retaining talented, experienced, and diverse staff, emphasizing a "participatory management style to improve internal communications and staff recognition," and creating "a working environment that encourages personal and professional growth." As one staffer said, "Friedman had a single, capital 'T' truth that he carried around in his head. Halbreich has many small 't' truths that emerge from her conversations with others. The difference is like night and day."

The test of this greater emphasis on participation was whether Halbreich could produce innovativeness. Some of Walker's supporters argued that Friedman had been successful precisely because he did not encourage participation. He did not want curators to stay too long, and he dominated the organization with a singular and powerful vision of modern art. Halbreich quickly proved that a more democratic approach could be equally successful. She produced a dramatic increase in the number of touring exhibitions—nine exhibitions were traveling in 1995 alone—as well as flashy shows on Jenny Holzer, Krzysztof Wodiczko, and Bruce Nauman, the last of which prompted a glowing *Newsweek* review describing it as an "engaging, if earsplitting, retrospective" (Plagens, 1994). If she had anything approaching a capital "T" truth, it was that the Walker mission had to reside in the entire organization, not just in her office.

Prime the Organization for Innovation

There is nothing quite like having a little extra money for a promising idea. Such resources, which organizational researchers call slack, make greater risk possible. Although some organizations believe that good ideas will find support on their own, all but a handful of the Surviving Innovation organizations had an innovation investment fund of some kind. Some of the funds were relatively small, providing a few dollars here and there for new software, a training program, or new materials. Others were fairly large, financing whole projects and staffs. But whether large or small, the effect of the innovation investment funds was the same: they stimulated ideas.

Indeed, an innovation investment fund is one of the most useful tools for transforming a well-performing public organization into an innovating one. It is a means of signaling the organization that innovative acts will be rewarded. And given the tightness of dollars in so many public agencies, even a little money can send a very loud signal.

Absent other efforts to address the ecological barriers to innovativeness, however, an investment fund will work only for a short time. Employees will certainly pick the proverbial low-hanging fruit in return for dollars and recognition, but their enthusiasm will slowly fade as they realize that innovative acts are just as risky and difficult with an investment fund as they have ever been. This is a common pattern in employee involvement programs in the private sector. By itself, an innovation investment fund is not enough to create sustainable change. As part of a broader effort, it is a very powerful device indeed.

It is also useful to note that there can be such a thing as *too much slack*. This point is well made by private-sector researchers Nitin

Nohria and Ranjay Gulati in a study of two multinational corporations (1996). According to the research, both too little slack and too much weaken the prospects for innovation: "As slack increases, the discipline that is exercised in the selection, ongoing support, and termination of projects becomes lax." More troubling perhaps, excess slack may reduce the pressure to shepherd resources wisely. As Nohria and Gulati conclude, "Excess slack can result in both type I (selecting projects that should not have been funded) and type II (stopping projects that should have been continued) errors" (p. 1249).

Organizations must answer two questions in creating an innovation investment fund. The first is how much money to put at risk. Here, all things are relative, and the answer will depend on the organization. A few hundred dollars might be more than enough in a small nonprofit such as CLUES or the Heart of the Beast Puppet and Mask Theater, whereas a few hundred thousand might be needed in a larger organization such as Anoka County, the Walker Art Center, or the Minnesota Extension Service. What matters is not so much the amount in play, for innovation investment funds can succeed with little more than pocket change, but the signal that new ideas will be supported. Innovation investment funds put the organization's money at risk. The bigger the organization's budget, the bigger the amount that will be necessary to send the message.

The second question is how to choose among competing ideas. Some organizations treat their innovation investment funds as little more than another source of petty cash, making decisions with casual abandon—that is, through a quick conversation in the hallway, a call to the executive. In contrast, the Surviving Innovation organizations tended to make much more deliberate choices, often following an investment banking model or establishing an internal foundation complete with calls for proposals.

The Minnesota Zoo's innovation fund is an example of the investment bank model. Created in 1992, the fund was administered by the zoo's Enterprise Programs Department, which had itself been created the year before to provide a concentrated focus on

making money. Built to oversee all revenue-producing activities—
marketing, fundraising, sales (food, souvenirs), and events (con-
certs, special exhibitions)—the department was headed by one of
the most entrepreneurial persons I have ever encountered in any
sector: Steve Ordahl. His investment fund was created with a simple mission well worth presenting here in full:

> In an effort to help generate funding for existing and
> new programs, the Zoo has adopted an entrepreneurial
> philosophy. That is, we support the taking of risks and
> seeking of opportunities to invest in and grow new busi-
> nesses which have a reasonable chance of success. We
> desire to use resources in new ways to maximize produc-
> tion, effectiveness and revenues to the Zoo. We recog-
> nize that inherent in risk taking is the potential for
> failure as well as great success. We hold the belief that a
> small percentage of failures is acceptable provided the
> business concept is sound, the business plan was fol-
> lowed, and reasonable attempts were made to modify the
> approach in response to changing market conditions.

The quid pro quo was clear: risk taking would be rewarded if it
involved careful planning, and failures would be accepted for the
right reasons. Employees certainly did not have to be perfect to get
a grant, but they had to think ahead and worry about results. In
return, their projects would get dollars for start-up, and their units
would get a 40 percent share of the net profits.

The actual investment decisions were to be made by the zoo's
management team on the basis of two relatively simple criteria.
First, the project had to have a reasonable chance of making *new*
money. It could not merely move existing dollars from one pocket
to another. Why fund a pretzel stand that puts the ice-cream cart
out of business? Second, the project had to be consistent with the
mission and vision of the zoo. The amount of the investment varied

from a few thousand dollars to much more, but whether big or small, all proposals had to have a detailed budget showing revenues, expenses, and net return on investment.

The investment fund clearly generated new ideas, some successful, some not. On the success side of the ledger was the Dolphin Overnight. Building upon the public's love affair with the zoo's "playful bottlenose dolphins," as the marketing brochure described them, these overnights invited children (and at least one parent/chaperon per group) to camp out in the dolphin observation chamber, watch the evening feedings, consume "an ample supply of pizza," "slumber beneath the watchful eyes of the dolphins" (meaning sleep on a concrete floor), rise to a "nutritious cold breakfast" (cereal and juice), and exit before the first daytime visitors arrived. All for $36 per child and $20 per chaperon. The program was an absolute hit, with space booked months in advance.

On the failure side of the ledger was the Coral Overnight, designed as a companion to the dolphin program. The only difference was that the children would slumber beneath the watchful eyes of patrolling sharks in the coral reef exhibit just around the corner from the dolphin tank. Same program structure, same fees, but very few takers. Apparently, sharks just are not as loveable as dolphins. There was no recrimination from the investment fund regarding the failure, however, for the coral reef staff had presented a solid business plan, designed an attractive brochure, and launched a broad marketing effort. Failures were seen as an inevitable part of success.

The Minnesota Extension Service is an example of the alternative innovation investment fund approach: internal philanthropy. A project certainly did not have to make money to get a *creative program grant*, but it did have to be clear in purpose and interdisciplinary in nature; it also had to contribute to the MES mission, have high potential for leveraging other funds, and include "clear, concrete anticipated outcomes and definitive plans for measuring impact." As with the zoo investment fund, the quid pro quo was clear: projects that fit the MES mission would be rewarded.

Unlike the zoo, MES had sharp restrictions on who could apply for the grants. Only collaborative teams of faculty and staff were eligible, and their proposals had to carry the signature of a cluster leader or other senior staffer. Maximum funding for any one project was restricted to $50,000 per year for up to three years. Created from internal reallocations and occasional windfalls, the amounts available were staggering. In 1995, for example, MES awarded twenty-three grants totaling $557,145; the projects ran the gamut, from teaching homeowners how to manage their septic systems to a round-the-clock fax-back service providing information on gardening, insect control, wildlife, and composting. The former dealt with an increasingly serious problem in rural communities, where homeowners often rely on wells for drinking water, and the latter freed employees from answering the telephones.

Create a Marketplace of Ideas

Carefully designed innovation investment funds not only stimulate new ideas, they can create a marketplace of ideas that improves organizational performance overall. By letting ideas rise and fall on their merits, rather than by accident or bureaucratic politics, innovation investment funds encourage the organization to be more rigorous in all its work, whether that work involves innovation or not. Investment funds become another way to reinforce organizational values such as honesty and rigor.

That is certainly how the Minnesota Zoo and MES designed their innovation investment review systems. At MES, for example, a series of questions had to be answered:

Is the project a collaborative effort?

Is there input from the people the project will affect?

What makes the need a high priority?

How will the project have a long-term institutional payoff for MES consistent with its vision and mission?

Is the budget reasonable? Does it match the work of the project?

Are other sources contributing to the project?

Again, such questions convey clear signals not just about what gets funded but about what the organization as a whole values. They also reassure the organization that ideas rise and fall on merit, not whim.

Also again, the amounts of money need not be large to create a marketplace of ideas. In fact, money is not even necessary to create the needed competition. At Heart of the Beast, for example, the marketplace formed around the proposals for new productions. To get on the production schedule, staff had to submit a brief narrative for further review. As at MES, new ideas had to answer a series of tough questions to move forward:

What is the vision of the project?

What is the prime metaphor of the work?

What is the process to be used (individual, collaborative)?

Who will be the coordinator, director?

How large a cast?

What is the anticipated length of the run?

Heart of the Beast also asked whether there were any aspects of a project that might be controversial—not to censor itself, but to prepare for hardball. The system became essential for setting priorities in what is a very small nonprofit.

The Dowling School created a similar marketplace around quality improvement. Launched in 1992, its Positive Action Request (PAR) system was designed to ask students, teachers, parents, and staff what might be getting in the way of good service. Each PAR statement asked for a description of the barrier to quality ("dust, dirt, cobwebs in classroom"), a suggested action ("need regular cleaning in addition to daily sweeping"), and a cost to quality ("dirty rooms are not good learning environments"). It was then up to a quality team to rank the requests and take action. In fact, it was a dirty bathroom that started the PAR process in the first place. How could Dowling honor its commitment to caring for its mix of children if the only bathroom available to the wheelchair-bound was filthy?

Although not an innovative act per se, the introduction of the PAR system was an expression of the ordinary good practice that creates space for innovation. Rather than struggling with how to keep the bathrooms clean, staff could think about how to teach children more effectively. Because Dowling did not have the resources to do everything, the PAR system was also a priority-setting device through which competing visions of the school could be assessed. At the beginning, most of the problems were dust-and-cobweb issues. As the system matured and the low-hanging fruit was picked, PAR became an increasingly important device for making decisions. As problems became more complex, costs to quality more diffuse, actions more far-reaching, and priority setting more central to Dowling's work, PAR became an internal marketplace for sorting the options.

Prepare for Stress

Innovating organizations are stressful places to be. Talking about missions, personal and organizational, can get uncomfortable, as can the competition for scarce resources. Shocks to the system and constant turbulence are unsettling at best, downright threatening at worst. Much as the experts remind organizations that stress is healthy and natural, it is stress nonetheless.

Consider WomenVenture as one example. Merging two radically different organizations into a new agency was anything but easy. Although CHART and WEDCO were both dedicated to helping women achieve, they had very different programs and targets. CHART was a career counseling agency for women struggling to reenter the workforce, whereas WEDCO was an economic development agency. CHART offered job search skills, WEDCO microloans. CHART appealed largely to women who wanted to get back into the workforce; WEDCO targeted women who wanted to start their own businesses.

Forced together in 1989 by financial circumstance, the two organizations were unwilling to give up their old identities or loyalties. For the first two years of the merger, the new organization was known as CHART/WEDCO, even though the executive director and most of the board came from WEDCO. "We took two very different systems, or ways, of operating organizations that had somewhat different missions and combined them in a very short time period," Kathy Keeley, CHART/WEDCO's president, told the *Minneapolis StarTribune* early in the merger. "We both thought we were doing the same thing. We both cared about women, but after that it was different about how we did that. Talk about all the issues like name and location, putting together budgets and staffing. Probably three-quarters of the staff jobs have changed as a result of the merge; the board, bylaws, articles, all of our policies and procedures internally had to be changed."

Renamed WomenVenture in 1991 to create a common identity among the CHART and WEDCO staffs the organization remained deeply divided. As one employee remembered, "We had our offices and they had theirs. There was really no effort to get ourselves around a common anything." Celebrated by ABC News and 60 *Minutes* as an engine of welfare reform only a few years before, WomenVenture, né CHART/WEDCO, seemed ready to collapse.

WomenVenture now began rebuilding under a new president, Kay Gudmestad. Her mission was definitely not to innovate but to manage a financial crisis that would cause a 60 percent staff cut in her first year. Stress was inevitable, as were complaints from the staff, some of which wound up on the pages of the *Minneapolis Star-Tribune*. "I think people are really stressed out and afraid," said the board chair at the time. "'Is it going to be me next?' It causes people to behave strangely." "We are focusing on end results, and certainly some people decided that's not for them," Gudmestad told the newspaper. "Things don't turn out the way people wanted and they say hurtful things."At the same time, something miraculous was happening. The number of clients served was increasing, and the budget was inching upward. WomenVenture was coming back to life. "We have really moved to more performance-based outcomes, so people know when they have succeeded," said Gudmestad early in her tenure. "We have moved to being very clear about when you had a goal and you achieved it. And when you have not, you also know that."

Having first visited WomenVenture in 1990, I can attest to the change. The agency seemed to cry out, "ENTER AT YOUR OWN RISK"—not exactly a healthy message for an organization dedicated to serving women who wanted to get back to work. By 1994, traffic was up, staff doors were open, the career counseling library was abuzz, and new programs were emerging around a common agenda. And by 1996, the payroll was back up to thirty full-time employees, the budget had increased by half, and WomenVenture had broadened its activities to include, among other things, an economic development program for Hmong refugees. Equally important, it had kept past innovations alive.

Project Blueprint is a case in point. A comprehensive preapprenticeship program to train women in the building trades and other nontraditional occupations, Project Blueprint reflected a synthesis of CHART's old commitment to career training and WEDCO's promise of new opportunities. Started under Keeley and expanded under Gudmestad, the project gave women access to much higher-paying jobs than traditional "women's work."

Not every innovating organization will experience the depth of despair and stress that faced WomenVenture. But it should not expect bliss either. Over half of the Surviving Innovation organizations reported conflict over ideas and decisions, and two-thirds reported both high staff turnover and high stress in their organizations.

Indeed, stress is both inevitable in an innovating organization and essential for keeping the mission true. "If you have consensus on an important matter, don't make the decision," writes Peter Drucker in *Managing the Nonprofit Organization*. "Adjourn it so that everybody has a little time to think. Important decisions are risky. They *should* be controversial" (1990, p. 124). Stress is the other side of the innovating coin. On one side is the joy that comes from accomplishing something worthwhile; on the other is the stress that results from challenging the prevailing wisdom, whether inside the organization or in the outside world.

Maximize Diversity

One of the great surprises of the Surviving Innovation project was the relatively limited use of diversity as a tool for innovativeness. Barely half of the organizations were connected to the communities they served through a diverse staff.

The Surviving Innovation sample itself was remarkably diverse. It included organizations dedicated to helping Chicanos and Latinos, Hmong, African Americans, Native Americans, gays and lesbians, the developmentally disabled, older citizens and teenagers, women, and the poor. If the twenty-six organizations and their ten thousand staff had been gathered together in an auditorium, the assembly would have been as diverse as any imaginable.

But within each agency, diversity was less apparent. Although many of the organizations actively sought intellectual and professional diversity, only a handful made racial and gender diversity a priority. I believe that was, and is, a fundamental mistake in terms of innovativeness. If innovative ideas are randomly distributed within an organization, it stands to reason that diversity is one way to increase the range of perspectives needed to innovate.

The problem for many organizations, whether innovative or not, is what might be called the *not like us* syndrome. Organizations tend to search for staff who fit a prevailing image of the good employee, and this is often based on the shared experiences of the people already employed. If most people in an organization are white or male, the prevailing image of the good employee will likely be white or male. If the only candidates that need apply look like *us*, diversity will be hard to achieve.

The not like us syndrome applies not only to race and gender but also to intellectual and professional history. If most people in an organization have a social work degree, the prevailing image of the good employee will likely be someone with a similar academic background.

Although intellectual and professional diversity is no substitute for racial and gender diversity, neither is racial and gender diversity a substitute for intellectual and professional diversity. It is in defining diversity to include the widest range of perspectives that an organization increases the odds of generating new ideas. Having female and minority versions of the prevailing intellectual and professional template will certainly increase the range of perspectives on which an organization can draw, but venturing beyond that template will yield far greater benefits.

Consider how the not like us syndrome affects academic recruitment. "The problem we face," I wrote of schools of public policy in 1994, "is less that *there aren't any minority candidates out there*, which is the most common refrain from search committees. Rather, the problem is more that *there aren't any minority candidates LIKE US out there*. By 'us,' I mean those who represent the prevailing patterns of training, career, and publication that tend to dominate most of our schools" (Light, 1994, p. 166). Success in recruiting women and minority employees depends in large measure on inviting and valuing candidates who bring new perspectives to the organization. Unfortunately, far too many organizations approach diversity as either a social obligation or a legal requirement—as a way to assuage their troubled souls or a response to extreme pressure, perhaps even a lawsuit. Neither approach is particularly effective in actually increasing diversity, for the dialogue that ensues rings false to candidates. "To really read someone's work and to ask a question about it demonstrates that you know something about what this person is spending all of his or her life on," one of my colleagues at the Humphrey Institute once remarked about what works in a search. "That's a big chunk out of your life to have worked on, to have produced a dissertation, to have produced a book and then another one, and you're coming to a place to interview and they're asking you about everything *but* your work. That would be a real disappointment."

Age Gracefully

Younger and older organizations clearly face different challenges in sustaining innovativeness. For young organizations, the challenge tends to be one of sheer survival. For middle-aged organizations, the challenge is to hold the edge as they gain a measure of financial security. For mature organizations, the challenge is to manage the natural transitions that are necessary for keeping the spark of innovativeness alive. As Chapter Seven suggests, the older an organization gets, the more it needs to stay young. Older organizations such as Luther Theological Seminary, St. Joseph's Home for Children, and the Minnesota Extension Service either reinvent themselves or fade into mediocrity.

Age is only a rough indicator, however, of an organization's position on its life curve. As nonprofit consultant Susan Stevens argues, organizations move through a series of distinctive stages: idea, start-up, growth, full development, decline, turnaround, and terminal phase (1992, p. 3). But as surely as night follows day, they must eventually renew themselves or face extinction. "Often organizations fail to recognize that they are terminal," writes Stevens. "Indeed many groups function in a marginalized capacity for a very long time before calling it quits. Many nonprofits in fact never formally close up shop, they just wither away" (p. 5). The challenge is to renew the organization before the decline accelerates too far, whether through new leadership, restructuring, or an infusion of fresh talent.

The Surviving Innovation sample included three housing development organizations that illustrate the lesson: Phoenix, Central Community Housing Trust, and Project for Pride in Living. Phoenix started out as the youngest of the three but accelerated rapidly through the life curve, dying an early and (I think) preventable death. It most certainly did not age gracefully. By accelerating so rapidly, Phoenix jumped directly from childhood into adulthood, with no intermediate learning. "Nobody there had a clue in my estimation of how to manage their way out of a paper bag," said the board chair in a candid postmortem interview with the *Twin Cities Reader*. "What Phoenix originally intended to do was to have the management emerge from *the people*, if you understand what I'm saying, but the people were unbelievably dysfunctional."

In contrast, CCHT was already well established by the time it became part of the Surviving Innovation project. It had gone through several years of learning and was well versed in how to raise and invest housing development funds. Its challenge was not to learn but to stay alive and innovative.

Indeed, CCHT had become so well established that it had started to attract criticism from neighborhood groups as being too conservative—and from corporate developers as being too liberal. *Corporate Report Minnesota* even described CCHT as "a business where you have no competitors, where you invest none of your own capital, where you, your lender, and, if you have one, your for-profit partner don't have to worry about failing because somebody else— the city, foundations, well-meaning corporations—will pay for your mistakes" (Weiffering, 1994). During this same period, residents of the Stevens Square neighborhood were arguing that CCHT was out of touch with the people.

CCHT answered its middle-age crisis by continuing to innovate. While expanding its innovative use of for-profit firms as managers of its more than six hundred apartments, it laid out plans for an integrated housing program in downtown Minneapolis for homeless youth, a long-neglected population in the housing development field. The organization's attitude to naysayers could be gleaned from an aphorism the CCHT executive director used as a computer screen-saver: "If 'ifs' and 'buts' were candy and nuts, every day would be Christmas." This is not to say CCHT ignored the press, but it was prepared for hardball and ready to keep innovating as a response to the criticism. It was aging gracefully.

Just across town, Project for Pride in Living was dealing with a very different challenge: how to manage the transition of Joe Selvagio into retirement. As the founder and chief fundraiser for the organization, Selvagio was essential to PPL's success, and PPL was essential to him. His was a unique voice in the Twin Cities community and a compassionate hand inside PPL.

To survive his retirement, however, PPL had to do the unthinkable and start planning for the separation. The key, according to Selvagio's successor, was an honest and explicit understanding of who was doing what as the transition began. "Some said it couldn't be done smoothly, that disaster was imminent, or that Joe would have to be pried out," he remarked. "But we made the steps clear and the goal obvious." It also helped that Selvagio and his successor were equally committed to making the transition work. Having founded the organization and nurtured it through the life curve, the last thing Selvagio wanted to do was destroy PPL on his way out. Just as he was aging gracefully, PPL was too.

Conclusion

At the risk of offending my colleagues in the structuralist community, I must note that the Surviving Innovation project suggests relatively low returns from structural reforms. Much as I believe organizations should flatten their hierarchies, rewire their organization charts, and generally make things fit, most of the Surviving Innovation organizations did quite well without such restructuring. For every Anoka County, Luther Theological Seminary, and Minnesota Extension Service that took on the hierarchy, there was a

Heart of the Beast, Walker Art Center, or St. Joe's that was highly innovative without flattening, rewiring, or refolding.

This does not mean structure is irrelevant to innovativeness. Even if they decide not to take on the hierarchy, for example, innovating organizations must keep the layers to a minimum. Some will opt for a *virtual* flattening by installing e-mail and other information technologies that snake around the layers; others will perform a bypass by creating *stovepipes* or *idea tubes* that pull ideas upward from the bottom. (We will return to these idea systems in Chapter Six.) And even if they decide not to rewire their organization charts, innovating organizations must push authority downward. Some will do so by giving their frontline employees real authority to spend money or make decisions; others will use innovation investment funds to prime the organizational pump.

The lesson is not to ignore structure but to work with it to create the freedom to imagine. Each organization has to deal with the structural barriers to innovation in its own way. No matter what the structuralists say, there is no secret organization chart that ensures innovativeness. Find some common space, push authority downward, create an innovation investment fund, and expect miracles. As the next chapter will argue, one of the key tasks of leadership is to decide just what comes first in creating the conditions for others to succeed.

5

Changing the Leader's Work

"Preparing to expect wonders" was the centerpiece of the Heart of the Beast Puppet and Mask Theater May Day Festival. Like the May Days before it, the 1994 festival emerged from a community brainstorming session. The theme, "Awesome Vessels of Power," was based on a simple statement by Henry David Thoreau: "Convince me that you have a seed there and I am prepared to expect wonders." One can never know exactly what will come of the seed planted in fertile soil. All one can do is prepare to expect the wonder that will eventually rise from the muddy ground.

For Heart of the Beast, every production was a seed to be nurtured into wonder. All of its work was original and refined in community workshops of one kind or another. Its productions were not so much written down as grown. All of its puppets were built by hand, from recyclable materials. Having started in 1974 as the Powderhorn Puppet Theater, Heart of the Beast had grown into a major force, not just for artistic expression but for community pride and renewal.

Its new theater building, located just three blocks from the Mississippi in east Minneapolis, was one tangible expression of its commitment to a vital and healthy culture. Having been evicted from its previous space by the fire marshal, Heart of the Beast raised the dollars to reclaim the historic Avalon Theater, which had been converted to a pornographic movie house in the 1960s. Not only would the art deco theater give Heart of the Beast a permanent home, its renovation would be a first step in rebuilding the East Lake Street corridor. (One reason Heart of the Beast painted its mission in bright colors on the building's outside wall was to make sure the neighborhood knew the Avalon's function had changed.)

Although Heart of the Beast was not an economic development agency per se, its future depended on the fostering of a vibrant community. "We believe that art and culture have the power to transform our lives and to play a crucial role in unifying and inspiring our community," declared the theater's mission statement. It hardly made sense to celebrate spring in a community cursed by perpetual economic winter. It also made little sense to have a community theater with ticket prices so high that no one in the neighborhood could attend. That is why the theater dropped its price from $9 to $5 in 1994.

Perhaps it was mere coincidence that the Surviving Innovation Project visited Heart of the Beast just after the festival's story board had been painted on an inside wall. "Hold eternity in your hand," it said. "Wake 'midst the rain and mud." "Sprout!" "Struggle to become." "Blossom in the community." "Give your seeds to tomorrow's garden!" "We are seeds," the festival proclaimed of the Powderhorn Park community, "we are awesome vessels of power!"

But the timing of the visit could not have been better. Whether by accident or divine intervention, the theme seemed to capture the general lesson of leadership that was already emerging from the other Surviving Innovation organizations. The vast majority of their leaders were prepared to expect wonders. They tilled the organizational soil, sowed the seeds of change, prayed for sun and rain, watched the ideas sprout, and protected the young crops as they began to grow. The leaders I came to admire most were planters who believed in the awesome vessels of power inside and outside their organizations. They did not have to do everything themselves in heroic defiance. They created the conditions for others to succeed.

Preparing to Expect Wonders

A half-century ago, the leader's work was easily described in a seven-letter acronym created by Gulick: POSDCORB. The seven key elements Gulick identified and his descriptions of each were (Gulick and Urwick, 1937, pp. 12–13)

Planning	"Working out in broad outline the things that need to be done and the methods for doing them"
Organizing	"The establishment of the formal structure of authority through which work subdivisions are arranged"
Staffing	"The whole personnel function of bringing in and training the staff"
Directing	"The continuous task of making decisions and embodying them in specific and general orders and instructions"
Coordinating	"The all important duty of interrelating the various parts of the work"
Reporting	"Keeping those to whom the executive is responsible informed as to what is going on"
Budgeting	"Fiscal planning, accounting and control"

In short, concentrate authority in the one true master of the organization, who would oversee a vast empire of subdivisions all designed to make the leader's work easier.

No one talks much about POSDCORB anymore—except to argue that it is essentially irrelevant. Although leaders are still responsible for many of the tasks outlined by Gulick, they must do so in a high-speed, information-driven world where no one master could ever hope to keep up. Moreover, as the thickening of government suggests, POSDCORB was not always healthy for organizational life. Concentrating authority at the top actually increased the likelihood that organizations would thicken with needless layers of oversight and control, becoming less and less efficient with the passage of time (see Light, 1995).

In today's post-POSDCORB world, it is not always clear what the leader's work is. Once again, where one stands on the issue depends on what one believes about the sources of creativity and new ideas. Leaders who believe that creativity is the gift of the special few would never push authority downward or democratize, for example. Because they already know who will innovate, they would concentrate authority at the very top, where they could use it for anointing stars and mad scientists. And because they would have achieved their leadership status by being brilliant themselves—or so they would tell themselves—they would make sure every last detail funneled to the top.

Leaders who believe that creativity is randomly distributed throughout an organization (or, for Heart of the Beast, a neighborhood) would take a different direction. They would spend their time creating conditions that allowed others to flourish. Because they could not know where an idea might develop, they would invite ideas upward from every corner of the organization. They would spread resources across a range of possibilities and would work to make sure their awesome vessels of power had the support, rain, and sun to flourish. They would see their work as being the creation of conditions in which others could succeed and the building of an organizational culture that supported risk taking and new ideas. (See Hatch, 1993, for a discussion of the elements of culture.)

At least for the Surviving Innovation organizations, preparing to expect wonders was the prevailing view of the leader's work. Those who led the twenty-six organizations were hardly naive about human nature. Most had stories of employees gone wrong and ideas lost to jealousy and bitterness. But they chose to see the positive potential in each employee rather than the negative. They designed for innovation, even as they made sure their organizations had the systems to limit damage. Call it a *rigorous optimism*. They created that optimism by adopting ten practices that helped them achieve a preferred leadership.

1. Change the leader's work.

2. Be clear about who decides.

3. Issue a call for ideas.

4. Give the permission to fail.

5. Communicate to excess.

6. Pay attention to sequencing.

7. Teach the organization how to say no and why to say yes.

8. Keep faith and intuition alive.

9. Stay balanced.

10. Keep innovation in perspective.

Change the Leader's Work

The first task for many of the leaders in the Surviving Innovation sample was to change the prevailing wisdom about their own work. They had to debunk the notion that good leadership means concentrated authority and tight subdivisions. They had to help their organizations get over POSDCORB, particularly its one true master ideology. They had to abandon the traditional images of compliance-based accountability in favor of accountability based on results. Their job was not to create new structure and control but to get rid of the old; not to create new barriers to creativity but to lower the old.

Many of the Surviving Innovation organizations allowed their leaders to do all these things. Recall that a very high percentage of the Surviving Innovation leaders had entered their posts as part of a transition from concentrated rule to democracy. Their boards either wanted something different from the traditional POSDCORB leader or, at the very least, were ready to try a new approach.

(Also note, from Appendix C, that 85 percent of the sample had a participatory/democratic leadership style.)

Kathryn Roberts is a perfect example. Roberts arrived at the Minnesota Zoo in 1986 on a temporary assignment. The first director had left, attendance was falling, and the state legislature was considering a cut in the zoo's annual appropriation. Having built her reputation in a series of similar assignments, Roberts's mission was to hold the organization together as the board began a search for a more traditional director—meaning someone with the proper credentials. Eleven years later, Roberts was still there.

Roberts clearly brought a different leadership style to the zoo. For starters, she was not a zoologist. She had earned her Ph.D. in educational administration and could barely tell the difference between a leopard and a lemur on her first day. Although she later adopted a chinchilla and several tropical fish, she had exactly the wrong degree to be easily accepted among the animal experts. Moreover, she had absolutely no experience with zoos of any kind—unless one characterizes state government as a zoo of sorts.

The only thing she had was a sense of how to rescue the zoo. "When I accepted the job, there was no shortage of really sharp people working here who knew everything they can possibly know about exotic animals and their care," she later told the *Minneapolis StarTribune*. "What was lacking was the ability to run the zoo as a business. I have channeled my energies into filling that gap."

Knowing that she could never challenge the expertise already present, Roberts began building a different kind of organization. Her job was definitely not to do the planning, ordering, or controlling but to provide the spark (or sun and rain, if you will) that would allow these awesome vessels of power already inside the organization to succeed. Her main strategy was to invite the market in for a permanent visit.

After weeding out the existing leadership team (no one ever said that innovating always means saying yes), Roberts spent her time letting business happen. She cleared the underbrush, then got out of the way. That meant recruiting a different kind of board, for example—one that did not care whether the zoo "used a hand pencil sharpener or electric as long as the points were sharp." It also meant getting the state legislature to give the zoo its gate receipts. "If the zoo didn't have its gate receipts," Roberts explained, "there would be no incentive for keeping the focus on increasing attendance. And without that focus, no one would care about making the zoo better. The market worked as a cold splash of reality."

Roberts was not the only liberator in the Surviving Innovation sample. There was Pat Borich at the Minnesota Extension Service, Carol Arthur at the Domestic Abuse Project, Kay Gudmestad at WomenVenture, Kathy Halbreich at Walker Art Center, Jim Walker at North Branch, Doug Goke at St. Joseph's Home for Children, the self-managed teams at Cyrus Math/Tech and the Minnesota Office of Waste Management   the list goes on and on.

Not all of the Surviving Innovation democrats arrived after a coup, however. At Episcopal Community Services, Carole Mae Olson had pretty much always run things democratically, and the same is true of Jeff Raison at the Dowling Environmental School and Alan Arthur at the Central Community Housing Trust.

Democracy was always a core operating principle for Mary Kay Kennedy, executive director of Advocating Change Together (ACT). To be true to ACT's mission, Kennedy had no other choice but to empower others. One need only page through ACT's annual reports, newsletters, and strategic plan to see the principle in action. Readers will never find a picture of the executive director or a summary of her role in tilling the organizational fields. She is completely submerged in support of the organization. Taking her post as ACT began to drift after its early legislative victories, Kennedy raised the dollars for a strategic planning process that redefined ACT as a consumer organization. Instead of talking about people with disabilities as victims or clients, ACT committed itself to "encouraging consumers to play active roles not only in ACT, but in their churches, neighborhoods, political parties and government." Said one of

ACT's board members: "Some people thought that because of my disability I would never amount to anything, that I didn't belong in the community. This hurts. I showed them that I am a good citizen and that I can make a difference in the community. I'm as good a citizen as anyone and I'm proud of it."

Be Clear About Who Decides

One of the greatest challenges in a democratic organization is to know who decides what. Employee involvement and participation efforts can create the expectation, whether correct or not, that employees should be allowed to vote on everything. There can also be a paralysis of consensus, in which endless discussion eventually ties the organization in knots.

There are at least two cures for decision paralysis in nonprofit and government organizations. The first is to establish the ultimate authority of the chief executive. At Chicanos Latinos Unidos En Servicio, that clarity came from the executive director, who left the organization in 1994 to become a Ramsey County Commissioner. His vision of the leader's work was to be the coach, with all that meant for both recruiting the team and designing plays. "I make the calls," he said of the inevitable problems that arise in a flat organization. "If I want to keep someone on the bench, that is where they sit. I'm not out on the floor passing the ball and making the shot. That's up to the players and depends on the opportunities that arise. I coach the best I can and give tight direction, but the players must make the plays."

At Chance to Grow, the clarity came from Bob and Kathy DeBoer. In a field flooded by innovations—from a hug machine for autistic children to colored glasses for the improvement of reading skills—the DeBoers had undisputed authority over all new initiatives. "We don't want to get the reputation for doing anything kooky," said one of the Chance to Grow staff. "We work in a very conservative domain. Therefore, everything we do has to have a strong chance of success."

For Chance to Grow, the challenge was to extend the invitation for new ideas without making any promises about the ultimate decision. The DeBoers would decide on the basis of the best available evidence. Hunch and intuition would have a role at the start of the review, but hard evidence would carry the day. The DeBoers were never arbitrary in their decisions. "Is it logical?" the DeBoers would ask. "Does it make sense with what we know about the brain?" If the answer was yes, Chance to Grow might launch a small experiment. The DeBoers clearly had a bias in favor of action. "Our staff doesn't always have the luxury of professional objectivity," said one of the senior team. "Every hour, the kids are further behind. We are not interested in wasting time on bad ideas." Even though they never adopted the hug machine as part of their program, they built one just to see how it worked. To this day, it is stored in the DeBoer garage.

The second cure for decision paralysis in nonprofit and government organizations is to create clear boundaries between staff and board. Lack of this clarity eventually led the Central Community Housing Trust to undertake a remarkably difficult yet productive division of responsibilities, which one staffer once described as like "dividing Siamese twins." At one point in its history, the board so dominated executive functions that it interviewed potential renters and read water meters in CCHT buildings. "We needed to move from a conversation about what the staff couldn't do," said a senior administrator, in looking back on his early discussions with the board, "to one about where the staff ended and the board began."

Working item by item through the organization's operations, CCHT developed a seventeen-point board-staff policy. This included a description of board governing style ("The board will approach its management task with a style which emphasizes strategic leadership more than administrative detail, clear distinction of board and staff roles, future rather than past or present, and pro-activity rather than re-activity"), a board code of conduct ("board members must represent faithfulness to the mission of CCHT"), and a deep list of limitations on the executive director's authority. The executive director was prohibited from violating commonly accepted business practices, jeopardizing the organization's financial integrity, or risking any losses beyond those necessary in the normal course of business.

Although detailed almost to a fault, the agreement was not self-executing. It all depended on the board's pushing authority down into the organization, which in turn depended on the organization's providing the kind of information that would satisfy the board. The key to success turned out to be Board Monitoring Reports, which covered everything from cash flow to occupancy rates, housing demographics, housing development updates, and recent press clips.

Nothing about the internal governance of CLUES, Chance to Grow, or CCHT was innovative in itself. But clarity about decision making is essential to the ordinary good practice that allows an innovating organization to prosper. A senior administrator at CCHT likens such clarity to fundamental maintenance in one of his rental properties: "When I go into a building, I always check the boiler room first. If it is clean, you can be pretty sure the rest of the building is working. If it is filthy, get ready for what you'll see inside the walls and behind the building." Cleaning that boiler room may not yield much glory, but it is an essential part of the leader's work.

Issue a Call for Ideas

There is nothing more important to an innovating organization than the signal that ideas are welcome. This may be conveyed either by a formal idea generator (suggestion box, innovation investment fund) or by a simple invitation. Innovating organizations rightly assume that many employees are just waiting to be asked.

The leadership challenge is to convey that new ideas will be not only welcomed but given a fair hearing. As far as the welcome is concerned, the organization must be ready to say yes to an idea. If its only responses to incoming ideas are "No," "Not ready," "Too big,"

"Too small," "Maybe later," and "No" again, the ideas will stop flowing. False invitations are easily detected.

As to the fair hearing, the organization must be clear about what it values in an idea. Just as it must ask how it will know if it is succeeding in its mission, an innovating organization must be clear on how it will value ideas. The minute employees detect a special pecking order, they will cease to offer their proposals. We will return to the question of how innovating organizations winnow ideas later in the chapter. For now, suffice it to note that the organization must make clear what it values in ideas *before* it issues the call for suggestions. Presented after the fact, such criteria almost always appear to be an ex post facto rationalization for decisions already made.

Organizations can go too far in issuing the call. Phoenix never said no to anything, opening new businesses and developing properties almost at random. The founders certainly had a vision of what a vibrant neighborhood would look like—a café, a grocery store, decent housing, and an auto repair shop. But this vision was in constant flux. It was never clear, for example, how an upholstering shop fit into the picture, except for the fact that it was a novel enterprise in an economically disadvantaged neighborhood.

Much as one can criticize its decisions in hindsight, Phoenix clearly created a bias for experimentation. The notion that any one person could change the organization was both a failing and a strength.

Other organizations in the Surviving Innovation sample subscribed to a similar, if more rigorous, approach. Their leaders expressed the same willingness to listen and the same obligation to say yes whenever basic criteria were satisfied.

The Dowling Environmental School is a case in point. Its principal, Jeff Raison, earned a reputation as both an effective listener and a strong champion for good ideas. He confirmed his commitment to both in his implementation of Total Quality Management (TQM). Everyone was allowed to participate in one way or another—parents, teachers, bus drivers, custodians, cafeteria workers, and students.

Although TQM may not be an innovation per se, Raison's definition of the participants most certainly was. The notion that first-graders might have a voice in deciding what the cafeteria serves for lunch or that fifth-graders might have as strong a voice in technology planning as the adults clearly challenged the prevailing wisdom in fundamental ways. Dowling was hardly alone in Minneapolis, let alone the rest of the nation, in establishing a site council to oversee the school, but it clearly violated conventions in giving students a voice as key consumers of the educational product. It is no surprise that teacher after teacher told me that the first thing they did with an idea was go to Raison.

Pat Borich played a similar coaching and cajoling role as the dean and director of the Minnesota Extension Service. Recruited as dean after spending thirty years in various MES posts, Borich's invitation to the organization was a variation of the common saying "'Tis better to have loved and lost than never to have loved at all."

Unlike Raison, who grounded his call in the effort to build a unique learning environment, Borich issued his call as a survival strategy. MES could either take control of its future or fade into irrelevance. Speaking to the MES staff at an administrative retreat just after his appointment in 1984, Borich called upon his colleagues to rebuild MES, not as it was in the 1950s but as it needed to be in the next century. "He got into a sailboat analogy," one of the senior staff remembered, "describing everyone as sailboats, all headed in the same direction. This was not to be a race. We were all welcome to stop along the way, but we all had to reach the other shore. He would do his best to support us if we did the best we could."

By 1991, when yet another budget crisis swept across MES, the time for leisurely sails had long passed. This time, Borich had to get all the boats to sail together—and fast. His challenge was to simultaneously flatten the hierarchy, root out the deadwood, formalize the county clusters, and innovate. "We're never going back to the past," said one senior manager in our interviews. "Change and ambiguity is now part of our mission. Some people are still looking for the one right way, but it doesn't exist anymore. We have to breathe confidence into the organization to deal with what will always be a fluid process."

Although the pressure clearly served as a wake-up call, it also raised the risks of innovating. Employees can easily imagine ideas that might help the organization—for example, streamlining the hierarchy or introducing labor-saving technology—but that also threaten their jobs. The fact that county clustering had involved some job losses certainly did not lessen the tension. The question for Borich and MES, therefore, was how to make the call for ideas *trustworthy*. How could Borich reassure employees that ideas (1) were welcome, (2) would be evaluated fairly, and (3) would not come back to hurt them?

Borich's answer was threefold. First, he tried to segregate the conversation about new ideas from the budget pressure. To the extent possible, therefore, he issued the call for ideas as part of a broad message about building an Extension for the 2000s. He talked of the whole organization, not its parts, even to the point of devoting a not-insignificant sum to a redesign of the MES logo so that every unit was linked to the whole, if not yet by a clear future, then at least by a common letterhead.

Second, even as he reinforced a common mission, he pushed enormous authority down into the counties. The clusters had authority to set their own program agendas, negotiate with their respective counties on staff allocations, and in at least one case, invent a new pay system to reward teams of employees rather than individuals with annual pay increases. Where he could, Borich gave the organization freedom to breathe, as did his key lieutenant, Gail Skinner-West.

Third, Borich was not afraid to take a stand on principle. Consider as one small example a speech he delivered in 1994 at the Cluster 29 picnic in Lake Crystal, a tiny farming town seventy miles southeast of Minneapolis. Standing in front of one hundred farmers gathered at the local American Legion post around plates of prime rib and marshmallow salad, Borich delivered an impassioned talk on the need to confront rural racism. He would have been on much more comfortable ground talking about the cluster's success in dealing with hog waste or crop stabilization, but he saw a more immediate task at hand. With corporate farms increasingly dependent on migrant labor, racism was on the rise in rural Minnesota. Borich called the farmers to take action against the narrowness. As stories of Borich's willingness to take hard positions with old friends worked their way through the organization, he built a store of trust that gave a ring of truth to his call for a new MES.

What Borich could not do was promise his staff that their good ideas would not hurt them. He could not adopt a no lay-off policy, as some nonprofit and government organizations do at the start of a reinventing process, nor could he guarantee even a token severance plan for those about to lose their jobs. No one can know whether MES would have done even better had it been able to protect its employees. Moreover, as Borich later argued, some cuts were essential for weeding the system of recalcitrant staff. Like the Minnesota Zoo and WomenVenture, the cuts created a heightened awareness of the need for action.

Give the Permission to Fail

Even as the leaders of innovating organizations invite ideas upward, they must simultaneously give the permission to fail. The old saying calls for trial and error, not trial and success. If innovation is a product of fine-tuning, groping along, and what Levin and Sanger call evolutionary tinkering, part of the leader's work is to send clear signals that mistakes are to be not merely tolerated but encouraged.

Error therefore is something to be valued. Consider for a moment how Levin and Sanger describe the process of innovating in nonprofit and government organizations: "Evolutionary tinkering—using bits and pieces of what is around in new ways to meet changing circumstances—is iterative, incremental, and disorderly. Failure—error—becomes the basis for evolutionary learning. Analysis occurs at the implementation stage, after a process that is begun to 'do the doable'" (1992, p. 101). Innovativeness occurs not through careful analysis at the front end of the idea process but through an aim-fire-ready process that is often born of crisis. The focus is on correcting errors, on speed and action, and on opportunism.

I am by no means convinced that all innovative acts are merely old stuff used in new ways. Surely, much of what we saw in Surviving Innovation organizations like Chance to Grow, Heart of the Beast, Advocating Change Together, the Walker Art Center, and the Domestic Abuse Project was new stuff, pure and simple. Nor do I believe, as Levin and Sanger do, that it is the leader's work to create the agency's mission and develop the organizational culture. The Surviving Innovation leaders did not so much substitute their vision for the organization's as ask hard questions about mission, focus attention on the outside world, and strip away the barriers to doing what comes naturally to highly committed organizations—that is, innovate. But I do agree that evolutionary tinkering is a critical piece of the leader's work. Inviting ideas upward without giving permission to fail ensures ultimate failure.

This permission can be given in many ways—for example, through an innovation investment fund that acknowledges a reasonable failure rate, a New Orleans funeral for a project that failed, an awards program for the year's most impossible dream, even for-giveness coupons and permission slips from the executive director. President Clinton's first secretary of education, Richard Riley, gave permission slips to every employee in the department. The slip read, in part, "Ask yourself: one, is it good for my customers? Two, is it legal and ethical? Three, is it something I am willing to be account-able for? If the answers to these questions are yes, don't ask permis-sion. You already have it. Just do it!"

The problem with such slips and coupons is that they are rarely accepted at all stores. If the legislature or board does not agree, the slips are not worth the paper on which they are printed. They can create a false sense of liberation. And they can trick employees into believing they, not their political leaders, are the ones most responsible for bringing innovation forth against the odds.

Whatever the device, experience suggests that the permission must be given over and over if it is to stick. Most of our nonprofit and government organizations are so utterly terrified of making mistakes that their first response to such permission is a big "Yeah, right!" Rare is the candidate who wins office by promising to make lots of mistakes or the new executive director who is appointed with a résumé of failure. Whereas private firms can advertise their commitment to trial and error, most nonprofit and government agencies do better by giving permission quietly or in response to specific requests.

In Anoka County, getting the permission to fail meant going directly to the County Board of Commissioners for prior approval. Not every county would have been willing to let the human services staff create the Parents' Fair Share Program, for example. It was risky at best and clearly violated the prevailing wisdom on child support enforcement. At least for the purpose of improving enforcement statistics, it would have been far better to put a father in jail for nonsupport than to find him a job. "Why bother with deadbeat dads?" one of the program designers asked rhetorically, mimicking the opposition. "Unemployed noncustodial parents were viewed as just another of many inevitable and unsolvable social conditions."

Anoka's Division of Human Services had a different view: instead of jailing the father, why not put him in a job training and parenting skills program? That way, the children would benefit. They would get their child support and, in theory, a more active parent.

The first stop in launching the program was the Anoka County Board of Commissioners. One could have predicted the questions from the county mission statement: "The Mission of Anoka County is to preserve the public trust by serving Anoka County citizens in a compassionate, innovative and fiscally responsible manner." The board wanted to know, first, whether the idea satisfied common sense and, second, whether it would cost money.

As one of the poorest of the metropolitan counties, Anoka spent less per capita than 90 percent of all counties in the state and had kept its tax levy virtually constant for the better part of two decades. "We innovate partly out of necessity," said one senior official. "Anoka County is very conservative fiscally, but the demands for social services are skyrocketing. Families that move to Anoka County are not like families that move to the richer suburbs. They are mostly blue-collar, on the margins. If we don't innovate, we cannot keep up."

The fact that Parents' Fair Share won a McKnight Aid to Families in Poverty grant in 1988 certainly helped reassure the board on the cost question. But the board had seen other front-end grants obligate the county to back-end funding. "How many times have we been forced to kill a special program that started with a grant?" one Anoka commissioner asked. "If the program doesn't have a good cost structure at the beginning, we'd rather not take the first grant." Luckily for Parents' Fair Share, the program clearly saved money. Factoring in county jail time, enforcement oversight, and general assistance, the program more than broke even.

Once the board signed on, the program had the freedom to do the evolutionary tinkering that eventually led to its Ford Foundation Innovations Award. In part because the board was so tax-sensitive, it had a reservoir of political capital with the public that could be spent in providing the space for new programs like Parents' Fair Share. Anoka was also blessed with a remarkably stable board. Four of the seven commissioners had been in office at least twelve years. Moreover, the board was part-time. Members served to serve, not to position themselves for statewide office. "The board gave us an absolute green light," said one of the Parents' Fair Share designers. "There was absolutely no money, but plenty of flexibility. God knows they micromanage some things like training dollars, but they never nitpick the big stuff. There were no hang-ups about credit, either. Once we got rolling, the entire focus was on whether the program would work."

Not all of the Surviving Innovation organizations required prior approval for evolutionary tinkering, however. Recall that the zoo made risk taking obvious in its business investment program: "We recognize that inherent in risk-taking is the potential for failure as well as great success." The zoo had the failures to prove it, too—in the coral reef overnights, a plan to rent video cameras, and an ant farm on the Northern Trail. Other organizations also had their share of failures, including an avant-garde video rental program at Walker. The Walker video rental business actually would have done quite well as a revenue producer had the designers been able to meet two challenges: parking and a late-night drop-off, which would have meant bulldozing the Sculpture Garden.

None of the Surviving Innovation organizations were more willing to give permission to fail than the American Indian Business Development Corporation. Although AIBDC hoped that each tenant in its business incubator would succeed, it accepted failure as a natural part of the process. Nevertheless, the organization sought to minimize risk whenever possible. In selecting tenants for its low-cost space, AIBDC's director, Brenda St. Germaine, relied on a mix of intuition and analysis. "In some cases, I've known the applicant and was willing to take a risk on a new start-up which in the end paid off," she wrote in a history of the Franklin Business Center. "You just 'click' with the personality of the applicant and you know that the tenant can make it *and* fit into the building. Other times, we might ask for a business plan, line of credit, credit references, and banking references." Sometimes, even the best informed decision goes wrong, as the following story illustrates:

> We had a tenant that I affectionately referred to as Dr. Pepper who produced products called herbal remedies. He was a highly creative, crazy kind of a guy who opened up shop and immediately employed six neighborhood people. He used his space to blend his herbs, package his product, and ship out across the country. However, what

I didn't know was that the main ingredient in his products was hot African cayenne pepper. When he would open a barrel of this stuff it would make its way through the air vents. It would not only stink up the whole building [all fifty-six thousand square feet of it], but caused tearing and burning eyes. Tenants would come into my office with tears streaming down their faces and threatening to move out if I didn't do something about Dr. Pepper. And I tried. We tried to block vents, we tried to contain the product in one area, and every morning I would spray the hallway by his door, but nothing worked. I finally had to relocate Dr. Pepper to another building down the street.

Part of the problem in giving the permission to fail, of course, is knowing just what failure is. "If you've never done something before," said one of the senior staff at Artspace, which develops combined housing and studio space for artists, "how do you know it's not a step you have to take to get to success?" Or as a sign on the Phoenix Group's wall said: "GOOD JUDGMENT COMES FROM EXPERIENCE. EXPERIENCE COMES FROM BAD JUDGMENT."

Once given, the permission to fail is usually tested when a failure actually occurs. It is one thing to whisper the permission at an annual retreat, quite another to celebrate a disaster when it happens. Leaders may be forgiven for getting angry when the organization makes the same mistake over and over, but they must learn to keep quiet when an experiment goes bad. To whatever extent possible, they should celebrate the mistake as a good faith effort, which is exactly what the zoo did when the coral reef overnights failed. That is arguably the strongest form of permission imaginable.

Communicate to Excess

Communicating is central to the leader's work in an innovating organization. Inviting ideas upward, giving permission to fail, asking questions of mission and outcome, and focusing the organization on the environment all involve communication. At least in the Surviving Innovation organizations, leaders communicated to excess. (See Ford and Ford, 1995, for a literature review and discussion of the role of conversation in creating momentum for organizational change.)

The first decision is what to communicate. Keeping secrets would not be a preferred state of being for an internal communications plan, for example. What if an employee asks about the pay raises in another department? What if someone wants to know about the latest budget crisis? What if there is a question about the rumored reorganization? One of the reasons leaders do not get out more is that they are scared about revealing secrets.

The easiest way to solve the problem is to reveal the secrets. Consider Anoka County, where one human services manager said, "We don't hide anything down here. If it doesn't fit under the protected data statutes, it's an open book. Nothing is secret anyway." Consider the zoo, where daily attendance figures were available through a recorded phone message, and where visitor complaints were posted in common areas for every employee to see. And consider MES, where budget information was available in such quantities that one senior staffer complained that "we sometimes knew too much. It would have been nice not to know how bad it was, but then again, we probably wouldn't have moved as far."

Once a leader decides what to reveal, he or she must decide how to communicate. Staff meetings? Most of the Surviving Innovation organizations had them. Retreats? Most of these organizations held them. Newsletters and house organs? Most published them. But by far the most important communication opportunities occurred through informal conversations and wandering around. Most of the Surviving Innovation leaders got out a lot. Brenda St. Germaine started each day with a walking tour of her building and strolled about frequently; Alan Arthur spent a great deal of time looking at boiler rooms with building managers; Jeff Raison wandered about, talking to students; Kathryn Roberts spent most of her days moving around, unpacking tropical fish for the coral reef exhibit one day, observing an unusual animal procedure another, greeting visitors another.

Communication also involves the outside world. Some of the Surviving Innovation organizations had nearly constant external exposure. Outreach was the very essence of Advocating Change Together, for example, which is why the organization spent so much time training consumers in how to write letters and make lobbying calls. It was also essential for Chance to Grow when it sought and won a charter from the Minneapolis School District. Not all the outreach was traditional, however. At the People Escaping Poverty Project in Moorehead, Minnesota, outreach involved organizing welfare mothers to engage with the governor in an Internet exchange on implementing the federal government's 1996 welfare reform.

A surprisingly high number of the Surviving Innovation organizations learned how to communicate as a result of some kind of crisis. Cyrus Math/Tech had the parents' phone tree incident, WomenVenture had the highly public complaints at a time of massive change, and the Minnesota Zoo had an intense controversy over a fireworks show during a winter festival.

In the zoo case, the enterprise staff had agreed to host the fireworks as part of a collaboration with the city of Apple Valley, its next-door neighbor. Although not a money-maker per se, the show was a good-faith gesture early in a relationship that would eventually lead to the Environmental High School. The only problem with fireworks is that they make noise, which in turn scares animals and birds. On hearing of the plans, the animal staff complained that they had never been fully involved in the decision, and they used the fireworks show as Exhibit A in arguing that the enterprise staff was overzealous. In the end, the zoo honored the commitment to Apple Valley. Backing out at the last minute would simply have been too drastic an action.

Pay Attention to Sequencing

Reading the scholarly literature on nonprofit and government innovation, one can easily conclude that success involves little more than opportunism and accident. Evolutionary tinkering and groping along are hardly terms that conjure up careful sequencing of change. Indeed, many of the scholars involved in the study of government innovation take a certain pride in puncturing the notion that planning and analysis have much to do with anything. Consider how Olivia Golden, who joined the Clinton administration in 1997 as an assistant secretary of Health and Human Services, summarizes a sample of early Ford Foundation award winners:

> In almost none of the cases did the innovation begin with a policy choice expressed through legislation.
>
> In many but not all of the cases, the innovative idea was not clear, complete, or well-specified at the beginning but instead evolved through practice. In these cases, the innovative idea was the culmination of the implementation process, not its starting point.
>
> Almost all of the programs were out on the street operating in some form very quickly, within a year. Thus they were characterized by very brief periods of prior planning, at least by the standards of large government bureaucracies.
>
> Typically, the programs were repeatedly modified in response to operation experience, reflecting managerial attention to the need for change [1990, p. 240].

This description of innovation as a blend of opportunism and accident resonates well in many, but not all, of the Surviving Innovation organizations. It accurately describes how the zoo's dolphin overnights emerged, but not Chance to Grow's brain gym. It helps to account for Heart of the Beast's May Day extravaganza, but not the Domestic Abuse Project's treatment program. It clearly captures the People Escaping Poverty Project's Internet dialogue with the North Dakota governor, but not the Dowling School's technology plan.

More important for the issue of changing the leader's work, the description relates only to the single act of innovation. Although groping along is a wonderful phrase for explaining how single innovations evolve into full-blown programs, it is exactly the wrong metaphor for describing how organizations create the freedom to imagine. Planning and analysis mattered very much to many of the Surviving Innovation organizations—and most certainly matter to the leader's work. The groping along did not occur in the dark.

The Surviving Innovation leaders clearly paid attention to the sequencing of organizational reform, a topic that Chapter Seven will deal with in detail. Suffice it to note here that although each of the Surviving Innovation leaders followed a somewhat different path, almost all laid out a broad vision of where they wanted the organization to go.

That is what Borich, Halbreich, and Kennedy did, for example, in taking the helm, respectively, at the Minnesota Extension Service, the Walker Art Center, and Advocating Change Together. Others used a less traditional *visioning* process, drawing broad images of what the organization might become. This was true of Nadya Reubenova at Heart of the Beast, Chuck Beattie and Bret Byfield at the Phoenix Group, and Kelley Linquist at Artspace.

Almost all of the Surviving Innovation leaders worked to develop an *itinerary* of sorts for their journey. Giving permission to fail was always an element of the trip, but that permission was almost always part of a broader map of how to get from A to B. (See Bryson and Roering, 1989, for a discussion of the role of strategic planning in shaping the innovation process.)

The Surviving Innovation leaders also paid attention to the type of innovation they pursued. As Appendix B shows, half of the Surviving Innovation organizations were *how* innovators, devoting most of their energy to changing the way a given service was delivered. Luther Theological Seminary is one example. With the Bible as a core text that would never change, the seminary focused on how to better deliver the curriculum in a changing world. The basic message remained the same.

Anoka County is another example. Although it certainly had some impressive *what* reforms, most notably the Parents' Fair Share program, most of its energy was centered on delivering existing services in novel ways, whether through unique collaborations (the Human Services Center), unique locations (a school in the juvenile corrections center), or unique exceptions (the merger of the auditor, recorder, and treasurer offices). Fond du Lac Community College is a third *how* innovator. Its very existence depended on changing how the community college worked. Students would still get a traditional education but in a very nontraditional setting.

The other half of the Surviving Innovation organizations were primarily *what* innovators, putting their energies into changing their basic product. The Walker Art Center is a perfect example. Its building was interesting, even novel, and the Sculpture Garden unique to the Twin Cities, but neither was particularly innovative in the arts. What Walker did was challenge the prevailing image of art itself, whether through its performing arts program, its film series, or its educational outreach.

The Domestic Abuse Project is also a *what* example. It had a fairly standard mix of individual and group sessions, all of which lasted a fairly standard number of minutes. Though it is quite appropriate to argue that DAP did innovate by chopping weeks off the standard treatment schedule—an act that created enormous criticism from entrenched programs—DAP's great innovation was in the substance of the treatment program itself and its willingness to present that program to batterers of any race, gender, or sexual preference.

As Chapter Seven suggests, the choice of *how* versus *what* innovation depends, at least in part, on the context in which the organization operates. Government agencies were much more likely to focus on *how* innovation, leaving the *what* to the legislature, whereas the nonprofits were much more likely to concentrate on *what* innovation, in part because they were more flexible organizationally to begin with.

The choice also involves a sense of which type of innovation comes first. Here, there is at least some scholarly research that suggests the following sequence: (1) the organization starts with a *what* innovation of some kind, which (2) forces it to consider a *how* innovation to keep the *what* innovation alive, which (3) creates even more opportunity for *what* innovation. (See Damanpour, Szabat, and Evan, 1989, for a report on sequencing in public libraries.) There is, of course, no hard-and-fast rule on which innovation to start with. The point here is merely to note that there is some reason to attend to both the type of innovation one desires and its sequencing. Piling one *what* innovation on top of another without any attention to *how* may spell eventual collapse.

Finally, the Surviving Innovation leaders paid attention to the overall level of innovation in their organizations. Contrary to the scholarly literature on public innovation, which seems to urge an unrelenting opportunism, most of the Surviving Innovation leaders had a sense of how much innovation was enough. Although they did not aim at some magic number of ideas, they did regulate the flow of pressure into the organization to make sure the level of activity was appropriate. They turned the pressure down when there were too many new ideas in play and pushed it up when there were too few. They became masters of timing.

The secret of timing is to maintain an innovation's upward momentum without overloading the organization. Leaders cannot delay the launch of a new idea too long without risking a complete loss of momentum, At the same time, they cannot put so much pressure on the organization that new ideas are coming on line so fast that they crowd each other. Such overproduction is a particularly virulent form of projectitis, the sickness that comes from unrelenting pressure to innovate at any cost. The result is an organization consumed with novelty and known for little else. The ideal scenario is to launch a new idea in time to capitalize on past momentum without diluting organizational focus.

Teach the Organization How to Say No and Why to Say Yes

The key to sequencing is knowing why to say yes and how to say no. Both responses must be based on considerations of mission. Organizations that do not know their mission will say yes to just about anything. They will constantly search for funding, no matter what the project, and will try one idea after another in an effort to stay current. They will worship innovation above all else, even to the point of diluting their mission in order to stay at the supposed cutting edge. External support will become the tail that wags the organization, eventually corroding any sense of purpose that might exist. Ideas that can attract funding will keep going regardless of their value. Afflicted with a bad case of projectitis, the organization will eventually become a novelty store, known more for funky programs than staying power.

The key question for an innovating organization, therefore, is how it will pick among competing ideas. Having turned itself toward the outside world, how will it know what fits and what does not? Having invited ideas upward, how will it pick and choose? The hotter the organization gets, the more it will be asked to do all things for all funders.

That was certainly the case at CLUES, which became the Hispanic organization of choice in St. Paul. Its leadership was under constant pressure to expand. "People come to you and want to give you more," said a senior CLUES administrator. "You have to know what you stand for or you end up being torn apart by the cause of the day." This does not mean an organization can never expand. Having started out providing mental health services to the Hispanic community, CLUES steadily expanded to a full service social security agency specializing in education and employment. CLUES simply came to see mental health in the Hispanic community as a problem of language and employment, turning to a prevention agenda designed to strengthen the community. CLUES decided that it was far better to have a healthy community in which families and individuals are equipped to deal with the normal stresses of life than to continue treating individuals after a breakdown. Although CLUES continued to offer basic mental health services, it began teaching English as a second language and providing basic job training. Just as St. Joseph's Home for Children decided to stop being the emergency room for Hennepin County families, CLUES decided to stop being the emergency room of the Hispanic community. By 1994, its mission had changed from a focus on individual mental health in West St. Paul to enhancing the quality of life for Hispanics across the entire metropolitan area. That meant new programs for HIV/AIDS and a new office in Minneapolis.

CLUES did not expand randomly, however. The senior staff set mission-based criteria for every decision, from where to locate to what dollars to accept. The decision to open the Minneapolis office, for example, was based on hard research about the market for services. In tracking client files, the CLUES staff noticed that a growing share of services went to the same zip code, 55404, which is in the heart of Minneapolis's Phillips neighborhood. "We just weren't accessible to the Hispanics on this side of the river," said the new director of the Minneapolis office.

Recall that CLUES was also remarkably discriminating with respect to sources of funds. "Some foundations will give $25,000 of funding that requires $250,000 of accounting," said a senior manager. "We don't want that kind of money and have turned it down." Although CLUES was quite willing to take government funds, including job training dollars under the Job Training Partnership Act, it did so with clear internal controls that made sure all contracts were signed before, not after, the first dollar was spent.

CLUES clearly knew why to say yes and how to say no, as did most of the Surviving Innovation organizations. As noted earlier, these organizations allowed ideas to rise and fall on their own merit. The question for the moment is just what *merit* means. Asked

point-blank how they judged new ideas, the Surviving Innovation
organizations said they posed four simple questions:

Is this faithful to who we are?

Can we do what we plan?

Will what we do actually make a difference in outcomes?

Can we get the dollars we need to act?

The first two questions involve mission and capacity. All but one
of the Surviving Innovation organizations said that mission was
central. The only organization that did not mention mission was
Fond du Lac Community College, which had such a tangible sense
of mission that it may have been an assumed criterion.

The rest of the Surviving Innovation sample were quite explicit
about the centrality of mission to the "go" or "no go" decision.
"What else is there?" said a senior staffer at Artspace when asked
why mission was so important. "If a project does not help artists, why
do it?" Indeed, the more I pressed for an explanation of why mission
was so important, the more puzzled the Surviving Innovation respondents became about why anyone would take a different view. "We
have the children in our minds on everything we do," said one of the
codirectors of Chance to Grow. "It is always there. Children are the
compass for our work." Of course, one can make mission the centerpiece of the organization only if one knows what the mission is.

All but one of the Surviving Innovation organizations made
capacity a top criterion, too. Their leaders worried about their ability to actually bring an idea to fruition. The only organization that
did not mention capacity was the Phoenix Group, which paid an
obvious price for this omission. The rest of the sample clearly worried about the impact of a new idea on existing capacity. They did
not expect their staff to add one new responsibility after another.

For at least a third of the Surviving Innovation organizations,
the question of workability was much less important. "If an idea

meets our mission and capacity," several leaders argued, "we have to believe it will work." For the Land Stewardship Project, everything revolved around mission. "For us, the spiritual component of agriculture is very important. There is a lot more to the land than nitrogen, minerals, and the soil to hold a root. There is a community of organisms—a life." More than any other organization in the sample, LSP believed in the action of grace. If it focused on mission and cared about capacity, if it nurtured ideas as things of wonder, workability would follow naturally. LSP simply believed that workability was more a consequence of belief than a product of analysis and planning.

Most of the Surviving Innovation organizations were not quite that confident. As we shall see shortly, most had faith in some greater power, but they did apply at least some minimal test of workability in sorting ideas. The zoo innovation investment process is a good example. If a project did not have a compelling business plan, it simply did not move forward. It also had to be able to pay back the initial investment.

At the very bottom of the list of Surviving Innovation criteria was cost. Even the leaders who mentioned cost tended to rate it as a secondary concern. Most of the organizations simply believed that the dollars would take care of themselves. Many also talked of the importance of keeping cost out of the conversation as long as possible. Cost gets in the way of mission, several argued, and ends up taking the organization toward fundable ideas. How can an innovating organization challenge the prevailing wisdom if its top worry is how to get funding from the very organizations that represent the prevailing wisdom? Although cost is something to care about at some point, organizations that base their innovation decisions on the availability of external funds will find themselves pulled and pushed by the latest fad.

Keep Faith and Intuition Alive

Some of the most delicate moments in my Surviving Innovation interviews occurred around questions of faith. When asked how they persevered in the face of opposition or failure, the vast majority of the Surviving Innovation leaders talked of their spiritual beliefs. But in doing so, they almost always asked for absolute confidentiality. They simply did not want others, inside or outside their organization, to know that they called on a higher power to help make innovation possible.

Whether expressed publicly or kept private, spiritual faith played at least three roles in the Surviving Innovation organizations. First, it provided a basis for endurance as the organizations and their leaders confronted the inevitable setbacks along the way. This role was especially important for those organizations engaged in very long-term change. Seeing one's own life in a broader context can provide the needed energy to keep plugging away, year after year, on what seem to be impossible problems. How does one keep going in the effort to clean up the environment or revitalize neighborhoods? How does one continue, day after day, confronting problems that seem impossible to solve? Faith in something bigger than oneself provides great comfort. "I could not keep going," said one of the Surviving Innovation leaders, "if I didn't believe in God. These problems are too hard to solve alone. We are only human beings."

Second, faith often instills a sense of one's own fallibility, which in turn engenders an awareness of personal forgiveness. That forgiveness is essential to the permission to fail that underpins so much public innovation. If one believes that human perfection is impossible, one will also believe that mistakes are inevitable. Where they talked of formal religious beliefs, the Surviving Innovation leaders believed in a loving God who accepts human beings as they are, not a vengeful God who casts sinners into a boiling pit. The challenge is to do as well as one can, not to achieve perfection. Believing in a loving God clearly helped many of the Surviving Innovation leaders forgive themselves for the mistakes they made in trying to do well.

Finally, faith often provides an opportunity to imagine a more hopeful future. As one of the Surviving Innovation respondents said, "We can sink into despair over many of the problems we face or create a renewal. In these times of great sadness, it is easy to imagine nothing but pain and suffering far into the future. My faith tells me that we have a chance to change and compels me to try." I believe part of the leader's work in innovating organizations is to provide hope—that is, a sense of the possible. Where hopelessness focuses on the impossible, hope focuses on an imagined future still within reach. Consider how theologian William Lynch explains the role of hope in human life:

> Hope looks to the next step, whatever it is, whatever form the step may take. If there is hope, I take it. We are too much inclined to think of hope as an emergency virtue that saves itself for a crisis (one that is really meant for use in moments when there is not much or any hope at all!). The truth is that it is present in each moment as it looks to the next. It is present everywhere, in the flowing of the bloodstream and in every small action. I would not breathe if I did not hope that the air around me would respond to my call [1965, p. 33].

As Chapter Seven suggests, faith is often a victim of growth and aging. The larger the Surviving Innovation organization, the less likely we were to find evidence of explicit conversations about faith. The faith may still exist, of course, but it may have gone underground. As organizations grow, they may also start displacing faith and intuition with analysis and evaluation. Over time, they may become addicted to measurement as the sole indicator of success.

This is not to argue that planning and analysis have no place in an innovating organization. They most certainly do. But they cannot be substitutes for faith and intuition. It is the combination of hard and soft, brain and heart, that appears to help an innovating organization stay on course. To supplant faith and intuition with analysis and evaluation is to risk a hopelessness driven by constant fear of failure. Part of the leader's work, therefore, is to keep faith and intuition alive, whether by talking openly about his or her spiritual values (even when it makes others nervous) or by encouraging others to do so in their own way.

None of this implies that innovating organizations should adopt a common religion or pray at the start of each day. For most of the Surviving Innovation organizations, keeping faith alive was not about formal religion. It was about acknowledging that success is often dependent on something bigger than the individual. At least for some, it was also about believing in luck, good fortune, grace, or magic.

For Heart of the Beast, faith in the possible even involved a bit of astrology. Early on in her tenure, executive director Reubenova ordered an astrological chart for the theater, mostly just for fun but also to show some of the staff that not everything in her transition was driven by hard-nosed budget pressure. According to the chart, the theater had the sun in Cancer and a T square to Uranus and Mars. "So there's lots of INNOVATION connected with the theater (URANUS SQUARE SUN)," said the interpretation. "The strongest foundation for the theater (4th HOUSE) is found in INNOVATION. (AQUARIUS ON THE 4TH HOUSE CUSP, URANUS IN T SQUARE). So, if you ever ask, to increase our SECURITY and STABILITY for the theater (4TH HOUSE CONCERNS), should we do the conservative thing, or should we do the unconventional innovative thing, the answer is the unconventional. Take the risks." Eerily accurate, the chart was one of several devices the organization used to remind itself of a higher power, not the least of which was the recurring theme of spiritual renewal in the annual May Day parade.

Stay Balanced

I saw many extraordinary leaders on my visits to the Surviving Innovation organizations. Some, like Bob and Kathy DeBoer, told moving stories of personal commitment to their cause. Others, like Kathy Halbreich and Kathryn Roberts, gave personal testimony about being the first women at the top of their organizations. Still others, like Pat Borich, Jeff Raison, and Doug Goke, spoke compellingly of the leader's need to listen. Overall, there is not a group of leaders anywhere in the country that I admire more.

That is why the following finding is so important for the leader's work: in all my visits, I saw very few heroic innovators. These were wonderful, dedicated leaders who kept their lives in balance. They worked hard, but they also had families, hobbies, friends, and lives outside the job. They were extraordinarily committed to mission, but they were not superhuman.

What made them special was not their great personal courage, though many had it, but their sense of self, their willingness to submerge themselves on behalf of the organization, their reluctance to claim credit for their work, and their remarkable staying power. These were not people always looking for the next job but individuals committed to the long haul. As a group, they were mostly ordinary people who were extraordinarily committed, indeed passionate, about their mission. And in that commitment, they found the energy and joy to keep going in spite of the barriers and myths that plague so many nonprofit and government organizations.

"I am a firm believer that the happiest and most productive people in their jobs are the people who balance work with family," said Kathryn Roberts. "I am committed to doing everything it takes to complete a job or task well, but I do not believe that you need to stay at work every evening in order to know you're doing a great job." Other Surviving Innovation leaders echoed the point, including Carol and Alan Arthur, two of my favorite executives, who happened to share a commitment to excellence in their respective organizations (the Domestic Abuse Project and Central Community Housing Trust) and to each other.

If there is one lesson I would draw from my observations of these leaders at work, it would be *stay human*. Although America is fascinated by heroic leaders, the Surviving Innovation organizations worked well precisely because their leaders were willing to let go. Where they had heroic passions, as many certainly did, they put that energy to work in lowering barriers and debunking myths. Rare was the leader who lifted the organization up alone. It was by calling others to a shared commitment to mission that these leaders did their best work. They did so, in part, by showing that one does not need to sacrifice all semblance of a normal life in order to succeed.

Keep Innovation in Perspective

One of the toughest challenges facing these leaders is knowing when to say "stop" to innovation. For roughly a third of the Surviving Innovation organizations, the ultimate goal was to make their innovation the prevailing wisdom. Once that was achieved, the innovating would be over. Chance to Grow, for example, certainly did not see itself as the educator of all brain-injured children in Minneapolis; if it did its work well, other schools would begin to change, installing their own brain gyms and biofeedback programs.

For another third of the sample, there was no stopping point. That was certainly the case at Theatre de la Jeune Lune. "The minute people start coming to our productions because we're safe," said one of the four artistic directors, "is the minute we will close." It was also the case at Heart of the Beast and the Walker Art Center, which shared a similar commitment to artistic edginess, and at the zoo, which felt innovation was essential to market share.

For the final third of the Surviving Innovation organizations, single acts of innovation were designed to respond to the needs of particular times. These organizations innovated to the extent necessary and were often quite uncomfortable calling what they did innovation. The only reason they were seen as innovative, several complained, was that the outside world was so out of step with good practice.

This was certainly the view of the three housing development agencies—the Phoenix Group, Central Community Housing Trust, and Project for Pride in Living. Providing social services as part of a housing program was hardly innovative except in the most relative sense, they all argued. It was the prevailing wisdom of isolating people's problems and assigning each to a separate government agency that was nonsense. Common sense, not a desire to be innovative, was at the core of these organizations' work.

Whatever the ultimate goal of the Surviving Innovation organization—whether to keep innovating as long as possible or shape the new prevailing wisdom—almost all of the leaders warned against innovating for innovation's sake. Some did so by refusing to label themselves or their work as innovative. "Are we innovative?" one of the housing executives asked. "I think we are just a bunch of people who work hard at what we do. We see a problem and work hard. I'd just as soon not label that innovation."

Others kept innovation in perspective by taking an occasional break from innovating. At WomenVenture, for example, Kay Gudmestad started her tenure by stopping the innovation. Her immediate goal was to shore up organizational morale and rebuild administrative rigor. "The cutting edge is not always good," one of the senior staff argued midway through Gudmestad's first year. "We had to start by honoring the commitments we had already made. We had to start generating cash flow statements and filing past-due grant reports. We didn't want to be innovative just then."

What WomenVenture needed, Gudmestad concluded, was not innovation but organizational therapy, which is exactly what she ordered. Working with a small grant from the McKnight Foundation, WomenVenture started asking hard questions about mission, both personal and organizational. It reworked its mission to focus more on the economic self-sufficiency of women, at the same time clarifying board roles and sharpening administrative systems. Only after stripping the organization down could Gudmestad start rebuilding.

Gudmestad also changed her language. She stopped talking about the need to "clean up" the organization and switched to a conversation about how WomenVenture could achieve a state of "well-being." She converted the CEO's office into a conference room as a gesture of good faith, taking a smaller office. She also leased out space to make ends meet.

Like Gudmestad, Halbreich also started her tenure by taking stock. She helped the Walker Art Center develop its first formal mission statement and began a dialogue with the community about future directions. "It has often struck me how few mission statements of museums include the word *people* in them," she wrote in her introduction to her first annual report in 1991. "Institutions such as this one have often functioned according to the Wizard of Oz model—you know, as though there is this great magician operating behind the white walls. I think it's time for the 'wizard' to come forward and show how human she is."

Despite a sharp drop in revenue caused by declining corporate and federal support at the time of the leadership transition, Halbreich chose to slow the institution down. Unlike Gudmestad, however, she did not have to rebuild the administrative structure: "The fact that this is such a well-managed and aesthetically vital institution allows me to think of the next evolution. It's not that we will radically transform our structure, but we will—at least metaphorically—build new entrances to it." Within two years, Walker not only had committed itself to asking the "questions that shape and inspire us as individuals, cultures, and communities," but had developed an elastic organizational structure to match. The innovation followed naturally.

Still others kept innovation in perspective by allowing programs to die. Although there are examples here and there in the Surviving Innovation files, the best illustration comes from the Illusion Theater of Minneapolis, which established one of the nation's first sexual abuse prevention programs alongside its more traditional performing arts projects. After working for years to teach children about good touch and bad touch, the Illusion Theater declared victory. Once thought of as a taboo subject, sexual abuse prevention had become the prevailing wisdom. Instead of expanding the program to cover other forms of child abuse, the theater let go. Painful as it was for those involved, the decision to stop innovating made sense. It was time to go back to being a full-time performing arts theater.

Conclusion

In a sense, the leaders of the Surviving Innovation organizations were awesome vessels of power in their own right. They made their greatest contributions in creating the conditions for others to succeed, eschewing personal credit for their organizations' advancement. They were generous in spirit, deeply committed to their organizations' missions, and well balanced in their personal lives.

Planting one of these leaders in an organization is the surest first step toward creating an innovating organization. Innovativeness is still possible in their absence—witness the Office of Waste Management—but it is so much easier with leaders who care most about the soil in which innovation and ordinary good practice grow—leaders ready to clean out the old roots and rocks that prevent other powerful seeds from sprouting into wonder. It is not the kind of work that earns awards, perhaps, but it is essential if our nonprofit and government organizations are to meet the growing demand for innovation in this rapidly changing world.

This is not to argue that individual heroism has no place in an innovating organization. But it is heroism used in tilling the fields that holds the greatest promise for the future. What greater expression of heroism could there be in a society fixated on individual glory than to submerge oneself for the public good? In this sense, there were numerous heroes among our Surviving Innovation leaders. Would that America had an award for them!

A Note on Wile E. Coyote Thinking

Most Surviving Innovation leaders did not look like the traditional heroic innovator. Their energies were devoted to the mundane tasks of stripping away barriers, encouraging participation, and creating conditions for others to succeed. Although they sometimes received appropriate credit for their work, they were generally the last people to be thanked. Perhaps I was just spending too much time watching Nickelodeon with my daughter, but the more I studied the Surviving Innovation files, the more I began to see these leaders as the antidote to Wile E. Coyote thinking.

Those who have not watched a Road Runner cartoon lately may need a reminder of the unvarying plot. Wile E. Coyote (also known as hardheadipus-ravinus, eatibus anythingbus, famishus outrageous, carnivorous vulgaris) has a single mission in life: to catch the Road Runner (also known as hot roddicus supersonicus, tastius supersonicus, birdibus zippidus, velocitus delectibus). Wile E. has many fine qualities, of course, which is why we all tend to identify a bit with him. "Genius by trade" reads his card. See Table 5.1 for a sampling of his strengths and weaknesses.

On the positive side, he is incredibly mission driven—he lives and breathes Road Runner. He also knows his environment (does anyone know the American Southwest better?) and knows the Road Runner's habits (has there ever been a situation when the Road Runner did not show up at almost the right moment?). Wile E. certainly challenges the prevailing wisdom of how the world works—he will paint a train tunnel on a mountainside and, *voilà*, a train will actually emerge from what was once (and will soon be again) solid rock.

He is ready to invest in new ideas (does anyone spend more money on gadgets?). And he uses old stuff in new ways: he puts a refrigerator on his back, using a meat grinder and electric motor to make snow for his skis (the motor gives up, where else, over a canyon); he attaches a street cleaner's wagon to a weather balloon driven by an electric fan in order to drop an anvil on the Road Runner (the balloon loses air, where else, over a canyon); he puts an outboard motor in a bathtub strapped to his back to better drive his roller skates (he is driven underground into a mountainside). Surely there is an award in there somewhere.

Table 5.1. Wile E. Coyote, Genius

Strengths	Weaknesses
Is mission-driven	Has picked an impossible mission
Pays attention to the environment	Finds that the world simply does not work as intended
Knows his adversary	Will not change diets
Challenges the prevailing wisdom of how the world works	Cannot turn corners
Is willing to invest in new ideas	Is addicted to novelty
Often uses old stuff in new ways	Relies on one source of stuff (ACME)
Has a definite bias for action	Never fine-tunes
Takes big risks	Always works alone
Has a very high tolerance for stress	Repeats the same mistakes over and over
Gives himself permission to fail	Does not know when to stop
Is ready to learn	Only reads the first page
Has enormous endurance	Will not accept the truth

He also has that bias for action Tom Peters writes about and takes very big risks (is anybody more willing to stand over the canyon?). He gives himself permission to fail and is ready to learn—he is a voracious reader of tomes like "How to Build a Burmese Tiger Trap" and "How to Tar and Feather a Road Runner." And he comes back time and again.

On the downside, he has simply picked the wrong mission. He can never, ever, ever catch the Road Runner. He is not operating in the zone of just beyond the possible. Furthermore, he expects to violate the rules of physics and get away with it. He will not change diets—anyone else would learn to like snake or cactus. He cannot turn the corners that pop up along the way—how many times does he find himself over the canyon in a cloud of smoke?

Wile E. is also addicted to novelty for novelty's sake and relies on one source of stuff (ACME) in creating his innovations. (Turns out, of course, that the Road Runner is the CEO of ACME.) He never fine-tunes—that refrigerator–meat-grinder package would work if he just had a backup motor. He invariably works alone—no other coyotes gang up with him to catch the Road Runner. Even though he never fine-tunes, he will do the same thing over and over—how many times has he pulled the same rock down on himself?

As for learning, he almost never reads past the first page or the large print—the earthquake pills that do not work on Road Runners, the ACME dehydrated boulders that expand too fast, the do-it-yourself exploding-camera kit that fails when Wile E. forgets to remove the lens cap. Most important, he is simply unwilling to accept the truth that he will never catch the Road Runner. (Truth be told, there is one cartoon in which Wile E. finally catches his prey. Unfortunately, he has shrunk to one-tenth of the Road Runner's size and cannot consume his prize!) He is not being honest about either why he exists or how he will know when he is successful. Although he tries to eat a Road Runner baked of clay, he ought to stop innovating.

The place to start abandoning Wile E. Coyote thinking is with honest questions about why the organization exists. The leaders I came to admire certainly made their share of Wile E. Coyote investments, but they learned from the results. Unlike Wile E. Coyote innovators, who spend much of their time inventing novel ways of failing, the Surviving Innovation leaders would, I am certain, have caught the Road Runner. (Kathryn Roberts came pretty close: the zoo has coyotes and free-range chickens.)

6

Using Management Systems That Accelerate Good Ideas

The North Branch School District was easily the most disciplined of the Surviving Innovation organizations at staying in real time. Virtually every management system in the organization was updated daily, with a premium placed on giving everyone the information he or she needed to act immediately. Grade school teachers did not have to wait a month to buy more construction paper or color crayons, the high school principal did not have to wait a quarter to know which students were absent or about to fail, and parents did not have to wait a year to find out how well their children were doing. The bells rang on time at North Branch, both literally and figuratively. Meetings took place when they were scheduled, budgets were updated daily, and phone calls were returned by the end of each day.

Staying in real time gave North Branch room to innovate. Because the superintendent could check the budget on a daily basis, he could actually delegate more authority to teachers. Because teachers could check their budget on a daily basis, too, they knew how much authority they had. And because both were able to track the impact of their decisions, students got what they needed when they needed it. Although providing budget innovation in real time was hardly innovative, except perhaps to nonprofit and government organizations, it created the confidence that the organization needed to take risks. Bad projects could be stopped early, and good projects could be accelerated.

Staying in real time was part of an overall commitment to use everyday effectiveness. North Branch was so concerned about time that it encouraged all staff to use Franklin Planners, a sophisticated time management system that blends a traditional calendar with a personal goal-setting and project management system (not to mention a list of frequently misspelled words and first-aid tips). North Branch purchased a Franklin Planner for any staffer who wanted one and provided the dollars for advanced training on using the system. North Branch was even willing to pay for the occasional substitute teachers to cover for this teacher training. North Branch simply saw the value in being disciplined about time, perhaps because its frontline staff had so little discretionary time to waste. By managing what is one of the most precious resources in a school, North Branch created the slack needed to develop new ideas, not to mention the accountability needed to give permission to make mistakes.

None of the Surviving Innovation organizations cared as much as North Branch about time. Some were strong on idea generation, others on personnel; some were disciplined about strategic planning, others about board development; some paid great attention to staying in touch with their external environment, others to learning. But to an organization, all worked to build management systems that served their mission, not vice versa. WomenVenture was particularly disciplined about building a financial management system that could track loan defaults, Episcopal Community Services about an evaluation system that could measure residential treatment success, Dowling Environmental School about a learning system that helped its teachers stay on the cutting edge, In the Heart of the Beast Puppet and Mask Theater about an accountability system that assured maximum community participation, and the Minnesota Zoo about a personnel system that linked pay and promotion to visitor satisfaction.

This chapter will examine the role of these and other management systems in creating natural innovation. As we shall see, rigorous management systems are absolutely essential if an innovating organization is to face the outside world, create the freedom to imagine, and change the leader's work. Organizations cannot pay attention to outcomes if they cannot define and track results, they cannot push authority downward if they cannot keep a budget in real time, and they most certainly cannot give permission to make mistakes if they cannot minimize the damage when mistakes are made. Rigorous management systems thereby give organizations the confidence to loosen the traditional command-and-control compliance systems that so often stifle creativity. And in doing so, they give the organization and its employees the confidence to challenge the prevailing wisdom.

Tying Management to Mission

Rigorous management systems are essential to any organization, be it high performing or innovating. Nevertheless, as already noted in Chapter Two, many nonprofit and government organizations believe that rigorous management systems are somehow incompatible with innovativeness. The reason is simple: they define rigorous management as synonymous with compliance. For these organizations, management systems exist not to create discretion or liberate the organization but to make sure that rules are written and enforced. The way to know if the organization is successful is to check how well it follows the rules. The way to keep it from failing is to detect mistakes *after* they occur and punish the rule breakers. Only by creating a "visible odium of deterrence," as one federal official once described the product of a good compliance system to me, can organizations hope to avoid catastrophe.

Innovating organizations choose another way, however. Instead of focusing on compliance, they focus on performance. For these organizations, management systems exist to help the organization track impacts, not compliance. The way to know if the organization is successful is to ask how well it is achieving its mission, which starts with knowing what the mission is in the first place and providing rewards for measurable progress toward a clearly defined goal. The way to keep the organization from failing is prevent as many mistakes as possible *before* they occur, and learn from the ones that are unpreventable. Only by deciding where it wants to go and creating incentives for getting there can the organization achieve the hoped-for result.

It does not take an organizational historian to know which of these two views has been favored over the years. (See Light, 1997, for a discussion of the different tides, or philosophies, of reform over the past half-century.) It has been compliance. Its impacts can be seen everywhere in today's public organizations: in the file drawers that house the paperwork on job classification, in the stacks of manuals that explain the internal rules on the budget, and in the recycling bins that contain the previous revision to the old bylaws. Despite five years of reinventing at the federal level, which has certainly reduced some of the red tape, America's nonprofit and government organizations are still keeping plenty of pieces of paper happy, as the Phoenix Group would have put it.

The way to reduce compliance is not to stop managing, however. It is to introduce a greater emphasis on performance.

An innovating organization can only push authority downward, for example, if it has good measures of performance coming back up. That means more than just assertions that the organization is doing well. At the absolute minimum, it means having up-to-date budget information so that the organization can stop the bleeding if a risky venture turns sour, as well as some kind of evaluation or monitoring system that defines and tracks program outcomes as a baseline.

Innovating organizations need not be perfect, however. An innovating organization can do many things imperfectly and still succeed. It can get by with too many job classifications or too few; it can survive with a state-of-the-art computer system or none at all; it can even endure the lack of Franklin Planners for its staff. What it cannot survive is poor financial management systems and a lack of concern for outcomes. The former is essential for both preventing financial disaster and creating room for investment, and the latter is an absolute requirement for changing from compliance-based to performance-based accountability.

The only Surviving Innovation organization that failed this test is the only one that failed overall. The other Surviving Innovation organizations persevered by adopting ten practices that helped them build a preferred set of management systems.

1. Downplay pay.

2. Measure performance.

3. Celebrate success.

4. Have fun.

5. Build mission into systems, not vice versa.

6. Be disciplined about management.

7. Reduce exposure to risk.

8. Listen to the audience.

9. Listen to the organization.

10. Keep learning.

Downplay Pay

Over the past thirty years, nonprofit and government organizations have probably spent more time and energy trying to implement pay-for-performance than any other management reform. It is a system for all ideologies: conservatives like it because it puts the emphasis on performance, not longevity or union contracts; liberals accept it because it actually provides pay increases, not freezes or cuts. What could be better for emphasizing performance than establishing a pay system that promises just that?

In reality, however, individualized pay-for-performance systems just do not work. It does not matter where they are tried; they do not work in government or nonprofit organizations, big corporations, or small businesses. "They should work," write public management scholars Patrick Larkey and Jonathan Caulkins, "but they do not." Pay-for-performance almost always creates more problems than it solves. (See Larkey and Caulkins, 1992, for a list of unintended consequences.)

Nevertheless, many nonprofit and government organizations persist in the search for the perfect pay system. The result is endless bitterness and frustration as employees fight over the tiny morsels available at the end of the year. Moreover, even if an organization could design a system that would measure performance perfectly, sort employees exactly, and put meaningful amounts of money in play, pay-for-performance would still not produce innovation.

The basic flaw in the idea is simple: pay is not a significant motivator for people who work in nonprofit and government organizations. Ask nonprofit and government employees what they value most in a job, and they will say challenging work, personal growth, pleasant working conditions, job autonomy, and service to society long before they mention pay, promotions, and prestige (see, for example, National Commission on the Public Service, 1989; U.S. Merit Systems Protection Board, 1994).

This is not to argue that pay is irrelevant to organizational performance. It is arguably one of the top sources of employee dissatisfaction. Scratch any organizational conflict and pay will be in the wound somewhere. But it is not a motivator for innovation. Asked if pay increases motivate employees, management guru Frederick Herzberg answered quite simply: "Yes, to seek the next wage increase. Some medievalists still can be heard to say that a good depression will get employees moving. They feel that if rising wages don't or won't do the job, reducing them will" (1987, p. 111).

Pay is certainly not the reason why the Surviving Innovation organizations succeed. It does not come up in the literature as a factor, nor does it come up in the Surviving Innovation sample. As Appendix C shows, less than 40 percent of the Surviving Innovation organizations had a pay-for-performance system to begin with, and even when these latter organizations had the dollars to fund their systems, the amounts of money involved were meager at best.

More important, there was absolutely no evidence that pay-for-performance had any impact whatsoever in producing innovative acts. As state agencies, for example, the Minnesota Office of Waste Management, the Minnesota Extension Service, and the Minnesota Zoo all had some form of merit pay linked to performance. During the three fiscal years covered by the Surviving Innovation project, 1992–1995, the state had two salary freezes and one 4 percent increase. The dollars involved were just not enough to matter. Pay was definitely a dissatisfier in these organizations but not a motivator. It could not be in such small amounts.

Indeed, if pay mattered at all to innovativeness in the Surviving Innovation sample, it mattered as an obstacle. At MES, for example, senior managers clearly worried about how the individual pay-for-performance system worked against the teamwork needed to survive. That is why the clusters began work in 1994 on designing a new performance appraisal system that would evaluate individual employees on their contributions to team success. Although it was not clear how much money MES was willing to invest in team-based pay, nor how much give the state personnel system would allow, the clusters were struggling with the barriers to collaboration created by the traditional pay-for-performance appraisal system. Merely asking questions about individual contributions to setting team goals, establishing effective coalitions, and communicating outcomes in terms understandable to citizens was a step in the right direction.

Just because pay was not a motivator for innovation does not mean the Surviving Innovation organizations gave increases capriciously. Most simply gave all of their employees the same percentage increase each year. However, at least one organization, the Domestic Abuse Project, decided to launch a new merit pay system in 1994, in an effort to move away from a seniority-based pay system in which pay increases were essentially automatic. Although DAP never expected the new system to produce innovation, its executive director, Carol Arthur, wanted to change the dialogue about what gets rewarded from one about length of service to one that at least considered performance. By linking the pay-setting dialogue to careful evaluation of each staffer's contribution to DAP's overall performance, Arthur hoped to create an organization-wide focus on mission as the central determinant of success, whether expressed in paychecks or client impact.

Nevertheless, the Surviving Innovation organizations offer a cautionary tale about pay as a motivator for innovation. Bluntly stated, creating a new pay system is absolutely *not* the first step in creating an innovating organization and may actually be a fundamental misstep. Whatever pay system an organization adopts, be it pay-for-performance, team-based pay, or some form of modified annual cost of living increase, it must be clear about who gets what and why.

Measure Performance

The way to honor performance is to talk explicitly about performance. Measure it, debate it, track it, and celebrate it. The Surviving Innovation organizations did just that. Without exception, they gave their employees an incentive to accomplish something worthwhile by tying pay, recognition, and promotion to just such accomplishments. They put the focus on performance not by creating complicated employee appraisal systems and unfathomable algorithms for distributing painfully small amounts of money but by talking about performance.

Moreover, these were not random conversations. For the most part, the Surviving Innovation organizations actively sought external evaluation of their programs and measured outcomes. Although they most certainly allowed for intuition and judgment in identifying success, they were often quite meticulous in measuring performance.

It was precisely this commitment to hard-nosed measurement that allowed Chance to Grow to flourish. In its early years, measurement provided a healthy defense against external critics. What better way to prove that a daily visit to the brain gym would improve reading skills than by showing the data? What better way to show that starting each day by tracing pictures, walking a balance beam, wiggling through a maze, and crawling through a tunnel would give students a chance to grow?

Over time, however, measurement created secondary rewards. It was careful measurement that led Secretary of Education Richard Riley to declare the Chance to Grow/New Visions School the most carefully documented example of charter school success in the country. It was also careful measurement that led the Minnesota State Department of Children, Families, and Learning to give Chance to Grow a grant to train five other school districts in the implementation of the brain gym curriculum. (Replication is also under way in North Carolina—Bob DeBoer's younger sister is a first-grade teacher in the state and served as the point of contact.) And it was careful measurement that led Chance to Grow to expand its biofeedback program to other schools. Slowly but surely, Chance to Grow was coming to represent the prevailing wisdom.

Measurement also paid off for the Domestic Abuse Project. By 1997, sales of publications were netting nearly $20,000 a year in a total organizational budget of $1.1 million, and training programs were generating nearly $30,000. That is precisely the kind of money that organizations like DAP can use for seeding new ideas or providing salary increases. The demand did not arise by magic—DAP's reputation for rigorous measurement helped create a market for its products. "If we couldn't say they work," said one DAP staffer, "they wouldn't sell. We have the data to back it up."

With the goal of making that data even more accessible, DAP redesigned its *Research Updates* publication to share information about the organization's training capacity and hired a new marketing director who was explicitly charged with generating more earned income. These steps, together with the existence of a stand-alone research and evaluation unit, gave DAP a special edge in gaining the trust of the outside world.

The Surviving Innovation organizations faced three basic questions as they attempted to measure performance. The first was, *What will be measured?* At Chance to Grow, for example, the brain gym (activity) was designed to improve vision scores (output), which were linked to vocabulary and comprehension scores (outcome). Measurement clearly helped discipline the Chance to Grow program as it experimented with new approaches like biofeedback, but it also challenged the prevailing wisdom. On the one hand, measurement showed Chance to Grow's deep commitment to doing what works. On the other, it put the onus on the opposition to do similar measurement of standard programs, thereby shifting the debate away from issues of school turf to what works for children.

The second question in measuring performance was, *Who does the measuring?* As a general rule, the Surviving Innovation organizations used independent evaluators to establish their credibility. At least two, St. Joseph's Home for Children and Episcopal Community Services, also called in outside accrediting bodies to provide an extra measure of review for their residential treatment work. St. Joe's used two accrediting organizations, the Joint Commission on the Accreditation of Health Care Organizations (JCAHO) and the Council on Accreditation for Services to Families and Children (CASFC), whereas ECS used just the council.

By itself, accreditation is much less a confirmation of overall performance than an assessment of how a given organization measures up against a set of standards. As an example, the JCAHO Accreditation Decision Grid covers twenty-one patient-level functions, such as patient care (treatment planning, nutrition, medication use), assessment (initial screening, laboratory services), and rights, and twenty-three organization-wide functions, such as leadership (organizational planning), management of the environment (measurement systems, therapeutic environment), human resources (orientation, training, and education of staff and care givers), management information systems, and surveillance, prevention, and control of infection. The focus is on compliance with a set of standards for good management.

Accreditation can therefore reinforce the very compliance-based mentality that innovating organizations need to avoid. It is a time-consuming, paper-heavy process that can require hundreds of hours of staff time. (Despite its reputation as the more rigorous of the two accrediting bodies, the JCAHO was, according to St. Joe's, actually easier to satisfy than the CASFC.)

Although the benefits of accreditation are not always clear (one staffer called it "the last refuge of weak organizations that can't get better on their own"), it can instill discipline in the internal systems needed for performance-based accountability. Tracking systems can be used to punish employees (compliance) or reward outcomes (performance); quality standards can be used to belittle programs (compliance) or pull them upward (performance). The question, as always, is how the systems fit into an overall strategy of accountability.

Used as a way to *benchmark* against similar organizations in the field, accreditation can improve the systems needed to reduce compliance-based accountability. Boards and legislatures are not going to reduce the rules without clear information in return. Moreover, accreditation may simply be good politics, not to mention a requirement for licensure. "Particularly during these times of cutback," said Carole Mae Olson, "you need to be able to show you are the best you can be in every way possible."

The third question in measuring performance was, *How hard should the measures be?* Almost all of the Surviving Innovation organizations used quantitative measures to track their activities and outputs—number of visitors at the zoo, reading scores at the Dowling School, citizen satisfaction in Anoka County.

Many also used judgment and intuition. Alongside an impressive portfolio of tests, the North Branch School District relied on "gut instinct" in evaluating outcomes. "We keep asking 'Do we have it right yet?'" said the district's superintendent. "We haven't answered yes yet. You can't come in here with a bunch of 'I thinks' this and that. We want something grounded. At some point, though, there is a gut check on what works and what doesn't. You have the permission to violate the rules as long as it is in the best interests of the child." It was hard measurement coupled with instinct that allowed North Branch to keep moving forward.

Luther Theological Seminary followed a similar approach. It was rigorous in measuring and evaluating its work, particularly in tracking the diversity of its students and the impact of its new Integrated Quarter. But it was not wed to simple measurement as the final arbiter of success. "We are a teaching institution that is trying to become a learning institution," one faculty member explained. "The overriding question is whether we are producing effective pastors in this changed world. We have always been good at training chaplains, but not so good at training leaders."

At least for Luther, faith clearly played a role in knowing what worked. "We don't fix things very fast here," said another faculty member. "We don't want to be super-responsive. A good pastor is not just what parishes *say* one is. Not everyone is raised in a Norwegian Lutheran home anymore. That's where our faith comes in. It is more than 'we'll know it when we see it.' We sometimes have to let God provide the insight."

No organization made intuition and judgment a more explicit part of its evaluation process than the Land Stewardship Project, however. "Grace is not found in an accounting system or an evaluation," said one senior manager. "These are just systems. They tell us where we have been, not where we are going. We name spirituality as the anchor for our work." LSP was just as rigorous in its evaluations as the rest of the Surviving Innovation sample but put a special emphasis on interpreting the results in a spiritual framework. It looked for evidence that its projects were, indeed, acts of stewardship, a term that does not yield so easily to simple quantitative evaluation.

Celebrate Success

If there is one thing the Surviving Innovation organizations did both well and often, it was celebrating success. And in celebrating success, these organizations provided an intangible benefit to employees—call it a psychic income—that far outweighed any pay-for-performance increase they could have awarded. They honored performance by acknowledging success.

At the Cyrus Math/Tech school, for example, success was celebrated by posting the names of all the former Cyrus elementary students who had made the honors list in middle school. Following the success of students allowed the teachers to claim some credit for doing their jobs well. Cyrus also posted a huge reproduction of the *Redbook* cover naming the tiny school as one of the fifty-one best schools in the country, plus countless reproductions of the school's mascot, Dr. Megabyte. All these things helped remind the teachers of Cyrus's core mission: educating children for a new world.

At the Minnesota Zoo, success was celebrated through a formal awards program for "outstanding efforts" in pursuing the seven parts of the organization's mission ("creating a magical experience, thriving as a special place for children, knowing our customers, managing moments of truth, linking revenues to results, building a premier service organization, and investing to keep the existing zoo great").

The process by which the award recipients were chosen made the program particularly powerful in reinforcing mission. Both individuals and teams were eligible, with seven awards available for each. The final award decisions were made by a joint labor-management team, not on the basis of the number of nominations an individual or team had received but on the basis of the quality of effort demonstrated by the nominee. Announced at the annual holiday celebration, the awards enabled the zoo to send a broad mix of signals. The labor-management team allowed two levels of the organization to work together, the team awards allowed the zoo to reinforce internal collaboration, and the awards themselves reinforced mission.

The Minnesota Extension Service and the Domestic Abuse Project both celebrated success in internal and external publications. The *MES Weekly*, a fax newsletter, provided regular opportunities for the organization to highlight particularly effective programs and congratulate individual staff and teams, and DAP's *Research Update* provided a quarterly platform for sharing evaluation results and celebrating impacts.

To remain authentic as a device for recognizing accomplishment, such celebration must be honest. DAP's celebration of a decade of *Research Update* is a case in point. "The findings have not always been complimentary and we have tried hard to change the way we intervene based, in part, on the information we have gained through our evaluation and research projects," the summer 1993 issue noted. "We hope that in the next decade we become just one of many programs across North America disseminating the results of its work and that we witness an explosion of shared knowledge. We will all benefit if this occurs, but most important victim/survivors and their children will become more secure when we learn from each other and improve the quality of our work." By simultaneously celebrating a decade of evaluation at DAP and embracing some less than favorable findings, DAP sent a powerful signal to itself, its field, and perhaps its own clients. Success sometimes involves small steps forward.

Other Surviving Innovation organizations celebrated success more loosely. At the American Indian Business Development Corporation, for example, celebrations of success included frequent centerwide coffee breaks, a pig roast, and a holiday party for tenants and staff. These celebrations served two functions: first, they provided a chance to acknowledge the real success of incubator tenants, and second, they reinforced AIBDC's mission by getting tenants to talk to each other. By increasing the flow of ideas through the organization, they improved the odds of another celebration in the not-too-distant future. Having a pig roast may not seem like a way to celebrate success, but as the director put it, AIBDC could not have a successful pig roast unless there were enough tenants willing to have a party. It was an indirect indicator of success, to be sure, but a valuable one nonetheless.

Have Fun

The Surviving Innovation organizations also honored performance by having fun. Although I did visit several organizations that were not particularly joyful places to be at the time, the vast majority of the Surviving Innovation organizations were alive with commitment and energy. Alongside the stress and conflict, there was a sense of excitement and passion. Call it the joy of innovating.

Wandering through the halls of Cyrus Math/Tech, for example, one could not help but be struck, both literally and figuratively, by the commitment to innovation. I arrived at Cyrus as the paper airplane contest was coming to a close in the long hallway of the school. The airplanes were designed with the help of a computer program, and the results were tracked on a simple, home-programmed spreadsheet. The learning was real and tangible, the students active and alert.

It is hard to say just which of the Surviving Innovation organizations was the most fun to visit. For all sorts of personal reasons that are difficult to articulate, I fell in love with Advocating Change Together for the joy of its members, Chance to Grow for its courage, Dowling for its enthusiasm, and the Domestic Abuse Project for its deep commitment to changing the prevailing wisdom. And I will always be drawn to Heart of the Beast, if only because I still do not know quite how those puppets do what they do.

As for my favorite interviews, none will likely ever top my conversation with the Minnesota Zoo's director of biological programs, which took place outside the coral reef exhibit. Truth be told, my notes are a bit unclear about just what he said, for everything in the exhibit had been designed to pull the visitor into the reef. The floor-to-ceiling curved glass of the tank (much more expensive than traditional flat glass) made me feel a part of the exhibit. Soft background music, low lights, and the lack of a railing between the viewer and the glass meant an even closer experience. Although there were signs describing every fish, they were tucked away where they would not distract the visitors. The point of the exhibit was not to teach visitors the difference between a puffer and a parrot fish but to create a connection with a distant and endangered world and, in doing so, increase support for marine protection. It most certainly worked.

To be sure, there were tough interviews. Several of the Surviving Innovation organizations were under great pressure at the time. Take the Walker Art Center as an example. My first visit occurred when the organization was brimming with excitement about the nationally heralded Bruce Nauman exhibit. My second visit occurred in the wake of Ron Athey's ritualistic bloodletting, which had quickly become a lightning rod for every complaint about the new regime—Walker was too politically correct, Halbreich was too brash, the performing arts curator, John Killacky, was too political. How the Walker handled the pressure would determine whether it remained a safe place for unsafe ideas. It was a particularly tough time to wander the halls, but the very fact that I was allowed in showed a certain hopefulness about the future. Though the Walker became just a little less safe for a time—organizations do not have a limitless store of social capital—it has since rebounded well.

Other organizations were having troubles, too. Chance to Grow was growing a bit too fast, Cyrus was locked in the phone-tree controversy, the Office of Waste Management was under fire from the Pollution Control Agency, MES was struggling to define itself, and the Project for Pride in Living was in transition. As noted earlier in this book, innovating organizations are often stressful places to work. Yet the conflicts were about the right issues. The people inside knew why they were there and accepted stress as the natural consequence of doing the right thing.

It is important to note that celebrating success and having fun are impossible unless people inside the organization know what success is and why they are there. Any organization can have a party, but innovating organizations do so when success is clear. However, they do not set the threshold of success so high that they can never celebrate, and neither do they wait for every last scintilla of evidence to come in to declare a celebration.

Organizations that do not measure outcomes at all cannot know whether success has been achieved, and organizations that become addicted to absolute proof may never reach a closure point where they can congratulate themselves on a job well done. Assuming that every act of innovation is a work in progress, these organizations may keep themselves in a constant state of anticipation without ever declaring a success. The first step in celebrating an achievement and having fun is acknowledging that progress is being made. The prevailing wisdom rarely changes quickly.

Build Mission into Systems, Not Vice Versa

One of the great mysteries about organizational life is how agencies manage to survive year after year without a clue as to their mission. Many public organizations do just that, enduring long after their primary mission has been exhausted.

Take the Federal Helium Reserve as an example. Created in the 1920s to ensure a steady supply of helium for the military's fleet of blimps, the organization persisted long after blimps went out of fashion. It was finally abolished by Congress in 1995, but only after a bloody battle.

The Federal Helium Reserve is hardly the only agency to linger on long after its mission is over. As political scientist Herbert Kaufman discovered in writing his book *Are Government Organizations Immortal?* agencies fight hard to stay alive. "They are not helpless, passive pawns in the game of politics as it affects their lives;" wrote Kaufman, "they are active, energetic, persistent participants" (1976, p. 9). Of 175 federal agencies that had existed in 1923, Kaufman found that 148 were still alive fifty years later, for a survival rate of 85 percent. Of the survivors, 39 had been merged, reorganized, or otherwise changed over the years, meaning that 62 percent of the sample had been untouched by history.

Lest anyone think that immortality is unheard of in the nonprofit community, a study led by University of Minnesota sociologist Joseph Galaskiewicz suggests that nonprofits may have higher survival rates than expected (Hager, Galaskiewicz, Bielefeld, and Pins, 1996). Of 229 randomly selected Minnesota nonprofits that had existed in 1980, Galaskiewicz and his colleagues found that 182 were still alive in some form by 1995, for a survival rate of just under 80 percent. Of the survivors, 19 had been merged, reorganized, or closed then revived, and another 16 simply disappeared. Putting all the numbers together, 147 of the nonprofits were still alive pretty much unchanged, yielding a survival rate of 64 percent. As such, the nonprofit survival rate was slightly higher than the federal agency rate, albeit over a shorter (but more turbulent) period.

If roughly two out of three nonprofits could survive the 1980s and the deep cutbacks that came with the Reagan Revolution, perhaps nonprofits are more durable than conventional wisdom suggests. (See Bielefeld, 1994, for a discussion of how the nonprofits died.)

Regardless of the subsector, however, far too many of the surviving organizations are merely on life support, awakening to protect their turf but otherwise in a vegetative state. They stay alive because their systems keep them running. They recruit employees, spend money, track expenditures, and train staff, but otherwise are adrift, waiting for the next request for proposal or new legislative initiative to provide a new reason for living. In essence, staying alive has become their mission.

The Surviving Innovation organizations clearly worried about how their management systems might eventually drive out mission. The Phoenix Group carried the worry to an extreme. Its unyielding focus on mission clearly made it the darling of the community. "What was unusual about the Phoenix Group was early, positive publicity and fundraising success," Jon Pratt, executive director of the Minnesota Council of Nonprofits, later told the *Twin Cities Reader*. "People really wanted the Phoenix Group to succeed. There was a willingness to suspend judgment. The organization argued from the beginning that it was different. And it *was* different. So some of the usual scrutiny that an organization was put through wasn't applied in the same way. The potential reward seemed so great."

Unfortunately, Phoenix picked an inherently risky mission—one in which strong systems were essential. "I saw them doing project after project, all of which were undercapitalized," the CCHT executive director later commented. "The question isn't if you're going to fall off the cliff, but when—and if you have too many of those types of situations, the cliff comes sooner."

Nevertheless, there was—and still is—something right on target about Phoenix's fear of systems. "Systems can take over," one of the cofounders argued during my site visit. "The worry is that some of these things will interfere with creativity. You get so hung up on satisfying the accountants that you can't breathe. We created Phoenix to bring the neighborhood back from the ashes, not to provide employment for accounting firms." In the end, of course, the accountants took control. Bills came due, money was misplaced, apartments and houses were neglected, and the Phoenix Group collapsed.

The lesson from Phoenix is not to let systems take over, however. Rather, it is to have systems serve mission, not vice versa. Had Phoenix imagined its accounting system as a device for freeing up dollars for creative investment and preventing disaster, rather than as a straitjacket, it might have survived. That is certainly how the two other housing development agencies in the Surviving Innovation sample, the Central Community Housing Trust and Project for Pride in Living, saw accounting.

That is also how most of the sample saw management systems in general. At Fond du Lac Community College, for example, serving the mission even extended to the faculty parking system. One of the first questions in moving to the new campus was where to let the faculty park. Although some of the faculty and administrators wanted the prime parking spaces, the mission of serving the students prevailed: students got the prime spaces, leaving the faculty to park at the far end of the lot.

At the Land Stewardship Project, considerations of mission extended to the investment of staff retirement savings. LSP made a deliberate decision early on to use a socially responsible investment fund. Although its rate of return was lower than a standard stock index fund, LSP made up the difference in psychic satisfaction.

Be Disciplined About Management

Even as they worried about not letting systems crowd out mission, the Surviving Innovation organizations were dedicated to rigorous management. They saw good management as an ally of innovation, not an enemy.

This is not to suggest that every system in every organization was perfect. Some of the organizations had serious financial problems during the period covered by the project, including one sizable embezzlement. Others had significant personnel disputes, including the highly publicized employee complaints at WomenVenture. Still others had problems with mission management; one organization had expanded so quickly that its frontline staff was mostly out of touch with the senior leadership.

Nevertheless, as a whole, the Surviving Innovation organizations were remarkably disciplined about management. Even if an organization was weak in, say, personnel management, it might compensate with exceptionally strong strategic planning. In another organization, a weakness in information technology might be balanced by strong learning systems. Thus the following report card shows unevenness across the sample, even as it confirms the importance of several key systems as essential to innovativeness.

Financial Management, A. Whatever the strengths and unevenness to be described later, none of the Surviving Innovation organizations would have survived without strong internal systems for tracking revenues and expenditures, tight cost controls, and real-time budgeting. They all also ordered regular audits. Except for Phoenix, all produced quarterly financial statements, and most had monthly information. For tight-budget organizations such as Theatre de la Jeune Lune, expenditure data could be generated instantaneously. Such information was particularly important as a device for preventing overspending on individual productions, where small purchases can add up in a hurry.

Real time budgeting was not just a way to prevent overruns, however. It also allowed the organization to push authority downward. At North Branch School District, for example, teachers could get information on their budgets the minute the accounting staff entered a transaction. That helped them make supply decisions quickly. "It makes no sense for us to wait until the end of the month to know whether we have the money to purchase supplies," said one teacher of the system. "The kids certainly can't wait."

It is impossible to overemphasize the importance of rigorous budget systems. But for Phoenix, the Surviving Innovation organizations were paragons of careful budgeting and internal financial control. This was not about compliance, but freedom and survival.

Idea Generation, A.   As noted in Chapter Three, the Surviving Innovation organizations had a mix of systems for stimulating ideas. They created upward momentum by pushing authority downward, providing the seed dollars needed for launch, and inviting ideas to rise and fall on their own merit. Although one can argue that such systems are unique to innovating organizations, well-performing organizations need ideas, too. Finding ways to get the front line to make suggestions for improvement may be as essential to running a well-performing organization as any other system.

Governance, A.   Governance systems were strong across the Surviving Innovation sample. For the nonprofit and government organizations alike, accountability started at the top, with a strong board. Three-quarters of the Surviving Innovation organizations had an active process for recruiting and orienting new board members, and most used a committee structure for channeling the board's energy into fundraising, financial management, and strategic oversight. Many had also gone through some effort to clarify board and staff responsibilities; among these organizations, the Central Community Housing Trust had the most rigorous discussion by far of the proper division of authority.

As in so many lessons from this research, the government agencies actually behaved more like nonprofits than like traditional agencies. All of the public schools (Chance to Grow, Cyrus, Dowling, and North Branch) had active, site-based management, which enabled parents to play a visible role in oversight, and the zoo had one of the strongest boards of any of the Surviving Innovation organizations. In Anoka County, of course, the elected county board was a key element in providing the protection and resources for innovative ideas. Only the Office of Waste Management appeared adrift, inventing its governance process in the midst of constant leadership turnover.

Fundraising, A.   Fundraising systems were strong and active across the sample. The Surviving Innovation organizations were simply unmatched in both finding and exploiting funding opportunities. Having written and reviewed my share of proposals over the years, I can say that the Surviving Innovation organizations did at least three things particularly well in their appeals. First, they made a clear connection between causes and effects. Though they might not always have used an outcomes chain, they were able to clearly explain how the infusion of funding would purchase a set of activities that would lead to a specific output and eventual outcome.

Second, they made their passion obvious but not oppressive. They were not afraid to say they cared about children or the land. Nor were they reluctant to express their strong views about the value of their work. At the same time, however, they did not overpromise. They kept their proposals balanced between fact and hope, project activities and mission-centered outcomes.

Third, they often showed remarkable creativity in their packaging. There is only so much an organization can do with a grant proposal to the National Endowment for the Arts or Humanities, for example. But all rules are suspended when raising endowment support. My favorite appeal came from the Heart of the Beast Puppet and Mask Theater, which assembled a spiral-bound notebook making the case for restoring the Avalon Theater as its new home. The booklet was filled with individually crafted puppets, hand-pasted photographs, cutouts, a pop-up mural, and a single nail taped onto the appeal page. It worked for me to the tune of $100.

Managing for Results, A−.   As already noted in this chapter, all of the Surviving Innovation organizations were committed to results-oriented management. Most conducted ongoing evaluations of their programs and used outcomes measurement as a centerpiece of ongoing conversations about mission. The very fact that they cared enough to measure performance sent a strong signal about what was valued inside the organizations.

Managing for results involves more than just collecting data, however. It also involves an effort to tie results to other management systems, most notably pay and budget. To the extent possible, the Surviving Innovation organizations tried to reward successful programs with additional funding or new staff. But some did better than others at this. At the very minimum, they tied results to organization-wide recognition, through awards or publications. At the maximum, they reallocated dollars to programs that demonstrated higher performance. "You can only stick with a failing program so long before you have to cut it loose," said one manager at Episcopal Community Services. "If you have three programs for families and one is doing better than the others, you need to push the dollars there."

Revenue Generation, B+.   Although generating revenue was never part of Luther Gulick's POSDCORB, it was an essential task in the Surviving Innovation sample. Almost all the organizations were working to create "products" that might bring in extra funding, thereby reducing dependence on government grants and foundation money. At the Land Stewardship Project, for example, the hope was to cut foundation support from 75 percent of the annual budget to just half. The only way to do so was to develop independent revenue streams, whether from the sale of publications or from more fee-for-service work.

To some extent or other, the Minnesota Zoo, the Domestic Abuse Project, the Minnesota Extension Service, the American Indian Business Development Corporation, the Project for Pride in Living, the Land Stewardship Project, In the Heart of the Beast, and Theatre de la Jeune Lune had already made significant headway in building independent revenue streams for the future. Some, like the zoo, had come to count on these generators for a substantial portion of their annual operating revenue, whereas others, like DAP, saw the sale of publications as a source of occasional discretionary support. What all the organizations shared was a desire to maximize independence by creating markets for their own products. (See Barzelay and Armajani, 1992, for a discussion of *enterprise management* as a new feature of public management.)

Learning Systems, B.   Traditionally defined as staff development or training, learning systems were uneven across the sample. As we shall see later in this chapter, all of the organizations were committed to learning at some level. None wanted to make the same mistake twice. But some were more systematic about learning than others. Far too many defined learning as a simple problem of spending a few dollars on training courses from time to time.

There is considerable evidence, however, that the Surviving Innovation organizations did learn. All clearly learned from their mistakes, whether through highly structured evaluations (Domestic Abuse Project) or more intuitive assessments. All provided training support for staff and board, some with dollars, others with peer learning programs, and still others with internships and apprenticeships.

Pay and Personnel, B–.   Most of the Surviving Innovation organizations had formal pay and personnel systems, using some form of job classification as a basis for hiring, promotion, and pay. The value of job classification is that it forces an organization to describe what a given job is supposed to do and how it fits into the whole. It also frames the conversation about what a given job is worth in pay and compensation and provides the basis for performance appraisal.

Where the Surviving Innovation organizations were uneven was in tying their pay and personnel systems to mission. Although some of the organizations were struggling to invent ways of using pay and personnel to reinforce innovativeness, others had given up. As a result, some of the pay and personnel systems operated in isolation from the broader effort to innovate, not doing damage per se, but not helping either.

Strategic Planning, B—. This was another area of unevenness across the Surviving Innovation sample. Some of the organizations were skilled in the technique—the Walker Art Center used it well, as did Luther Theological Seminary and St. Joe's. Others were much less formal about planning. Although almost all made forecasts of the future and thought about stakeholders, most did not have the dollars to engage in formal strategic planning efforts.

Where they were able to mount such efforts, however, the results were plainly clear. At DAP, for example, a 1991 strategic plan committed the organization to an even more intense focus on outcomes and drove its treatment programs more aggressively into all communities experiencing domestic abuse, including communities of color, the gay and lesbian communities, and low-income populations. The plan was so effective in shaping internal priorities that DAP raised the money for another five-year planning effort in 1997.

Information Systems, C. Information resources were much more uneven across the sample. Some of the Surviving Innovation organizations had state-of-the-art computers, whereas others were still using notepads and adding machines. Anoka County, Cyrus Math/ Tech, and Central Community Housing Trust were the most advanced of the sample, investing heavily in technology. The sell was also relatively easy in Anoka County. "As long as it comes in a computer box," said one senior county official, "most county boards will buy it. They don't want to spend another dime on staff but just love new computers." Size clearly has its advantages, too. Anoka had a specific budget for technology and a Department of Information Services underneath its Division of Finance and Central Services.

Interestingly, one of the technology leaders was the People Escaping Poverty Project, a tiny nonprofit dedicated to helping welfare recipients win a place at the policy debate. It is one of the few Surviving Innovation organizations with a web page (http://rrnet.com/~pepp1) and has even started to generate revenue by designing web pages for other organizations. As noted earlier, PEPP used the web to stimulate an electronic dialogue about welfare reform with the governor of North Dakota.

Time Management, C.   Tracking and shepherding time was another mixed commitment among the organizations. Some, like North Branch School District, made time management a top priority. Other organizations simply did not keep track of time at all, the Phoenix Group being example number one. The problem with lack of time management comes when grants must be renewed, bills paid, and audit reports filed. Although the vast majority of the Surviving Innovation organizations did just fine in meeting deadlines, some of their success was more accidental than deliberate.

Reduce Exposure to Risk

However contrary it may sound, one of the best ways to increase risk taking is to reduce exposure to risk. By insulating itself against financial loss, an innovating organization can actually increase the size and range of its bets. It can also be more confident in giving the permission to fail.

All of the Surviving Innovation organizations tended to use general operating support as a hedge against risk. The more heavily the organization is leveraged to project-specific funding, the less flexibility it has to support high-risk/high-gain ventures. Whether the money comes from an endowment campaign (Project for Pride in Living, Episcopal Community Services), a small revenue generator (Domestic Abuse Project), bake sales and auctions (Cyrus), cash awards such as the Ford Foundation's $100,000 Innovation Award (Anoka County), or creative management of financial windfalls such as the 1994 flood grants at the Minnesota Extension Service, the extra cash can provide the breathing space, if not the seed funding, to allow experiments to flourish.

Just over half of the Surviving Innovation organizations put this operating support into a reserve fund of some kind. At CLUES and MES, for example, the money went directly into a rainy-day fund for use in lean times. Once the clouds lifted, both organizations were able to redeploy the dollars for new ventures. CLUES used its rainy-day fund, in part, to open its Minneapolis office, whereas MES converted its dollars into an innovation investment fund.

Also as a general rule, all of the Surviving Innovation organizations stayed in close touch with particularly risky projects. Almost three-quarters had some formal policy for reducing exposure in the event of a project collapse. For Theatre de la Jeune Lune, that meant staying in touch with every project, of course. Having been so close to death early in its life, the theater maintained tight control over every cost. "People still look at us and ask, 'Will they be here tomorrow?'" said one of the cofounders from the kitchen of the new theater. "If we were to die tomorrow, which we're always ready to do, we know we've done what we wanted. Thus far, knock on wood, we have been in the fortunate position that we decide to do something and there's always been support. That can change instantly."

This history produced an organization that was both extraordinarily creative and exceptionally disciplined about costs. Every production was carefully budgeted and tracked using a *red-flag* system designed to trigger spending freezes when productions exceeded budget. In general, the only way to remove the flag was to reprogram the budget. "They trust me to do the job," said the business manager of her relationship with the artistic team. "When I say stop, they usually, but not always, stop."

Such red-flag systems depend on real-time budgeting, of course. "We know exactly what is leaving the company each day," said the business manager. "We can tell exactly where a production is at any given moment." To keep track, the business office established a sign-out process for purchase orders. Staff still had the freedom to buy materials on short notice but could do so only through a signed purchase order. Vendors were told that the business office would not provide payment without a purchase order, and this created even more pressure for careful budgeting. "We do not get in anyone's way," said one administrative staffer. "However, we do require that people tell us what they are spending. We have to cut down the 'oh-by-the-way' spending. Someone has to make an affirmative decision for a project to go over budget." At the start of a production cycle, the process was very flexible. As costs tightened near the end, the real-time system kicked in to limit exposure to risk.

If the red-flag system sounds like compliance, it is. This is one area where tight compliance is essential for organizational survival, but it is compliance based on mission, not on mindless rules. Theatre de la Jeune Lune could lower the flag if the artistic directors felt the risk was worth taking. The point is not to avoid risk but to take risks wisely.

As a final general rule, almost all of the Surviving Innovation projects used the budget process as a way to impose discipline on the range of risks taken. No one was better at doing so than the Land Stewardship Project, which operated with two formal budgets. One budget was built on a most-probable estimate of revenues and expenditures, whereas the other was built on the worst case scenario. LSP stayed with the most-probable budget unless events dictated a switch. It hoped for the best but had a contingency budget for the worst. "The big problem is predicting the revenue stream," said one senior LSP manager. "You start each year with a list of likely grants and only switch to the conservative budget if the revenue projections fall below a certain point."

Like Theatre de la Jeune Lune, LSP developed its process after a financial crisis had forced staff cutbacks in 1991. "Once you've been through layoffs, you never want to do it again," said one LSP staffer. "It is expensive to do, including severance and unemployment insurance. There is also enormous pain involved in letting friends go. These were people we knew and cared about." Under the worst-case budget, LSP could more easily stop spending money on "luxuries" such as new computers in its Lewiston and Monte offices. The problem in 1991 had not been the revenue shortfalls per se but the fact that LSP did not have a real-time budget and therefore did not know about the shortfalls in time to stop spending. The new budgeting system was not only in real time but had a series of clearly identified *triggers* that would allow LSP to downsize without cutting staff. The key was to know in time.

Listen to the Audience

The Surviving Innovation organizations were remarkably good listeners. They paid attention to their audiences through a host of devices, both formal and informal, including opinion surveys, focus groups, complaint programs, suggestion boxes, and conversations at the local café. The Surviving Innovation files contain dozens of surveys and feedback mechanisms designed to help the organizations orient themselves to the outside world. They never gave the audience a veto over their work, but they did care enough to listen.

Interestingly, some of the best listeners were organizations that could just as easily have taken a head count of attendance as a sign of audience enthusiasm. Heart of the Beast, for example, listened to the audience at the front end of the production cycle by inviting community members into the design process, and at the back end by conducting a simple survey. At the end of each performance, staff would distribute a flier that said: "Our approach to play-making is akin to that of an inventor—we tinker with our work over a long period of time. You can be part of the process if you give us feedback on today's performance." What followed was a short list of simple questions, with space for answers:

> What about the production did you like most?
>
> What did you like least?
>
> Would you recommend this production to your friends and family?
>
> What do you think the children in the audience got from this production?
>
> On a scale of 1 to 10 (with 1 being worst and 10 being best), please rate the following components: Puppetry, Script, Music.

Audience members could drop the finished surveys in a box clearly marked "What About . . . [Production Name]" on the way out. The surveys were read each day as the artistic staff fine-tuned that night's production.

Like Heart of the Beast, the Minnesota Extension Service knew exactly how many people were attending its programs and calling in for advice from faculty. But starting in 1995, it began listening more carefully to people who were not attending. The first step in the effort involved a series of focus groups across the state. "The purpose of this study was to find out how the Minnesota Extension Service could improve," said the study director. "We asked people to talk about needs, concerns, and problems. Therefore, much of the information contained in this report focuses on weaknesses rather than strengths. . . . It takes a healthy organization to look inward, reflect, discover areas of concern and then share those findings publicly."

Listening often means hearing difficult messages. One of the key findings of the MES research was that many people who could benefit from its programs simply did not know what MES was or did.

"The organization lacks visibility," concluded the report. "And even when visible, images of MES are often stuck in stereotypes or limited to a person's experience." At the same time, MES also confirmed its decision to build new programs from the bottom up, not from the top down. "People want to be listened to, recognized, invited and encouraged to participate, acknowledged for their contributions, and encouraged and supported to continue involvement." The MES challenge was not so much to listen to its current audience; if it wanted to survive, it had to listen to and activate the unconverted.

The Office of Waste Management, a tiny state agency, was particularly effective at staying in touch with its audience. Its very reason for being was to reach out to the public. It used surveys, focus groups, advisory groups, and informal wandering about to listen to its audience. Its goal was to craft messages around its "three Rs" mission: reduce, reuse, recycle. Only by listening could OWM make the messages resonate.

Indeed, concerns about sending the right message to the outside world led OWM to ask the legislature for a name change late in life. Its new name, the Office of Environmental Assistance, was designed to make clear that the organization existed not to punish polluters—be they mom-and-pop dry cleaners or large industrial plants. "I'm from the Office of Environmental Assistance and I'm here to help you" seemed a better door-opener than "I'm from the Office of Waste Management"—and infinitely better, or so the OWM staff thought, than "I'm from the Pollution Control Agency and I'm here to help you."

Other organizations listened in less formal ways. Early in its effort to focus on the visitor, for example, the Minnesota Zoo created the Greet the Visitors program, which required all employees, from top management to the front line, to spend at least three hours a month welcoming visitors. The point was to get employees in touch with the source of their survival, as well as to provide visitors with a warm smile at the door. Other organizations had similar programs. The Domestic Abuse Project required its staff to spend at least one hour a week answering the crisis lines, and the North Branch School District had a call-back system for making sure parental complaints had been answered.

Many of the Surviving Innovation agencies also listened to the audience by making the audience part of the board. The Land Stewardship Project reserved space for local farmers and community members, the Domestic Abuse Project provided a slot for one of its first clients, the Central Community Housing Trust had formal rules guaranteeing a sizable share of seats to community members and residents of its properties, and Advocating Change Together had a board composed almost entirely of the developmentally disabled.

Listen to the Organization

Just as they listened to the outside world, the Surviving Innovation organizations had a variety of formal and informal systems for listening to their own employees. Some used a variation of managing by wandering around (see Peters and Waterman, 1982), encouraging senior staff to get out and about. Most created stovepipes or idea tubes to speed ideas upward from the bottom of the organization.

These stovepipes often took shape as formal suggestion programs. "Don't hit your head against a brick wall," the zoo suggestion flier told employees. "We are giving you a guarantee in writing." According to the guarantee, the zoo promised to acknowledge the suggestion within two weeks of receipt, forward it for review by a special advisory committee within four weeks, keep the employee informed of the zoo's response, and respect the employee's right to either public recognition for the suggestion or anonymity.

St. Joe's used a similar system for listening to itself: the "Hey, Doug Goke!" form. Available throughout the organization, the form invited participants to declare whether they were impressed, pleasantly surprised, satisfied, a bit annoyed, or angry, and to tell the administrator why. "I need the benefit of your viewpoint, needs, observations and impressions," Goke wrote in his preface to the form. "If you've been let down, please tell us. If you are pleased, we would like to know this, too. We do care."

Similar suggestion and complaint programs existed across the sample of Surviving Innovation organizations, most notably at Dowling (recall the Positive Action Response system and the commitment to Total Quality Management). Although these systems rarely generated innovative ideas on their own, their existence was essential in reinforcing the call for ideas. It is one thing for an organization to invite ideas upward, quite another to reinforce the invitation with systems that give employees at least one path. Moreover, the systems did produce small ideas for making life better, which in turn might give employees greater confidence in collaborating toward innovative acts.

Ultimately, no organization was better at listening to its own people than the Phoenix Group. In pursuing its vision of a healthy community, it designed its businesses to provide employment opportunities for neighborhood residents, who in turn provided guidance to Phoenix on future initiatives. "The combination of attempting to develop businesses and use businesses in a therapeutic kind of way, in a life-changing way with and for inner-city residents, is cutting-edge stuff," said Jim Nelson, the president of Change, Inc., a nonprofit consulting firm that tried to help rescue Phoenix as it came apart in late 1995. As one of the cofounders told the *Twin Cities Reader* in a retrospective after the collapse, "You could say that Phoenix got bottom-heavy real fast, because the people with the most need came regularly and those who probably should have been participating and helping with those people of great need ended up standing back, looking and judging."

Along with its financial management weaknesses, Phoenix's willingness to listen proved to be its downfall. Organizations that allow anyone who comes in the door to change the mission have to be particularly careful about who walks in the door. Having defined itself as an organization of and by the people it served, Phoenix was victimized by residents with serious personal problems, most notably chemical and alcohol dependencies. Being a good listener does not mean always saying yes. Sometimes, it is just enough to listen.

Keep Learning

As noted earlier, many organizations define learning in the narrowest terms. They maintain tight control over what employees should and should not learn, decide from above who gets what information, and see knowledge more as a *thing* to be stored than as an *energy* to be harnessed. The organization, not the employee, decides who learns what. Knowledge is allocated on a need-to-know, not want-to-know, basis. If an employee wants to take a course or seminar that does not fit the training czar's manifest, it does not get taken.

Often, what employees learn most from these systems is how not to take risks. They learn to think in narrow terms of what they need to know—secretaries need to know only about word processing and travel vouchers, not what the organization does; executives need to know about strategic vision and financial management, not what the front line does. It is a classic expression of old-time machine thinking.

The Surviving Innovation organizations had a different model. They saw learning as a compact among employees. Staff played the key role in learning by defining what knowledge they needed and recommending ways to acquire it. They took primary responsibility for seizing opportunities that would advance their own learning. Most important, these organizations ceded authority for learning to the employees. It was not up to a single person to *train* the organization, but the responsibility of everyone to *learn*, whether through formal course work or informal conversation.

As a general rule, the Surviving Innovation organizations openly encouraged employees to determine their own learning needs and provided the resources to do so. Even in organizations with extraordinarily tight budgets, there was almost always a little money available for a conference, training seminar, or book. St. Joe's even had a mini-grant program to encourage staff to become their own teachers. Under the program, staff could submit proposals for small grants ($100 or less) that would be used to prepare in-service training programs for the rest of the staff. The relatively short proposals stated the agency need, the goal of the training, the particular curriculum to be used, and the teaching method, and the final decision was made by a representative committee of employees.

Cyrus used a somewhat different process. It would scrape together the dollars for staff learning as long as the employees involved agreed to come back and teach the rest of the staff. It was a teach-the-teachers model in which very scarce resources were leveraged by making sure knowledge did not reside just in the one person who got to attend a given program. A similar approach was followed in many other Surviving Innovation organizations, including North Branch, Chance to Grow, and Advocating Change Together.

The teachers at ACT—who ran seminars on subjects such as legislative lobbying, letter writing, and media relations—were almost never outside experts; they were generally ACT members who had learned from experience. For the purpose of sharing that knowledge with others, ACT produced a video titled *Four Easy Pieces* designed to teach other teachers. With segments on assertiveness, making decisions, knowing rights, and participating in the community, the video was accompanied by a training manual developed and tested by the ACT members. "People with disabilities can use their wisdom in ways that help other people with disabilities," said one ACT founder, Gloria Steinbring. "Self-advocacy is normal. We're teaching others, breaking down the barriers, so that other people understand our disabilities. Helping people is a natural thing to do."

This is not to argue that traditional training programs should be dropped in favor of a more fluid learning system. Learning does take place in formal courses. Equally, I am not suggesting that an organization let employees take whatever courses they wish. Organizations have a stake in employees' learning certain things—for example, budgeting, diversity management, human resource management, supervision. The challenge is to frame such knowledge in a way that gives employees a stake in learning, too.

At the Minnesota Zoo, this challenge was met through Zoo University, an internal training platform for traditional and nontraditional learning. Zoo U was structured with seven units:

1. An introduction to the zoo

2. A first-day orientation on pay, benefits, and zoo policies

3. A "safari your zoo" course, looking at the zoo's history and offering a comparison with other zoos across the country

4. A pair of short seminars on service strategies, including how to manage visitor moments of truth

5. A set of longer courses on environmental stewardship and an introduction to zoo animal management for staff not involved in animal care

6. A series of courses on communication, employee recognition systems, and conflict resolution

7. Two longer courses on managing change, with a particular emphasis on cultural diversity

Although Zoo U did very well in its first years, in part because of the energy of its dean of instruction, Lucinda McCandless (or as some employees described her, Lucinda McVision), it eventually faded from prominence. Much as the zoo wanted to act as a nonprofit, it was still a state agency with very little employee turnover. After several successful years, most of its students had either taken the courses or dropped out.

Perhaps not surprisingly, Luther Theological Seminary was among the most deeply committed to learning. Indeed, part of its long-range plan for the future was to "incorporate all at Luther Seminary into a community of learning which is spiritually, physically, mentally, and emotionally healthy." That meant more than just a new curriculum and governance structure, however. It also meant a focus on a healthy community life. People cannot learn, the seminary's strategic plan argued, if they do not have a community that allows "gathering for worship, learning to care for others, becoming physically healthy in an environment which is physically safe, respecting diverse opinions and viewpoints, understanding and accepting cultural differences and assumptions, balancing solitude and silence with community and speech, and providing adequate facilities for all who teach, study and work here." Learning is not just a function of good classes and distinguished faculty. It depends on an organizational setting that celebrates learning as an essential product.

Probably none of the organizations in the Surviving Innovation sample would call themselves learning organizations, but many were headed in that direction. (For appropriate definitions of the term, see Marquardt, 1996; Cohen and Sproull, 1996; Senge, 1990.) At The Pew Charitable Trusts in Philadelphia, where I wrote this book, the effort to become a learning organization has followed many of the lessons outlined here. Employees have been given more freedom to chart their own directions in learning, and the organization as a whole has made a series of commitments to making that learning easier. It has recommissioned its evaluation unit to become a source of learning resources, launched the first courses at Pew University (on general orientation, introduction to philanthropy, grant crafting, and personal development), and changed its basic decision-making systems to provide opportunities for greater learning across programs. Like Luther, it is working to create a community of learning, not just a better inventory of training experiences.

Conclusion

The Surviving Innovation organizations resolved one of the great tensions in contemporary management: they were mostly able to use management systems in support of mission, not vice versa. They clearly believed that good management is essential to maintaining the edge but did not allow the systems to drive out mission. Instead, they used good management to reinforce performance as the measure of success. Again, none of the Surviving Innovation organizations were perfect. As the inventory presented earlier in the chapter clearly demonstrates, they managed to maintain their edge in spite of weaknesses in a variety of systems. They did so by focusing on assets, not liabilities. Although all of the organizations but the Phoenix Group were strong on financial management, all also had some weakness somewhere. It seems reasonable to infer that an innovating organization can do just fine with relatively weak pay and personnel systems, strategic planning, information management, and time management.

This is not to argue that organizations should abandon these systems altogether; strategic planning, for example, clearly helped the organizations that could afford it. Rather, the findings suggest that the journey toward becoming an innovating organization begins with strong financial management and continues with strong idea generation, governance, fundraising, and managing for results. Organizations on this path can tolerate fairly weak information management if they have strong idea generators, for example, and can go some distance without strategic planning if they manage for results.

If there is any one system that was surprisingly weak given my early hunches on how one might manage an innovating organization, it was the learning system. The Surviving Innovation organizations were clearly learning organizations at some level, but the challenge they often failed to meet was to *learn the right lessons*. Much as they tried not to repeat the same mistake twice, they were not very deliberate in chronicling their mistakes. Aside from St. Joe's and Episcopal Community Services, which created critical incident tracking systems as part of the accreditation process, the organizations in the sample learned mostly by accident.

Perhaps it is the academic in me, but I believe good learning systems are as essential to innovating organizations as is sound financial management or governance. They can certainly increase the chances that good ideas will rise on their own merit, and they can also reduce the odds that the same mistake will occur over and over as board members, legislators, and employees come and go.

7

Confronting Real Life
in Nonprofit and
Government Organizations

The challenge in searching for preferred states of being among the Surviving Innovation sample, indeed any sample, is that not all organizations are created equal. Some are big, others small; some are young, others older; some specialize in changing how they deliver services, others in what they deliver; some work in human services, others in economic development.

The variations in the Surviving Innovation sample are substantial. The biggest organization (Anoka County) had a $130 million budget, whereas the smallest (People Escaping Poverty Project) had one just under $100,000; the youngest organization (Phoenix Group) was barely 3 years old when the Surviving Innovation project began, whereas the oldest (Anoka County) was 137 years old; half were primarily *how* innovators and half primarily *what* innovators; and as Appendix B shows, the range of issues they dealt with ran the gamut from arts and culture to special education, environment, and social services.

When compared with the universe of *government* organizations, the Surviving Innovation sample favored relatively small government agencies. Hennepin County government, which covers Minneapolis and its suburbs, is almost ten times as big as Anoka, most Minneapolis public schools dwarf tiny Cyrus Math/Tech, and the Minnesota Office of Waste Management is but a rounding error on the Pollution Control Agency's organization chart.

This bias was an almost inevitable product of the search for innovating organizations. Although single acts of innovation occur in large government agencies every day, it is difficult to find many such agencies that could be remotely described as innovating organizations. At least in Minnesota, the search for organizations that were large, governmental, and innovating produced an empty set.

Not so for the nonprofit sector. When compared with the universe of *nonprofit* organizations, the Surviving Innovation sample appears to be a representative collection of large and small, young and old. There is nothing in the literature on nonprofit organizations to suggest that the typical Surviving Innovation nonprofit is radically different from the typical nonprofit nationwide (see Powell, 1987; Salamon, 1992).

Whether typical, as in the case of the nonprofits, or atypical, as in the case of the government agencies, the Surviving Innovation sample conveys a cautionary tale about fitting preferences to realities. If not all organizations are created equal, perhaps not all preferences fit so tightly. It is one thing to recommend a small innovation investment fund to a $130 million county government and quite another to recommend such a fund to a small nonprofit. It is one thing for a small nonprofit to adopt a flat organizational structure and quite another for a heavily scrutinized government agency to stay lean.

Thus organizational self-knowledge is an essential step in picking among the preferred states of being outlined in this book. Whether an organization is young, small, and nonprofit or old, large, and governmental, it will certainly find some preferences that fit and others that do not. The rest of this chapter will examine the fit of preferences to reality using the data summarized in Appendix C.

Know Thyself

That the preferred states of being for organizational innovativeness might vary by the size, age, sector, and issue focus of a given organization is as close to a truism as the research on innovation gets.

Scholars may not agree on much about innovation, but they certainly agree that organizations vary (see Downs and Mohr, 1976, for a classic statement of the issue). They have dealt with the one-size-fits-all problem either by narrowing their focus to one particular type of organization (small or old or social service) or by making the differences within their samples of organizations more explicit. Because the Surviving Innovation sample was designed to cover a range of organizational sizes, ages, and types, the latter approach is the only one feasible here.

Before turning to differences among the Surviving Innovation organizations, it is important to note that not all the preferred states of being are conditional. There are clear preferences that hold for all of the Surviving Innovation organizations, regardless of size, age, sector, emphasis, or issue focus. As Exhibit 7.1 shows, there was unanimity in answering yes to five of the eighty-four questions listed in Appendix C, including two concerning the importance of mission to innovativeness. There was near unanimity (90 percent agreement or above) on another twelve questions, including those on the subjects of gathering ideas, giving permission to make mistakes, and managerial rigor. And there was close agreement (80 percent plus) on fourteen questions important in connection with leadership and paying attention to the outside world. Finally, there was unanimous, near unanimous, or close agreement in answering no to five questions, including an absolute 0 percent on using merit pay as a contributor to innovativeness.

Even where there is close agreement, however, there can still be important differences among the Surviving Innovation organizations. As we shall shortly see, the smaller and older organizations were more likely than larger and younger ones to use intuition and judgment in measuring success. Smaller organizations (whether measured by staff or budget) may not have the dollars to purchase the prevailing substitutes for intuition—for example, analysis and evaluation—whereas older organizations may face less external pressure to measure their performance in hard numbers.

Exhibit 7.1. An Inventory of Agreements

Unanimous "Yes" (100 percent)

1. Does the organization worry about its mission?
2. Do the staff and the board identify with the mission?
3. Does the organization support training for the staff and the board?
4. Does the organization appear to learn from its mistakes?
5. Is the organization disciplined/rigorous about its governance systems?

Near-Unanimous "Yes" (90–99 percent)

1. Is there external political support for innovation?
2. Does the organization scan the environment for new funding?
3. Are there informal lines of communication within the organization in support of innovation?
4. Is communication of decisions clear?
5. Does the leadership give permission to make mistakes?
6. Does the organization enjoy its work?
7. Are new ideas gathered throughout the organization?
8. Does the organization judge new ideas by fit with mission?
9. Does the organization judge new ideas by organizational capacity?
10. Are there strong internal financial controls?
11. Is the organization rigorous/disciplined about its personnel systems?
12. Is the organization rigorous/disciplined about its budget systems?

Close Agreement "Yes" (80–89 percent)

1. Is the market a contributor to innovativeness?
2. Does the organization collaborate with other organizations?
3. Does the organization have unpaid volunteers?
4. Does staff work across bureaucratic boundaries?
5. Does the organization provide resources for idea development and launch?
6. Is the organization headed by a single executive?
7. Is there clarity about who makes what decisions?
8. Is leadership a contributor to innovativeness?
9. Is the general leadership style participatory?

10. Does the organization pay attention to its audience, customers, or clients?
11. Does the organization actively seek evaluation of its programs?
12. Is there a role for intuition and judgment in measuring success?
13. Does the organization trust its members?
14. Is there an orientation for new board members?

Unanimous, Near-Unanimous, or Close Agreement "No" (80–100 percent)

1. Is there external opposition to innovation?
2. Is the environment rule-laden against innovation?
3. Have there been more than two executive directors in the past five years?
4. Is the general leadership style heroic?
5. Is merit pay a contributor to innovativeness?

Moreover, once past the unanimous and near-unanimous preferences, the Surviving Innovation organizations showed significant differences by sector (nonprofit or government), type of innovativeness (*how* or *what*), size (measured by staff and budget), and age. (Unfortunately, there were simply too few organizations in the sample to distinguish preferred states of being by issue focus.) The analysis that follows suggests that innovating organizations pick and choose among the preferred states of organizational being according to circumstance. Although some preferred states are absolutely essential—for example, strong internal financial controls—others are more elective. One size definitely does not fit all.

Nonprofit Versus Government

Even though the eight government organizations in the Surviving Innovation sample often behaved very much like the eighteen nonprofits, there is ample evidence in Appendix C that the two sectors are different. Although the relatively small sample size suggests caution in interpreting the data, there are a number of divisions that suggest different paths to innovativeness in the nonprofit and government sectors.

Before turning to these lessons in more detail, it is important to note the differences between the two sectors in type of innovativeness, size, and age. The government agencies tended to be older than the nonprofits (fifty-three years, on average, versus thirty-two years), larger (346 full-time staff versus 47; $28 million budget versus $2.6 million), and much more likely to focus on innovations in how they did business than in what they produced. Seven of the eight government organizations were primarily *how* innovators (meaning they focused primarily on changing how they delivered services), whereas twelve of the eighteen nonprofit organizations were *what* innovators (meaning they focused on changing what they delivered). It is no surprise that government agencies would mostly emphasize *how* innovation, if only because legislative bodies have such a significant say in what those agencies do.

The two sectors also differed in their external environments, internal bureaucracies, leadership, and management systems, each of which will be discussed in brief. With respect to *environment,* the nonprofit organizations were much more likely than the government ones to have unpredictable environments, less likely to have a monopoly in their fields, and more likely to have a waiting list for services. These organizations existed in permanent white water, and experienced far greater uncertainty than their government counterparts. For them, the problem was not so much to invite the market in for a visit but to manage the intense competition for scarce funds and visibility.

At least one of the government agencies, the Minnesota Zoo, witnessed a dramatic change in its environment after the field work for this project was completed. The Mall of America opened a new aquarium in 1996, complete with a shark exhibit and coral reef, in direct competition with the Minnesota Zoo and its dolphins. The zoo did not, however, passively stand by as the mall siphoned off its attendance. Instead, it raised $25 million to build its own new marine science center.

Government organizations are hardly immune from external pressure, however. As Appendix C also suggests, it was the government agencies, not the nonprofits, that were more likely to receive a wake-up call from their environments. Six of the eight government organizations had been shocked by crisis within the previous five years. Four of the six were public schools, startled into alertness by public school choice; another was the Minnesota Extension Service, shocked by a deep budget crisis; and the last was the Minnesota Zoo, also shocked by state budget cutbacks.

Although both sectors found external political support for innovation, they differed sharply in the extent to which the environment contained more tangible rewards and punishments for innovativeness. Government agencies were far more likely to exist in a rule-laden environment, presumably driven again by legislative bodies, less likely to exist in fields with histories of innovation, yet quite clearly concerned about their basic survival as sources of innovativeness.

These data point to the barriers facing innovation in government agencies. In a sense, the nonprofit organizations studied here were already more naturally oriented toward innovativeness, led more by general turbulence and a history of innovation, whereas the government agencies had to be shocked awake with threats to survival in order to counteract their sluggishness.

This general sluggishness is equally apparent in *internal structure*, where the government agencies were more likely than nonprofits to pay attention to the thickness of their administrative hierarchies. Although both worried about their general shape—trying to avoid the middle-level bulge that comes with organizational aging—the government agencies worked a bit harder at staying thin. Staying thin was clearly a concern for Anoka County and the Minnesota Extension Service, both of which worried about remaining relatively flat in spite of their relatively large staffs. But largeness was not the only determinant of worries about thickness. With a staff of less than one hundred, the Dowling School also worried about its hierarchy, in large part because it was so concerned about keeping the distance between top (principal and parents) and bottom (students) short.

Although size was mostly a barrier to innovativeness in the government setting, it did allow the bigger agencies in the Surviving Innovation sample to put money into promising ideas. The three largest organizations (Anoka County at 1,550 full-time employees, Minnesota Extension Service at 600, and the Minnesota Zoo at 250) all had innovation investment funds, two of which (at MES and the zoo) were allocated through internal competitions. This is hardly an endorsement for increasing organizational size as a sure path to innovation, of course. After all, none of these organizations begins to approach the immensity of even the standard big-city bureaucracy, let alone a major department of state or federal government. Size here is obviously relative. Larger size means extra resources, but also demands a more conscious effort to cultivate ideas and create internal competition.

Diversity is also relative. The eighteen nonprofit organizations were more likely to mirror the ethnic and racial diversity of their communities than were the government agencies, in part perhaps because they were more directly accountable to the neighborhoods and clienteles they served. This was particularly true of the economic and community development organizations, which saw ethnic and racial diversity as essential to local credibility. Hence, CLUES was heavily staffed by Chicanos and Latinos. Other nonprofits maintained clear ties to their communities through income and/or residential diversity. The Phoenix Group drew heavily on staff from its predominantly poor neighborhood, as did Project for Pride in Living, while Artspace had a staff active in the arts.

Interestingly, however, many of these organizations were anything but diverse professionally. It was not unusual to find an ethnically diverse social service agency in which all staffers had master's degrees in social work. Here, it was the government agencies that did better at recruiting diversity.

The data on *leadership* suggest more agreement than disagreement between the two sectors. The major difference concerned the degree to which an organization encouraged dissent. The leaders of the government agencies may have said they wanted strong points of view, but their staffs often reported a rather different attitude. Creating an environment in which frontline staff felt comfortable voicing their differences appeared to be easier in the nonprofit sector, perhaps because the barriers to such honesty are so high in government agencies. Another possible explanation is the greater tendency of nonprofit leaders to believe in luck, good fortune, grace, and intuition and to build spiritual concerns directly into conversations about work. Such conversations may create a sense of forgiveness within the organization that allows individuals to voice their concerns honestly.

Indeed, despite the general agreements on most of the leadership items, nothing is so different in the two sectors than this readiness to trust instinct and faith. The depth of faith-based conversation within most of the nonprofits studied here was unmistakably uplifting to those involved. This faith was explicitly proclaimed in organizations such as Episcopal Community Services, Luther Theological Seminary, and St. Joseph's Home for Children, all three of which had obvious religious ties, and was more subtly revealed in organizations such as the Land Stewardship Project or Project for Pride in Living, both of which had close ties to the Catholic tradition, PPL having been established by a former priest.

Although no one can be certain that these organizations performed better because of their faith, few could visit these organizations and not sense a shared vision that allowed staff to take greater risks with each other and with ideas. In the obviously more secularized government agencies, faith and intuition were often replaced by policy analysis and evaluation, which can sometimes discourage staff from taking the risks needed to innovate. It comes as no surprise, therefore, that the nonprofits put less of an emphasis on dollars and workability in evaluating competing ideas. They tended to believe, even assert, that the dollars would come to ideas that work.

This is not to suggest that government is filled with faithless leaders and staff. But public conversations about faith in something greater than self are mostly off-limits. Government must build its momentum around technique and analysis, which may weaken the ultimate perseverance of the organization. As noted earlier in this book, faith plays several important roles in innovating organizations, not the least of which is providing a sense of place in history and a readiness to forgive the small mistakes that occur in the natural evolution of ideas. Technique and analysis are poor substitutes for the basic faith needed to keep the edge in spite of inevitable setbacks.

The data on *internal management systems* fit well with the different environments in which the two sectors operate. The Surviving Innovation nonprofits were more likely than the government agencies to have a reserve fund or other cushion for lean times, in part because they are more vulnerable to temporary shortfalls in cash, in part because government agencies operate under a spend-it-or-lose-it budget system. The nonprofits were less likely than the government agencies to push budget authority downward, perhaps because of this greater vulnerability, and were less likely to have formal systems for provoking ideas, probably because they were smaller, flatter, and more oriented toward coughing up ideas in response to their environments.

Looking back over the data, one is prompted to ask whether it is easier to maintain an innovating organization in the nonprofit sector or government. The answer appears to be that innovating is easier in nonprofits—a conclusion warranted perhaps by the fact that seven of the eight government organizations behaved more like nonprofits than government units. As of this writing, the zoo has been struggling to convert itself into a nonprofit for the better part of nine years, believing that nonprofit status would give it enormous freedoms to innovate more naturally. The only obstacle is the high capital cost of maintaining the zoo infrastructure.

This is not to suggest that the life of an innovating nonprofit organization is easy. But the bias toward innovating appears easier to create and maintain in nonprofits. All the more reason, one might argue, for urging heroic government leaders to focus their energies on tearing down the barriers to a similar orientation in government.

How Versus *What* Innovativeness

Innovations in what an agency does (sometimes called *technical innovation*) are closely related to innovations in how it does it (*administrative innovation*). Some researchers argue, for example, that technical innovations almost always provoke administrative innovations, which in turn create the administrative capacity needed to provoke further technical innovations, and so on. (See Daft, 1978, for the classic statement of the difference between the two types of innovation.)

The power of sequencing has been studied in two very different government settings: public libraries and hospitals. In the libraries, the adoption of administrative innovations such as computer-based accounting and personnel systems, strategic planning, and new staff training curricula produced technical innovations such as computer-based cataloguing, automated circulation control, and book-by-mail service (Damanpour, Szabat, and Evan, 1989). In the hospitals, the introduction of new medical technologies such as the ultrasonic nebulizer and blood gas electrode system created pressure for new administrative procedures such as electronic data processing, which in turn produced secondary effects that enhanced a hospital's sensitivity to market pressures (Kimberly and Evanisko, 1981).

Obviously, it is not clear which type of innovation should come first. Should a new nonprofit or government agency focus on nurturing a technical innovation, such as welfare reform, in the hope that the organization will have to change its administrative procedures as a result? Or is it best to start with an administrative innovation, such as a laptop-based case-management program, and wait for the technical innovation to follow?

As argued earlier in this book, administrative procedures in many government agencies are so resistant to innovation that no amount of technical innovation may be enough to disturb the prevailing system. There may be a tipping point below which single acts of technical innovation and the heroic innovators who produce them are mostly defeated by bureaucratic resistance. At least in Minnesota, therefore, government agencies have tended to start with administrative innovation, whereas nonprofits have been oriented more toward the technical.

Moreover, despite the unmistakable symbiotic relationship between *how* and *what* innovativeness, the Surviving Innovation cases tended to specialize in one or the other. Luther Theological Seminary is a case in point. There is only so much a Lutheran seminary might do to create technical innovation in what it teaches, but much it might do to invent new ways to deliver its message.

With the Bible as its core text and a long history of doctrinal debates that framed its theological positions, Luther focused on how to better deliver its curriculum rather than on how to radically change its overall message. It worked on bridging the gap between theory and practice, moving toward an integrated curriculum, changing its governance structure, introducing new courses that applied traditional teachings to contemporary issues such as human sexuality, and drawing on alternative teaching media. The gospel of Jesus Christ remained at the center of the curriculum but was to be taught in new and imaginative ways.

As this example suggests, nonprofit and government organizations do not always have a choice between *how* and *what* innovation. The environment may preclude technical innovation in government agencies, in large measure because of tight political oversight or other legal, regulatory constraints, even as it discourages administrative innovation in nonprofit organizations, in large part because external funders have proven so reluctant to cover the overhead costs of such reforms. It is no surprise, therefore, that so many of the Minnesota nonprofits focused on developing ideas that met a market test for funding or that government agencies focused on administrative reform. Both were reasonable paths given the prevailing incentives.

Appendix C reveals a number of differences in the preferences of *how* and *what* innovators. The former were more typically found in rule-laden environments with less history of innovation. They were more likely to collaborate with other organizations and had significantly less internal conflict over competing ideas, less exposure to internal reorganization, less internal stress, more intellectual and professional diversity, more internal collaboration, and significantly lower turnover.

Organizations that were *how* innovators were often less stressful places in which to work, in part because so many focused on administrative innovations that created greater employee participation and trust. Unlike the *what* innovators, who sometimes used stress and high staff turnover to ensure a supply of fresh ideas, the *how* innovators worked with calmer external and internal environments. Although these patterns reflect the high number of government agencies in the pool of *how* innovators, the trends also reflect the competitiveness that characterizes the world in which many nonprofits operate.

The *what* innovators clearly lived on the organizational edge. Not only were they buffeted by an unpredictable environment and more stressful working conditions, they relied on somewhat different kinds of leadership. Their leaders were more likely *not* to come from the professional field served by the organization, a fact that suggests a greater focus on maintaining an edge almost against the prevailing ideology of the environment. The *what* leaders were also somewhat more likely to operate with a heroic, against-the-odds leadership style; to put more focus on luck, intuition, and faith in creating an organizational culture in support of innovativeness; and were less likely than their colleagues to worry about dollar cost and workability of ideas. Their organizations were somewhat less sensitive to audience, more likely to have internal systems for red-flagging problems, twice as likely to have budget information in real time, half as likely to have a formal system for provoking ideas, and much less sensitive to managing time, all of which fit with a pressure to stay ahead of the market.

It is no surprise, therefore, that the *what* innovators were stressful organizations in which to work. Although they were just as likely to enjoy their work, they tended to thrive on pressure, even to the point of actually manufacturing stress to keep the organization alive and vibrant. It was just this churning, for example, that made Theatre de la Jeune Lune so successful in maintaining its artistic edge. Although the theater was remarkably rigorous about internal systems, maintaining tight control of production costs through a single business manager, its artistic vision was in constant flux as the four artistic directors pursued new ideas.

Recall that the team often did its best work while cooking in the on-site kitchen, which served as the theater's executive conference room. Because the four founders played some role in every performance, rotating among writing, directing, performing, choreographing, building sets, raising funds, and taking tickets, there was no shortage of conflict over time. Indeed, it was in the conflict that came from this constant shifting of roles that the theater found energy to create new visions of classics such as *Germinal* or invent new works such as *The Green Bird*.

Small Versus Large

Size is a double-edged sword for innovating organizations. On the one hand, size creates internal resources that can be invested in promising ideas. It can also insulate the organization from political opposition and allow somewhat greater control of the environment. (All of the large organizations in the Surviving Innovation sample held monopolies in their fields—at least until the Mall of America challenged the Minnesota Zoo's marine monopoly.) Size can also increase the odds that a good idea will find a champion.

On the other hand, as already noted, size can create distance between top and bottom, thereby increasing the transaction costs of moving ideas up the hierarchy and sending guidance down. Size can also create internal barriers that work against collaboration. Furthermore, although bigger organizations may have more money to invest, they may face greater obstacles to successful implementation and monitoring. And finally, size can generate a rise in formal work rules, which may reduce risk taking by frontline employees.

Both edges of the sword are apparent in Appendix C, which breaks down the Surviving Innovation sample by budget and staff. Size works its will in all four areas of organizational life.

Start with *environment*, where the bigger Surviving Innovation organizations experienced less turbulence but a greater incidence of shocks. In one of the most curious twists in the data, the larger organizations were simultaneously much more likely than their smaller peers to have a monopoly in their fields and more likely to use the market as a contributor to innovativeness. One possible explanation lies in the higher incidence of external shocks among the bigger organizations. Big or not, monopoly or not, these organizations were quite aware of the world outside, perhaps because they had so much organizational weight at risk of budget cutbacks.

Moreover, many of the monopolies were very narrow. The fact that the Minnesota Extension Service had a monopoly as the only land-grant university extension service in the state did not mean it faced no competition for citizen attention. As attendance at its myriad events around the state continued to fall during the 1980s, MES received a very significant wake-up call. The mere fact that it held a seminar on sustainable agriculture did not mean farmers would attend. It had to fight for audience share against a host of other claimants, not the least of which were prime-time television and the Minnesota Vikings professional football team.

Similarly, the fact that the Minnesota Zoo had a monopoly as the only zoo in the state with dolphins and timber wolves did not mean it faced no competition for the entertainment dollar. In fact, the zoo defined its competition broadly to include amusement parks, the Minnesota State Fair, the annual Renaissance Fair, and the Mall of America's indoor amusement park, Camp Snoopy, all of which were closer to the metropolitan audience than was the zoo. As the zoo's costs went up during the 1980s, so did its ticket prices, leading to a slow but steady erosion of audience base. Only by competing for the entertainment dollar with more attractive exhibits, better food, ample and free parking, and friendlier staff could the zoo hope to survive.

So, too, with the Walker Art Center, which held a Minnesota monopoly as a home for modern art, be it painting, sculpture, film, or performance. Like the zoo and other theaters, the Walker could survive only by making itself *the* destination for art-goers. Although hardly willing to mold itself into Disneyland North, the Walker clearly worried about how to position itself as a safe place for unsafe ideas. Sometimes, doing so meant great controversy, as in its decision to present HIV-positive performance artist Ron Athey.

Interestingly, these bigger organizations tended to operate in less appreciative environments, whether manifested in a lower level of political support for innovation (perhaps because bigger organizations are rarely the new kid on the block that captures the funder's fancy) or a heavy thicket of rules governing action. Perhaps big organizations only get to be big by surviving year in, year out in relatively noninnovative environments. Hence the need for some shock to wake them from their slumber and the tendency to rely more on basic survival needs as the driver for innovativeness.

Size also had an impact on *internal structure*, not surprisingly creating significant challenges for the bigger organizations. Bigness also meant a certain thickness of hierarchy—which I define as the height (number of layers) and width (number of employees in each layer) of the organization. Although there were only four organizations that had more than two hundred employees, two had a substantial middle-level bulge, occupied by managers who had either aged or been promoted into midlevel management. If size was a contributor to innovativeness in these less wieldy organizations, it was only apparent in one, the Minnesota Extension Service, which used its size to create a large innovation investment fund. At least as it affected the shape of the organization, size acted more as a barrier than a help to innovativeness.

Size also appeared to increase the level of internal conflict and stress. At the Minnesota Extension Service, for example, budget cutbacks simultaneously created an intense interest in innovation and deep fears of downsizing, both of which occurred. Similarly, concerns about market share prompted great discomfort at Luther Theological Seminary, which suddenly went from being one of three seminaries serving the American Synod of the Lutheran Church to one of seven serving the newly merged Evangelical Lutheran Church of America. Because the new church could not possibly support all seven, the threat to Luther was quite real.

Size produced expected impacts on internal demographics and boundaries. The bigger the organization in this sample, the more difficult it was for it to be demographically matched to its community. Big organizations may have more than enough turnover at the bottom to recruit racial and ethnic diversity, but they may find it difficult to change the middle and higher levels, particularly in government agencies with strong career service protection.

It is in generating internal slack for innovation that big organizations have their greatest advantages. The small Surviving Innovation organizations seemed to be more agile, diverse, and likely to solve problems collaboratively, but they had less funding to deploy at the early, crucial stage of idea development. As the data in Appendix C suggest, the challenge for the big organizations lay much less in inviting ideas up from the bottom and much more in choosing among the competitors. With strong bureaucratic champions ready to systems for winnowing the field of possible innovations. The Minnesota Zoo required that every new idea be presented with a business plan, complete with market projections, profit-and-loss statement, and payback plan for returning the initial investment. Artspace used an equally rigorous assessment process for its housing investments, as did the Central Community Housing Trust for its expansion plans.

Investment planning was hardly absent in the smaller Surviving Innovation organizations. To the contrary, their size made most of these organizations acutely aware of the cost of things. Moreover, some of the very best business planning systems could be found in the smallest organizations. The three-person American Indian Business Development Corporation was particularly sensitive to preventing loss and was anything but gentle in making project decisions. Allowing Coyote Chile to take space in the AIBDC small business incubator depended just as much on an analysis of rates of return as on the taste of the salsa.

However, the smaller organizations as a group had greater difficulty enforcing financial controls, in part because they were often so close to the communities they served. The Phoenix Group made the decision to open the Phoenix Cafe because it simply believed a strong neighborhood had to have a good place for breakfast and lunch. It used the same logic in leasing the space for a grocery store, believing that neighborhood residents should not have to take a bus to the suburbs to get a decent price on bread and milk. Both were very risky ventures that drew heavily on the organization's vision of the neighborhood and its faith in the possible, and as noted earlier, the grocery store played a central role in creating the financial crisis that eventually caused the organization's demise.

Size also matters to *leadership*. The smaller organizations in the Surviving Innovation sample were more tolerant of a nontraditional leadership structure. Cyrus Math/Tech was led by a self-managed team composed of six teachers, Theater de la Jeune Lune by a four-person team, and Chance to Grow/New Visions School by codirectors. Recall that Cyrus created its team to save money, believing that a full-time principal was simply not worth the cost. The school used the dollar savings to invest in capital equipment for new technologies.

The smaller organizations also appeared to be more tolerant of dissent and less likely to depend on leadership as the source of innovativeness. This latter point does not mean that leadership was irrelevant but rather that the lines between leader and follower were somewhat difficult to discern. Where did leadership begin and end at Cyrus or at Theater de la Jeune Lune? Moreover, as the figures on leadership strategy in Appendix C suggest, smaller organizations were much more likely to believe in luck, fortune, and grace than their larger peers. One of these smaller organizations actually used astrology as part of its planning process, and another repeatedly emphasized its belief in magic.

Finally, the smaller organizations were also more likely to embrace conversations about faith and spirituality. As noted earlier, larger organizations are much more likely to substitute analysis and evaluation for luck and faith, in part because they have the dollars to buy the analysis and evaluation in the first place, and in part because conversations about faith can be more difficult in larger organizational settings.

Just because smaller organizations did not have the dollars for evaluation does not mean they ignored outcomes. As we shall see, they actually worried more than the bigger organizations about measurable indicators of performance, perhaps seeing them as selling points for generating funder interest in a turbulent environment.

This focus on luck and faith helps explain the relative lack of concern for dollar cost and workability as criteria for sorting new ideas in smaller organizations. At the Land Stewardship Project, for example, there is a palpable sense that God will provide. The best the organization can do is live in a state of grace—that is, be conscious of its mission and ready to act when opportunity arises. Everything else takes care of itself as a result.

Believing in luck and good fortune does not mean sloppy accounting systems, however. Small organizations and large alike worry about keeping track of their funding. It is mostly in the relative availability of organizational slack that size mattered to *internal management systems*. Thus only a handful of the smaller Surviving Innovation organizations had merit pay or a formal idea-generating system, and a majority could not find the dollars for a reserve fund. Nevertheless, as suggested earlier, the smaller organizations were hardly undisciplined about their financial performance. They were the most likely to have a stop-spending policy to reduce exposure from high-risk ventures and were actually the most committed to measuring the outcomes of their programs. They also gave their employees greater access to full budgetary information, even though they were less likely than larger organizations to give front-line employees budgetary authority. Part of this caution may relate, of course, to the lack of real-time budgeting. However boring they may seem, rigorous accounting systems are one means of making trust possible.

Young Versus Old

Age and size are clearly related. As an organization ages, it often tends to get bigger, attracting new programs and responsibilities. Organizational demographics may also conspire to increase size over time, particularly in government agencies. Employees advance up the career ladder, building seniority and creating a natural tendency toward middle-level thickening.

The relationship between age and size is hardly perfect, however. One of the oldest Surviving Innovation organizations, the Minnesota Extension Service, actually declined in size during the 1980s in the wake of budgetary pressure. In fact, as the data in Appendix C suggest, it was the smaller organizations that were actually growing the fastest. During the period covered by the Surviving Innovation Project,

CLUES began expanding its social services from West St. Paul to Minneapolis.

The Domestic Abuse Project began offering counseling services to gay and lesbian abusers and their partners.

The Phoenix Group bought its grocery store and increased its housing development goals.

Artspace extended its operation to Duluth and began planning for a national launch.

Theatre de la Jeune Lune moved from a high school auditorium to a newly renovated warehouse-district theater and a full season of production, complete with subscription ticket sales.

Chance to Grow/New Visions School became a contract, or charter, school in the Minneapolis School District.

Such growth offers great challenges, of course. In dealing with the *environment*, the younger Surviving Innovation organizations were much more likely to face external competition in their fields, greater opposition to innovation, and significant threats to survival. They also had fewer buffers against turbulence. They were less likely than the older organizations to have a monopoly in their fields or to have the kind of membership base that sometimes protects an organization against lean times. New theaters, for example, are less likely to have stable subscriptions; new schools may have greater difficulty drawing students.

Moreover, even as they were buffeted by a turbulent environment, these young organizations experienced a surprisingly high incidence of shocks. For the Phoenix Group, at least, this combination eventually meant collapse.

Yet what made these organizations more vulnerable to the environment may also have made them particularly exciting places to work. Even though they lived close to the organizational edge, they were not particularly stressful or conflict-filled workplaces, and these organizations clearly enjoyed what they were doing. They were mission centered and appeared to motivate their employees by calling on mission. Given a choice between young and old, the graduate students who worked with me on the Surviving Innovation Project were invariably drawn to the young. They saw the chance to make a difference more clearly there than anywhere else.

Other blessings of youth were apparent in *internal structure*. The younger organizations were more likely to be demographically connected to their communities, more likely to use overall diversity as a contributor to, yet less likely to have high turnover than older organizations. Staff were more likely to work collaboratively and face fewer bureaucratic boundaries. In this sample, the younger organizations were also thinner, at least in part because they experienced internal turbulence in addition to external white water. They were exactly twice as likely as the older organizations to have experienced a major reorganization within the previous five years, perhaps giving them a chance to clean out unnecessary layers.

Youth also affected the *leadership* of the Surviving Innovation organizations. The younger organizations were less likely to have the traditional single leader and were more likely to have high executive turnover. Although these organizations clearly survived, leadership turnover cannot be characterized as a preferred state of being for innovativeness. The Office of Waste Management, for example, innovated in spite of unrelenting turnover at the top. With strong adversaries in the Pollution Control Administration, OWM was in constant distress, yet persevered in rolling out one innovative pollution prevention effort after another. At least in this one organization, a single-minded focus on mission was enough to overcome external hostility and leadership instability that might have killed lesser agencies.

The hazards of youth can be summed up in a single word: *money*. As a general rule, the younger Surviving Innovation organizations lived under constant cost pressure. One of the reasons they used external funding as an incentive for innovativeness, for example, was that they did not have internal funding as an alternative. They knew the cost of everything, did not have money for merit pay, made the availability of funding a top criterion for evaluating new ideas, had less opportunity to create a reserve fund, and had very strong systems for preventing financial disaster.

Like the older organizations in the sample, the younger organizations worried about whether the source of funds (for example, from Honeywell, Inc., once an international weapons maker with a generous philanthropic program) would somehow carry strings or taint their mission, but they seemed somewhat more willing to set aside those worries in the interests of survival. At the same time, however, they were moving so fast that they could not provide information in real time. It could be said that they did not need formal systems for forcing ideas up from the bottom, in part because the bottom was closer (they had less thickening), and in part because they were properly oriented to pay attention to their audiences, customers, and clients. They did, indeed, live closer to the edge.

As far as *internal management systems* were concerned, age had its advantages in almost every area, in part because budget size and age were closely related. The bigger the organization became, the more likely it was to have the financial systems to provide information in real time and to have the flexibility to create reserve funds for lean times. Ironically, the older Surviving Innovation organizations also had the dollars to reduce exposure to risk—ironic because the younger organizations may have had the greatest risks (recall that the younger organizations faced significantly higher external competition). Furthermore, the older organizations had money for external evaluation but appeared much more likely to temper that evaluation with intuition and judgment, perhaps because of their greater financial security.

At the same time, older organizations had a much greater tendency to use formal systems for provoking ideas from within, perhaps because, over the years, they would drift somewhat from mission. As the memories of their foundings faded, they sometimes forgot why they existed and whom they served. In sum, what age provides in terms of financial security may be lost through a narrowing in the flow of ideas. As organizations age, they risk a kind of idea sclerosis, a hardening of the innovation arteries. It is a disease well worth preventing by focusing on mission.

Thus aging appeared to produce greater bureaucratic boundaries, less connectedness to the community, more need for formal systems to provoke ideas, and more need for shocks to jump-start the organization's interest in innovativeness. Although older organizations were more comfortable places to work perhaps, greater age brought its own share of challenges, not the least of which was a certain complacency. If the task of leadership in the young organizations was to survive, the task in the oldest was to wake up.

Interestingly, the data confirm the balancing act of middle age. No longer quite so agile, but not yet quite so seasoned, the middle-aged organizations in the Surviving Innovation sample followed a less predictable path to innovativeness. Although they suffered the fewest shocks by far and operated in a less rule-laden environment, they had the greatest amount of internal conflict over ideas and the highest levels of stress. They also were more likely to invite the market into the organization, perhaps as a revitalization tool. At the same time, they gave their staff greater access to information, worried about recruiting effective board members, and were most likely to focus on mission and internal capacity in evaluating new ideas. Caught between youth and older age, perhaps it is no surprise that they believed so much in luck and good fortune and were so much more likely to make questions of faith and spirituality prominent in their ongoing work. Perhaps one needs to have faith to endure the loss of agility that comes with age.

Lessons Learned

This brief analysis only scratches the surface of how innovating organizations might apply the preferred states of being outlined earlier in this book. It is possible, for example, that large government organizations would apply a rather different set of preferences from those applied by large nonprofit organizations. (See Roberts and Wargo, 1993, for a discussion of how large government agencies might use strategic planning to compensate for size.) It is also possible that small government organizations have considerable advantages over small nonprofits, particularly in terms of long-term budgetary security.

Unfortunately, the Surviving Innovation sample cannot provide insights on such subgroups. Multiplying two categories of sector by two types of innovation, three rough levels of size (small, medium, large), and three levels of age (young, middle, and old) produces thirty-six categories, a number that exceeds the total sample size by ten. There are simply not enough data to warrant firm conclusions about the interactions between sector, type of innovation, size, and age.

Nevertheless, this overview suggests four simple lessons for starting the journey toward innovation. The first, obviously, is *know thyself*. Although innovating organizations share many characteristics, they do vary. Sector, type of innovativeness, size, and age do matter. Small organizations should be careful about how they emulate large ones. Large organizations should be circumspect in following the example of smaller ones. Self-assessment is a critical first step in becoming an innovating organization, and this can be facilitated by asking the questions summarized in Appendix C.

Second, small organizations should be very deliberate if and when they decide to grow. Largeness has serious consequences for organizations, not the least of which is a natural proliferation of internal barriers and hierarchy. Although large organizations have clear advantages in the innovation process, not the least of which is the ability to place larger bets on promising ideas, they also have serious liabilities, including a thicker hierarchy. Small organizations should think hard before they trade their flexibility and speed for the greater security that comes with size.

Third, all organizations, small and large, young and old, should worry about the substitution of analysis for faith, judgment, hunch, and intuition. This is not to argue that analysis has no role in an innovating organization. As noted earlier, analysis informs judgment, complements intuition, and disciplines hunch. Even great prophets prepare for their journeys. But organizations can go too far, asking analysis to make decisions that are best left to judgment. Though a good cost-benefit analysis can reveal the dimensions of a leap, it is faith that propels us forward. Organizations substitute for faith at very great risk. It is faith combined with analysis that appears to provide the best guidance on when and where to take a new idea forward.

Finally, older organizations would do well to find a fountain of youth. There are grounds for arguing that mature organizations do just that in shaking off the layers, rules, and myths that block innovation. Although humans may be unable to turn back the hands of time, organizations most certainly can. To the extent possible, they should try to recapture a simpler time, taking advantage of their considerable expertise even as they free themselves of the less desirable consequences of the years.

8

The Core Values of
Innovating Organizations

Organizations about to start the journey to innovativeness can draw considerable comfort from the Surviving Innovation sample. If these twenty-six organizations can survive the journey, one can argue, so can any organization. They were not blessed by divine providence, although at least two, the Land Stewardship Project and Luther Theological Seminary, certainly tried to create a state of grace. They did not live charmed lives, although at least two, Artspace and In the Heart of the Beast Puppet and Mask Theater, believed in magic.

In fact, the Surviving Innovation organizations were not so radically different from thousands upon thousands of nonprofit and government organizations across the nation. Half of the sample came late to innovation, starting out as steady, even unimaginative organizations until the shocks or turbulence became unbearable. Anoka County was mostly a rural county until the late 1970s, when the Twin Cities expanded out to meet it, and the Minnesota Extension Service was mostly an agriculture–home economics–4-H operation until the problems of the cities also expanded out to meet it.

The Surviving Innovation sample certainly shows that organizations do not have to be perfect to be innovative. As a group, the Surviving Innovation organizations were very well run, suggesting that high performance is a necessary, if insufficient, prerequisite for innovativeness. As individual organizations, however, each had its blemishes. The leaders and staff were only human. Even setting aside the Phoenix Group, the sample had an assortment of weaknesses that would hardly be seen as harbingers of success—an embezzlement at one, falling morale at another, absent leadership at a third, poor planning at a fourth.

Yet succeed these organizations did, largely by focusing on assets and mission rather than liabilities. They did not allow their internal weaknesses to become an excuse for inaction, nor did they waste time and precious resources building systems they did not need. Some were strong on job descriptions and pay systems but weak on learning; others were strong on strategic planning but weak on evaluation; still others were strong on reducing financial exposure but weak on fundraising. Weakness was almost always balanced by strength. That is how so many of the organizations managed to survive the ordinary (and sometimes extraordinary) setbacks encountered in their work.

The Surviving Innovation organizations also show that there is no one true path to innovating. They mixed and matched preferred states of being as needed. If you have seen one path to innovativeness, you have seen only one. Thus the best the Surviving Innovation sample can do is provide a broad inventory of preferences that can be drawn on when designing and operating an innovating organization. Sometimes an organization will adopt a particular preferred state, other times not, depending on its circumstances.

Other things being equal, for example, it would be nice to have a resource-rich environment, a lean bureaucracy, talented leadership, and strong management systems. But as noted throughout this book, other things are not equal. Although the Surviving Innovation organizations clearly shared some very strong preferences, each one took a slightly different route to innovativeness, and each had its own way of maintaining the edge once innovation began to occur.

Although the Surviving Innovation organizations varied in the choice of preferred states, there are several rules that hold good throughout the sample—with the single exception of the Phoenix Group. There is no question, for example, that strong financial systems are essential to innovation. Innovating organizations can tolerate a variety of managerial weaknesses, but not poor financial controls. There is also no question that mission was central to ultimate success. Innovating organizations do not always have the mission just right, but they do ask the right questions on a fairly steady basis.

Finally, the Surviving Innovation sample provides ample evidence that organizations do not need superheroes to create innovativeness. Most of the people I met in my travels across Minnesota kept innovation in perspective and their work lives in balance. They were highly dedicated to their careers, intensely committed to making a difference in the world, extraordinarily loyal to their clients, customers, or audience, and they were often exceptionally creative people, but they were not superhuman. They were not willing to sacrifice all to bring innovation forth against the odds. Where they were heroic, it was almost always in service to the mission, not in innovating against the odds within their own agencies.

Where the Surviving Innovation organizations differed, perhaps, from other organizations in Minnesota and elsewhere was in their commitment to a set of core values that helped guide their decisions about innovation. These core values of honesty, trust, rigor, and faith clearly shaped their choice of preferred states of being. No single organization adopted all forty of the preferred states described earlier in this book. Rather, they picked those that fit their core values.

An Update on the Surviving Innovation Sample

Before turning to these core values in greater detail, readers might want to know what happened to the Surviving Innovation organizations once the project was over. After all, most of the fieldwork for this book was completed in early 1995, two years before I put pen to paper. Given the book's title, it seems perfectly reasonable to ask how the sample did subsequently. The answer, in classic Minnesotan, is "pretty darn good." Most of the organizations were still innovating as of 1997, some with a little less of an edge, some with a little more.

Just because an organization is still innovating does not mean it either can or should live forever. Innovating organizations, even in Minnesota, are certainly no less mortal than other organizations and may actually be more vulnerable to early demise. Pushing against the prevailing wisdom is a sure way to get pushed back.

As of 1997, at least two of the Surviving Innovation organizations were either dead or virtually dead. The Phoenix Group was gone for good, its offices boarded up, housing sold or condemned, and meager assets long exhausted. The Office of Environmental Assistance, né Waste Management, was also gone as an independent agency, buried in the Pollution Control Agency, awaiting a new governor who might give it new life.

At least four other Surviving Innovation organizations were in various states of transition. The Minnesota Extension Service, Project for Pride in Living, and Heart of the Beast Puppet and Mask Theater had all hired new executives—a long run was not in Nadya Reubenova's astrological chart—and Cyrus Math/Tech had replaced over half of its self-managed team with new teachers and staff (low pay and a lack of health benefits eventually led two of the founding teachers to leave).

For three of the four, the transitions had no discernible impact on innovativeness. After years of fretting about Joe Selvagio's retirement, PPL emerged stronger than ever; staff and revenues were up sharply. Heart of the Beast had a smooth transition, too, in large part because its artistic staff remained stable. The May Day festival could not have come sooner after what had been a long, brutally cold winter. Most surprisingly given the degree of turnover, Cyrus came through the 1996–97 school year with top grades. Not only did overall enrollment inch up slightly, but the number of students from outside the district grew substantially, yielding more money for computers and networking.

That these three organizations did so well in transition times speaks to the importance of both mission and systems. Organizations that live by the heroic leader often die by the heroic leader. Truth be told, there may be leaders out there who would be offended if their organizations did not collapse on their departure.

In an innovating organization, however, part of the leader's work is to prepare for the inevitable transitions that come with time. At PPL, for example, that meant several years in which Joe Selvagio worked side-by-side with his chosen successor. However uncomfortable that might have been for the two individuals, it certainly allowed PPL to withstand the departure of its truly mythic founder.

Of the four transitioning organizations, MES faced the greatest uncertainty as it grappled with its leadership handover. Although Pat Borich did not create the MES, he had calmed the organization during a remarkably turbulent time. Having been inside the MES system for thirty years before his promotion to the deanship, Borich had a deep reservoir of political capital that protected the organization as it expanded beyond the traditional extension agenda. His departure gave opponents an opportunity to renew the old debates about just how far to venture outside the box of agriculture, home economics, and 4-H. Although the new dean came with all the right credentials, she was also the first woman to head the system and quickly attracted fire from a state legislature that began asking hard questions about the odd MES organization chart.

Such stresses are hardly a harbinger of failure, however. Witness WomenVenture's turnaround in the wake of Kay Gudmestad's arrival. She spent the better part of three years fixing things— rebuilding the financial systems, confronting staff, and taking political hits. Since then, the organization has taken off. Project Blueprint is still running strong, as is the micro-loan program. WomenVenture has also launched a new program for daughters of women on welfare to break the cycle of poverty that persists from generation to generation. By 1997, the budget was up 40 percent, and the staffing complement was back to the pre-crisis level.

Even though the vast majority of the Surviving Innovation organizations were still alive and innovating in 1997, many will eventually stop innovating—some of them against their own wishes. Anoka County is only two or three board members away from the second-guessing and bitter politics that have infected so many other counties as the devolution revolution reaches bottom. A handful of board retirements, a scandal of some kind, perhaps a conversion of the board from part-time to full-time status could easily produce a much more hostile climate for innovation.

Others will simply run out of energy as senior staff move on. It is not clear how Theatre de la Jeune Lune will handle the eventual transition of its four artistic directors. Sooner or later, they will decide to step down, at which point the theater must find new energy or ring down the curtain. Nor is it clear how the American Indian Business Development Corporation will handle the sudden departure of its founder-leader Brenda St. Germaine.

My sense, however, is that the majority of the Surviving Innovation organizations will not stop innovating unless or until they come to represent the prevailing wisdom. If they do their work well, what was once innovative will become standard good practice; what was once on the leading edge will become routine.

Setting the standard for ordinary good practice is precisely the goal of Chance to Grow. At some point, Bob and Kathy DeBoer will succeed in changing the paradigm of how brain-injured children learn. When they do so, they will likely stop innovating, turning more to fine-tuning and replication than innovation.

The Domestic Abuse Project has a similar goal. For some time now, Carol Arthur and Jeff Edleson, the director of evaluation and research, have been working more on fine-tuning DAP's treatment curriculum than on creating entirely new initiatives. Although the organization is best described as a *what* innovator, with a primary focus on changing the basic approach to treating batterers and victims, DAP has been evolving into a *how* innovator in recent years, extending its already-proven treatment program to a wider community (gay and lesbian, minority).

At the Dowling School, Jeff Raison's goal has always been to create a racially mixed school where all children, whether severely disabled or not, could participate in a unique environmental curriculum. At some point, telling students that they are the solution will not be an innovation. Raison's aim is not to make Dowling the most innovative school in America but to prove that a school can do well while doing good, mainstreaming a very high number of disabled students into a successful magnet school under a public choice system.

The point here is that there is nothing wrong with slowing down. To be successful, innovating organizations need not continue innovating for all time. It is perfectly reasonable, therefore, to imagine that a well-performing organization will occasionally transform itself into an innovating organization and later transform itself back. It may decide that innovation is essential for reaching the next plateau in performance. Perhaps it needs a new way of delivering services to absorb the latest devolution from Washington, or perhaps its audience is changing to the point where it needs a new kind of program.

It is also quite conceivable that an innovating organization will decide to change direction for the same reasons. That is certainly why Episcopal Community Services decided to merge its Putting It All Together (PAT) program and Fathers' Program into a single Families That Work Together initiative in 1996. With twelve years of experience in helping unemployed and underemployed single mothers gain the skills and confidence to move from welfare to work, PAT had clearly succeeded. Nearly 2,500 women had graduated from the program, often doubling their income as a result. The Fathers' Program was much younger but had also demonstrated growing success in helping fathers support their children, both financially and emotionally.

Although each program could have continued pretty much as it was, funding was increasingly tenuous. With the state of Minnesota pursuing a major welfare reform experiment designed to help single mothers simulate the presence of a second wage earner, ECS concluded that its best future work involved holding families together. Preventing the dissolution of the family seemed to yield higher returns than repairing it afterwards.

Ultimately, therefore, the greatest challenge facing an innovating organization is to know when to start innovating and when to stop. This is a question that reinforces the very first lesson of this book: center on mission. Organizations that do not know why they exist, whom they serve, and how they will know they are successful turn innovation on and off like a light switch. They move from fad to fad with ease, jumping for the latest bait, be it a new funding stream or an award. Innovating becomes just another thing to do in keeping the organization going, with or without purpose.

As the following pages suggest, however, the way innovating organizations pursue their missions depends on four core values that guide their preferences: honesty, trust, rigor, and faith. Asking about mission is utterly useless if the organization is not honest about answers. Pushing authority downward is a shallow gesture if the organization does not trust its own people. Measuring performance is a waste of time if the organization does not do so with rigor. And successfully challenging the prevailing wisdom without faith in the possibility of success is impossible.

Again, building an innovating organization involves more than just lowering barriers and debunking myths. The absence of barriers and myths is not the presence of innovation but the possibility. The key to converting possibility into action involves four core values of organizational life. If the organization cannot trust its employees or itself, if it cannot be honest and truthful, if it has no interest in rigor, and if it has little faith, the organization simply cannot succeed. If it is honest, trusting, rigorous, and faithful, it cannot fail. It will know when to innovate and when to stop. (See Figure 8.1 for

Figure 8.1. The Core Values of Innovating Organizations

TRUST	HONESTY
Use the market as an ally	Center on mission
Lower the barriers to	Create a marketplace of ideas
external collaboration	Age gracefully
Push authority downward	Be clear about who decides
Lower the barriers to internal	Give the permission to fail
collaboration	Communicate to excess
Democratize!	Teach the organization how to
Prime the organization	say no and why to say yes
for innovation	Stay balanced
Change the leader's work	Downplay pay
Issue a call for ideas	Celebrate success
Listen to the audience	
Listen to the organization	
Keep learning	

RIGOR	FAITH
Beware the source of funds	Operate just beyond the possible
Pay attention to outcomes	Embrace the volatility
Harvest external support	Prepare for hardball
Stay thin	Change the prevailing winds
Pay attention to sequencing	Create the space to experiment
Keep innovation in perspective	Prepare for stress
Measure performance	Maximize diversity
Build mission into systems,	Keep faith and intuition alive
not vice versa	Have fun
Be disciplined about management	
Reduce exposure to risk	

an illustration of the relationships among these four core values in innovating organizations.)

This chapter explores these four core values in more detail, using them as a way to sort the various lessons provided in the book. The chapter concludes with a brief discussion of the sequence of change that might help an organization move from mediocrity to high performance to innovation.

The Core Values of Innovating Organizations

If innovating is neither the product of perfection nor at the end of one true path, organizations must have some means of judging the relative merits of different preferred states. It is certainly helpful to heed the admonition "know thyself"; knowing where to go requires at least some understanding of where one is. It is also helpful to benchmark, or measure, oneself against other organizations in the same field, though such an effort can sometimes reveal more about how those organizations sustain the prevailing wisdom than about how they challenge it.

Such benchmarking cuts against the balkanization of nonprofit and government organizations. Surviving Innovation organizations in the same field rarely talked to each other, for example. The housing agencies—Artspace, Central Community Housing Trust, Phoenix, and Project for Pride in Living—knew about each other but did not have routine contact, even though at least two, Phoenix and PPL, were located in the same neighborhood. The schools also knew about each other but had accidental contact at best, even though at least two, Dowling and Chance to Grow, were in the same city.

If like organizations in the sample did not talk to each other, it should not be surprising to find that unlike organizations did not talk either. Kathryn Roberts and her team had much to share with Kay Gudmestad, and vice versa, but neither had the time to talk; Bob and Kathy DeBoer had much to teach Katherine Halbreich and her deputy David Galligan, and vice versa, but there seemed to be no opportunity for an exchange. Though many of the organizations collaborated with other organizations in their environment, such joint efforts were mostly designed to exploit opportunities, not to discuss issues of organizational innovativeness. The opportunities to intersect and share preferences are rare indeed.

Given these realities, how might an organization know which of the preferred states of being fit? Despite their general lack of contact, all of the Surviving Innovation organizations used a similar compass for guiding their journey toward innovativeness. As Figure 8.2 shows, it is a compass that might help organizations sort the preferred states of being into a more accessible inventory of options.

Thus, even if an organization does not have the money for an innovation investment fund, for example, it can still express trust in its employees by pushing authority downward or by issuing a call for ideas. Even if it sometimes gets confused about who decides

Figure 8.2. Sorting the Preferences

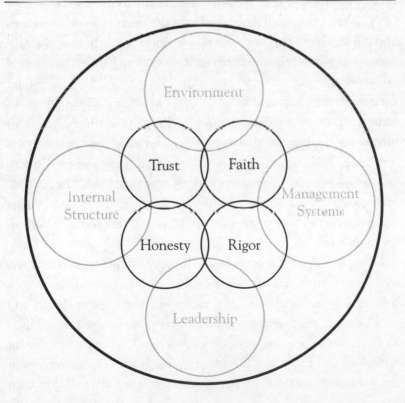

what, it can still express its honesty by asking hard questions about mission. Even if it cannot flatten its internal hierarchy or afford a strategic planning consultant, it can still express its rigor by paying attention to outcomes or reducing exposure to risk. Finally, even if it is unable to change the prevailing winds that buffet the agenda, it can still express its faith by giving permission to fail.

Trust is the logical place to begin. As noted earlier in this book, one of the defining issues in building an innovating organization is what it believes about people. Does the organization believe creativity and high performance are concentrated in the special few or more evenly distributed throughout the organization? The Surviving Innovation organizations had little doubt about the answer. Although none were so naive as to trust everyone equally (Phoenix, of course, came very close to doing so), they were not so jaded about human nature that they demanded constant control.

This trust extended downward into the twenty-six organizations and outward into their environments. Internally, there was a willingness to push authority downward, lower the barriers to internal collaboration, democratize, prime the organization for innovation, issue a call for ideas, and listen to what was being said at all levels. Externally, these organizations were willing to use the market as an ally, lower the barriers to external collaboration, and listen to the audience. Whichever direction they faced, they were willing to imagine a different role for the leader—one that would concentrate on creating the conditions for others to succeed, particularly by lowering the barriers to collaboration and giving stakeholders authority to innovate.

Trust was not without its limits, however. The focus on learning involved an effort not to make the same mistake twice. Even as they tolerated a great deal of groping along, evolutionary tinkering, and trial by error, the Surviving Innovation organizations worked hard to learn from their mistakes. Some, such as St. Joseph's Home for Children and Episcopal Community Services, conducted formal debriefings on particularly significant incidents. (Recall that such screening of critical incidents is part of the accreditation process.) Others, such as Chance to Grow and the Domestic Abuse Project, stressed rigorous evaluation and monitoring. But most adhered to a more informal quid pro quo: the organization would push authority downward provided the authority was wisely used.

One of the Surviving Innovation leaders pointed out that *honesty* is the twin sister of trust. "Trust is not something easily given if people are not honest with each other," she said. "I can't have any surprises. If a project goes wrong, I need to be the first to know, not the last." In a sense, trust is validated as well as earned through individual acts of honesty. Willingness to tell the truth becomes the key that unlocks the needed authority to act.

At the same time, honesty stands on its own as an essential commodity of mission-driven innovation. When an innovating organization asks hard questions about why it exists, whom it serves, and how it will know if it is successful, it must be willing to give honest answers. For example, one can legitimately assume that most employees work to get paid; being committed to mission does not suddenly render employees immune to self-interest. However, if pay is the only interest at work, and if there is no calling to mission, an organization will find it extraordinarily difficult to sustain innovativeness.

Honesty concerns more than mission, of course. It requires clear communication on how a marketplace of ideas might work, open conversations about organizational reality (subsector, age, size, type of innovation desired), clarity about who decides what, and candor about pay and success. And for leaders and frontline staff alike, part of staying balanced and aging gracefully is honest dialogue about where the organization is at a given point in time.

Just about the worst thing an innovating organization can do is give *false* permission to fail. It should invite risk taking only if it is ready to tolerate mistakes. Similarly, it should ask for dissent only if it is ready to hear criticism. What matters most is how the organization handles the first few mistakes and dissents. If the first mistake is greeted with fury, it will likely be the last one an employee admits. And if the first dissent is met with indignation or ridicule, it will likely be the last dissent an employee expresses publicly. Keeping an open door only for those who say what the organization wants to hear is hardly a way to foster honest dialogue.

Being honest also involves a confrontation with the role of secrets in organizational life. If an organization cannot reveal the substance of decisions on matters such as pay, for example, it should at least be candid about the process used. In large organizations, that might mean disclosing average pay increases by department and employee grade. In small organizations, it might mean open conversations about the basic criteria used in making pay decisions. The assumption should always be that secrets will not be secrets for long. If a given decision cannot be defended in public, perhaps it should not be made at all. "I always like to imagine how a decision will look on the front page of the paper or as the lead in an I-team investigation," one county administrator once told me. "I don't like to be the scandal du jour."

It is easier to be honest, perhaps, if the organization brings *rigor* to the task. Teaching the organization how to say no and why to say yes is impossible if the organization does not have a clue about how to measure results; celebrating success is impossible, or at the very least rings false, if the organization has no ability to tell whether success has actually been achieved. To paraphrase Senator Daniel Patrick Moynihan, organizations are entitled to their own opinions but not their own facts.

The need to be disciplined about one's work is relevant to a host of lessons offered earlier in this book. Being wary about the source of funds requires rigorous (and honest) conversation about what a given dollar requires. Being effective in harvesting external support demands a commitment to careful scanning and thoughtful fundraising. Staying thin means measuring the specific cost of each layer of management in dollars and distraction. Paying attention to sequencing means careful assessment of the life cycle of innovation. Measuring performance means astute evaluation of the outcomes chain. And reducing exposure to risk means hard-nosed forecasting of revenues and costs.

The goal here is not to seek perfection. Rather, it is to contradict the notion that the act of innovation is best done casually. Just because the act of innovating involves tinkering and groping along does not mean it is accidental. If not exactly like assembling a 2,500-piece jigsaw puzzle in an hour, innovating does entail plenty of sorting and fitting. Efforts to innovate through essentially random trial and error will likely produce more error than success.

Rigor also reinforces trust and honesty. It allows innovating organizations to give the permission to fail as it also helps them separate truth from illusion about mission. It also undergirds the effort to liberate organizations from needless rules and regulation. One reason compliance-based accountability is so common is that performance-based accountability is so difficult. It requires a commitment to careful measurement, thoughtful tracking, and a strategic plan of some kind. Furthermore, it requires reasonably precise statements about cause and effect—that is, if the organization puts X dollars and employees into a set of activities, it will get Y measurable results and Z outcomes.

Short of such measurement, it is not clear what might lead funders, boards, and legislators to liberate their organizations. I used to believe, for example, that giving organizations the best and the brightest people, state-of-the art technology, comparable pay, and strong leadership was the answer. Trust would flow from confidence in the basic capacity to do well. Over time, however, I have concluded that this capacity-based accountability is not enough. "Trust us" does not carry much weight if it is not backed up by the invitation "Measure us, too." Funders, boards, and legislators will likely cut their organizations free only if there are outcome measures showing clear links to the inputs funders care about most—dollars and staff. If the measures are neither honest nor rigorous, why let go of the rules?

Letting go of rules, taking risks, and trusting others involve a leap of *faith*. That faith may be deeply grounded in rigorous analysis and tightly linked to past experience, but sooner or later, every innovation involves a decision to take the organization beyond the realm of known experience. If the organization has been disciplined about its work, there should be relatively few surprises as it makes the leap, but under no circumstances should the organization expect no surprises at all. The leap of faith may be informed, but it is still a leap. Having done everything possible to minimize risk and calculate odds, some organizations will take that leap only to find themselves in a cloud of smoke over the canyon. What will distinguish them from Wile E. Coyote, one hopes, is that they will have done their homework, learned as much as possible, and picked a goal not too far beyond the possible. It also helps enormously if they have packed a parachute.

As Figure 8.2 shows, faith expresses itself in many ways. It allows the organization to confidently stand up to hardball and stress; it encourages the organization to celebrate success and have fun; and it permits the organization to believe in itself as it faces into the winds of change. It also allows the organization to consider diversity not as a social obligation but as a cornerstone of innovativeness. Although becoming more diverse certainly involves elements of trust (Are we really ready to work with people not like us?), honesty (Are we willing to debunk our own myths about diversity?), and rigor (Are we doing everything possible to increase the effectiveness of our searches or just the bare minimum to satisfy our equal opportunity officer?), diversity is very much the product of faith in the basic human capacity to grow and adapt.

Luckily, one does not need to be a great prophet to create an innovating organization, for such prophets come along all too rarely. But one does need to believe that the prevailing wisdom can be changed. No matter how much cost-benefit analysis the organization pours into its decision, no matter how many evaluators and auditors it brings to the task, it must eventually make a leap of faith.

Together, trust, honesty, rigor, and faith provide the context for the courage necessary to act. Although courage is rarely mentioned in the literature on innovativeness and will always be difficult, if not impossible, to quantify, it is central to the act of innovation. One simply cannot challenge the prevailing wisdom if one does not have the courage to try. Trust, honesty, rigor, and faith may be essential core values for designing and running an innovating organization, but courage is the essence of the enterprise.

It is courage, for example, that led Bob and Kathy DeBoer to act on behalf of their daughter and other children in creating Chance to Grow. Yes, Chance to Grow is deeply committed to rigorous analysis. Yes, it is honest about results. And yes, Bob and Kathy have a profound faith in the possible. But the decision to take on the special education establishment, to dare to challenge the prevailing wisdom about how brain-injured children learn, involved something deeper than good statistics and faith in the possible. Bob and Kathy had the courage of their convictions, as did so many others across the Surviving Innovation sample.

Although one does not have to sacrifice all semblance of a normal life to create an innovating organization, it would be naive to suggest that innovating organizations are blissful places to be. They exist in challenging, stressful environments and experience plenty of hardball. Not everyone will have the temerity to stand up to the prevailing wisdom and articulate an alternative future. Not everyone will have the courage of conviction to persevere as the prevailing wisdom strikes back. Some, like the DeBoers, will find courage in love for their children. Others, like the faculty at Luther Theological Seminary, will find it in role models. Still others, such as the Walker Art Center, will find it on their walls. But find it the organization must.

The Sequence of Change

Using trust, honesty, rigor, and faith as the four points of its compass, each Surviving Innovation organization took a somewhat different path toward innovativeness. Asked where other organizations might begin the journey, the Surviving Innovation organizations appear to answer, "Anywhere." If the organization waits for the perfect moment to begin, it will wait forever. Nevertheless, just as we can detect preferred states of being in the Surviving Innovation organizations, we can also suggest preferred steps in the journey. Consider five conclusions about the appropriate sequence of change.

First, no organization can take advantage of the market, build a reserve fund, invest in promising ideas, or give permission to make mistakes until it creates the management systems needed to track and control its financial and organizational future. There is no substitute for good management systems as a precursor to high performance and innovativeness. Those who doubt it should visit the former Phoenix Group headquarters in South Minneapolis. It is not only vacant but an eyesore, a sad monument to the myth that good management is mere enslavement to wasted paper.

For those who believe that markets are the first step toward excellence and innovativeness, the Surviving Innovation organizations offer a different sequence. Organizations cannot sense the market, manage the market, or otherwise use the market as a lever if they do not have the management systems to see, manage, and exploit. The first step in becoming an *innovating* organization, therefore, is to become a *well-performing* organization. Simply stated, all innovating organizations must be well performing. Helping nonprofit and government organizations become rigorous about management is an essential step toward innovativeness (not to mention toward higher public confidence in whatever they do).

Second, there is also no substitute for a focus on mission. Without exception, the Surviving Innovation organizations centered on mission—they talked about whom they served, why they existed, how to know when they were succeeding. They could measure outcomes, for example, because they knew what the valued outcomes were. They could celebrate success because they knew when it occurred. Without a strong sense of mission, nonprofit and government organizations cannot long sustain innovativeness. They will have no basis on which to say either yes or no.

It is important to remember that mission is much more than a set of written words. It is a spirit, a focus, a sense—something to be felt rather than read. Thus mission need not be painted on an outside wall, built into a blueprint, or enshrined in legislation to have meaning. Indeed, drafting a mission statement may be exactly the wrong thing to do in starting the journey toward innovativeness, particularly if that statement becomes some kind of sacred text that can never be questioned or changed. The Surviving Innovation organizations did not always have the answers right, but they never wavered in challenging themselves to ask why they existed and whom they served. They always reserved the right to ask the core questions. If that meant penciling in a few new words here or there on the mission statement, those words were penciled in. If it meant erasing the statement entirely, then that was done.

Third, even if markets are not necessarily prior to good management, they are nevertheless essential to both higher performance and innovativeness. The organizations I came to admire most were unafraid of the market. If a market did not exist, they created one; if one did exist, they harnessed it as a lever for innovation. Turning toward the outside world is part of building an innovating organization.

This is not to be done casually, however, for an organization can tear its sails in effecting such a turn. As already noted, the market must be noticed, cultivated, managed, and harnessed as a force for innovation through management systems. For example, public executives must be taught how to make the market an ally, not an adversary, in their efforts to improve organizational performance and innovativeness.

Fourth, even as an organization builds a strong management system and harnesses the market as an ally, it can take a few simple steps to increase the odds that acts of innovation will occur and endure. Lowering the barriers to external and internal collaboration, providing the space to experiment, and issuing the call for ideas are all simple steps toward innovativeness. The Surviving Innovation organizations also did exceptionally well with innovation investment funds. The key in launching such a fund is not so much the money—the Surviving Innovation organizations did well with both large amounts and small—but the willingness to say yes to something.

Finally, organizations cannot underestimate the importance of faith as a core value for sustaining innovativeness. There is simply no way to persevere in the face of the stress and uncertainty associated with true innovation without faith in something larger than oneself. Faith gives organizations the ability to forgive, endure, and imagine, and is an essential ingredient in the conditions for sustaining innovativeness over time. Whether rooted in formal religion (as at Luther Theological Seminary), culture (Fond du Lac Community College), a vision of a just society (Land Stewardship Project), or simple confidence in basic human capacity (Advocating Change Together, Chance to Grow, Dowling), faith provides the extra element that keeps an innovating organization vibrant even as it confronts the ordinary disappointments involved in challenging the prevailing wisdom for the public good.

Conclusion

If there is one lesson that should rise above the others as readers page back through this book, it is that innovativeness is possible. Any organization can innovate once—that much is clear from the hundreds of "How did it happen here?" acts of innovation that take place every day in America's nonprofit and government organizations. The challenge remains to innovate twice, thrice, and more.

I believe it is a challenge that can be met only by organizational design. Even as we admire and celebrate those who struggle against the odds today, we must also begin the hard work needed to reshape our nonprofit and government organizations so that innovation becomes easier, even natural, tomorrow. The nation's future heroes deserve no less. They should put their considerable talents to work in creating the innovations and high performance that this nation so desperately needs as the new millennium begins, not in fighting their own organizations. If redesigning these organizations means that today's public servants must stop innovating for a moment or two, it is a delay worth bearing. Investments made today in creating nonprofit and government organizations that innovate naturally will pay off a hundredfold tomorrow.

Appendix A

The Surviving Innovation Cases

Advocating Change Together	Created in 1979 to help disabled individuals become advocates on their own behalf
American Indian Business Development Corporation	Created in 1975 to encourage economic and community development in the Native American community of Minneapolis
Anoka County	Created in 1857; one of seven counties in the Minneapolis-St. Paul metropolitan area
Artspace	Created in 1979 to provide living and working space for artists
Central Community Housing Trust	Created in 1986 to develop housing for individuals and families displaced by the construction of the Minneapolis Convention Center
A Chance to Grow/ New Visions School	Created in 1983 to develop new teaching curricula for brain-injured children; became a charter school in 1995
Chicanos Latinos Unidos En Servicio (CLUES)	Created in 1981 to enhance the quality of life for Chicanos and Latinos in the St. Paul metropolitan area; expanded to include Minneapolis in 1989

Cyrus Math/Science/ Technology Elementary School	Created in 1988 as a magnet school to elementary school students in northwestern Minnesota
Domestic Abuse Project	Created in 1979 to assist victims/survivors of abusive relationships and to treat batterers
Dowling Urban Environmental Learning Center	Created in 1920 as a school for physically disabled children (Dowling School for Crippled Children); became a magnet school in 1988
Episcopal Community Services	Created in 1963 to provide residential treatment and family support services on behalf of the Episcopal community in Minnesota
Fond du Lac Community College	Created in 1987 as a joint Tribal Community College/Minnesota State Community College
In the Heart of the Beast Puppet and Mask Theater	Created in 1974 as a neighborhood-based theater
Land Stewardship Project	Created in 1982 to promote an ethic of farmland stewardship and sustainable agriculture
Luther Theological Seminary	Created in 1869; became part of the newly created Evangelical Lutheran Church of America in 1989
Minnesota Extension Service	Created in 1909 as an outreach arm of the University of Minnesota; reorganized following the farm crisis in the 1980s to provide broader social and community support
Minnesota Office of Waste Management	Created in 1989 out of its predecessor, the Waste Management Board, to encourage

	pollution prevention by the Minnesota private sector, governments, and citizens
The Minnesota Zoo	Created in 1978 as the first state-run zoo in the country
North Branch School District	Created in 1909; reorganized in the late 1980s
People Escaping Poverty Project	Created in 1986 as a community organizing agency to help poor people in Fargo-Moorehead, Minnesota, be advocates on their own behalf
The Phoenix Group	Created in 1991 to provide low-cost permanent housing and strengthen economic development in a historically underserved neighborhood of Minneapolis
Project for Pride in Living	Created in 1972 to provide housing services to poor citizens of Minneapolis; expanded in mid-1980s to include social services for housing residents
St. Joseph's Home for Children	Created in 1886 to care for orphaned children; reorganized in mid-1980s to provide deeper services to disadvantaged juveniles
Theatre de la Jeune Lune	Created in 1978 as an ensemble theater in Minneapolis
Walker Art Center	Created in 1927; redirected in 1960s to focus on modern art, including performance art, film, and nontraditional media
WomenVenture	Created in 1989, through a merger of two other organizations, to promote economic development opportunities for women

Appendix B

An Overview of the Surviving Innovation Sample

Characteristic	Cases
Total cases	26
Sector	
Government	8
Nonprofit	18
Type of innovativeness	
How (process)	13
What (product)	13
Budget	
Less than $1 million	9
$1–7 million	9
Greater than $7 million	8
Staff	
Fewer than 40	12
40–200	10
More than 200	4
Age	
Less than 15 years old	9
15–30 years old	9
Over 30 years old	8

Primary field of interest	
Arts	3
Children	1
Community development	3
Domestic abuse	1
Housing	3
Education, special	2
Education, K–12	2
Education, higher	3
Environment	3
Social services	3
Comprehensive/mixed	2

Appendix C

An Overview of the Surviving Innovation Data

Organizational Attribute	Total	Subsector		Type of Innovativeness		Budget (in Millions)			Staff (Total Full-Time)			Age (in Years)		
		Non-profit	Government	How	What	<$1	$1-7	>$7	<40	40-200	>200	<15	15-30	>30
External environment														
External turbulence														
1. Is the environment predictable?	50%	28%	100%	77%	31%	33%	44%	75%	42%	60%	75%	56%	33%	63%
2. Does the organization have a monopoly in its field?	46	33	75	46	46	22	44	75	33	40	100	33	44	63
3. Is the market a contributor to innovativeness?	85	83	88	92	77	67	100	88	75	90	100	78	89	88
4. Is there a waiting list for services?	54	61	38	46	62	44	78	38	50	60	50	56	56	50
Shocks to the system														
1. Has there been a recent and sudden change in the environment?	50	39	75	69	38	33	33	88	25	70	100	56	11	88
2. Is external funding an incentive for innovation?	54	56	50	54	54	67	22	75	50	40	100	44	44	7

Organizational Attribute	Total	Subsector		Type of Innovativeness		Budget (in Millions)			Staff (Total Full-Time)			Age (in Years)		
		Non-profit	Govern-ment	How	What	<$1	$1-7	>$7	<40	40-200	>200	<15	15-30	>30
External resources														
1. Is there external political support for innovation?	92	94	88	85	100	100	89	88	100	90	75	89	100	88
2. Is there external opposition to innovation?	12	11	13	8	15	11	11	13	8	20	0	33	0	0
3. Is the environment rule-laden against innovation?	10	22	75	54	23	22	44	50	17	50	75	44	22	50
4. Is there a history of innovation in the field?	69	78	50	54	85	89	67	50	75	80	25	89	56	63
5. Is the basic survival of the organization a contributor to innovativeness?	39	28	63	38	38	56	22	38	42	30	50	56	33	25
External boundaries														
1. Does the organization collaborate with other organizations?	85	78	100	92	72	89	67	100	83	80	100	78	78	100

Organizational Attribute	Total	Subsector		Type of Innovativeness		Budget (in Millions)			Staff (Total Full-Time)			Age (in Years)		
		Non-profit	Govern-ment	How	What	<$1	$1–7	>$7	<40	40–200	>200	<15	15–30	>30
External slack														
1. Does the organization have unpaid volunteers?	85	83	88	77	92	89	78	88	92	70	100	78	89	88
2. Does the organization scan the environment for new funding?	96	100	88	100	92	100	100	88	100	90	100	89	100	100
3. Does the organization have a membership base?	38	50	13	23	54	44	22	50	33	40	50	22	44	50
4. If yes to question 3, has the organization expanded its base in the past five years?	90	89	100	100	100	100	100	75	100	75	100	100	100	75

Internal structure

Shape

Organizational Attribute	Total	Subsector		Type of Innovativeness		Budget (in Millions)			Staff (Total Full-Time)			Age (in Years)		
		Non-profit	Government	How	What	<$1	$1–7	>$7	<40	40–200	>200	<15	15–30	>30
1. Does the organization have a pyramid shape?	65	67	63	69	62	78	67	50	67	80	25	89	44	63
2. Does the organization worry about its thickness?	58	50	75	62	54	44	67	63	42	70	75	56	56	63
3. Is thinness a contributor to innovativeness?	62	61	63	69	54	78	56	50	67	60	50	89	56	38
4. Is size a contributor to innovativeness?	35	28	50	38	31	44	17	50	42	30	25	33	33	38

Internal turbulence

Organizational Attribute	Total	Non-profit	Government	How	What	<$1	$1–7	>$7	<40	40–200	>200	<15	15–30	>30
1. Has the organization been reorganized in the past five years?	54	56	50	46	62	55	44	63	58	50	50	67	56	38
2. Has there been rapid growth or decline?	73	78	63	69	77	100	67	50	92	50	75	100	89	25
3. Is there internal conflict over ideas, decisions?	53	56	63	46	69	44	56	75	58	50	75	44	78	50
4. Is internal stress high?	58	61	50	31	85	33	67	75	50	60	75	44	78	50

Organizational Attribute	Total	Subsector		Type of Innovativeness		Budget (in Millions)			Staff (Total Full-Time)			Age (in Years)		
		Non-profit	Government	How	What	<$1	$1–7	>$7	<40	40–200	>200	<15	15–30	>30
Demographics														
1. Is the organization demographically matched to its community?	54	61	38	54	54	78	44	38	75	40	25	78	44	38
2. Does the organization cultivate intellectual, professional diversity?	77	67	100	85	69	67	78	88	67	90	75	100	56	75
3. Is overall diversity a contributor to innovativeness?	42	44	38	38	46	56	22	50	50	40	25	67	33	25
4. Is staff turnover high?	65	78	38	38	92	44	78	75	58	80	50	56	67	75
Internal boundaries														
1. Does staff work across bureaucratic boundaries?	80	82	75	77	83	100	56	88	100	60	75	63	78	100
2. Does staff solve problems collaboratively?	52	59	38	62	42	88	33	38	82	30	25	75	56	25
3. Are there regular staff meetings?	76	71	88	77	75	75	78	75	82	80	50	75	78	75
4. Are there informal lines of communication within the organization in support of innovation?	96	94	100	100	92	100	89	100	100	90	100	89	100	100

Organizational Attribute	Total	Subsector		Type of Innovativeness		Budget (in Millions)			Staff (Total Full-Time)			Age (in Years)		
		Non-profit	Government	How	What	<$1	$1–7	>$7	<40	40–200	>200	<15	15–30	>30
Internal slack														
1. Does the organization provide resources for idea development and launch?	81	72	100	85	77	44	100	100	58	100	100	56	89	100
2. Is there internal competition among ideas?	23	11	50	31	23	0	11	63	0	40	75	11	11	50

Organizational Attribute	Total	Subsector		Type of Innovativeness		Budget (in Millions)			Staff (Total Full-Time)			Age (in Years)		
		Non-profit	Govern-ment	How	What	<$1	$1-7	>$7	<40	40-200	>200	<15	15-30	>30

Leadership

Clarity

1. Is the organization headed by a single executive?	85	83	88	85	85	67	89	100	75	90	100	67	89	100
2. Is there clarity about who makes what decisions?	81	83	75	85	77	78	89	75	83	90	50	78	78	88
3. Is communication of decisions clear?	96	94	100	100	92	100	89	100	100	90	100	89	100	100
4. Has there been a communication "accident" in the past five years?	38	39	38	31	46	33	44	38	42	40	25	44	44	25
5. Is dissent actively encouraged?	56	61	38	62	54	63	56	50	67	70	25	55	44	63
6. Is leadership a contributor to innovativeness?	85	83	88	92	77	78	89	88	75	90	100	78	78	100

Durability

1. Have there been more than two executive directors in the past five years?	8	6	13	0	15	11	0	13	8	10	0	22	0	0
2. Has there been a major leadership crisis within the past ten years?	65	67	63	62	69	67	67	63	75	60	50	67	67	63

Organizational Attribute	Total	Subsector		Type of Innovativeness		Budget (in Millions)			Staff (Total Full-Time)			Age (in Years)		
		Non-profit	Govern-ment	How	What	<$1	$1-7	>$7	<40	40-200	>200	<15	15-30	>30

Style

1. Is the leadership drawn from the professional field served by the organization?

| | 46 | 44 | 50 | 62 | 31 | 56 | 33 | 50 | 42 | 50 | 50 | 33 | 33 | 75 |

2. What is the general leadership style?

| A. Heroic | 15 | 17 | 0 | 8 | 23 | 22 | 22 | 0 | 17 | 20 | 0 | 11 | 33 | 0 |
| B. Participatory | 85 | 83 | 100 | 92 | 87 | 78 | 73 | 100 | 83 | 80 | 100 | 89 | 66 | 100 |

Strategies

1. Does the source of funds for a given innovation worry the organization?

| | 77 | 72 | 88 | 85 | 69 | 78 | 78 | 75 | 67 | 90 | 75 | 78 | 78 | 75 |

2. Does the leadership believe in luck, fortune, grace?

| | 54 | 67 | 25 | 46 | 62 | 78 | 56 | 25 | 75 | 50 | 0 | 56 | 78 | 25 |

3. Does the leadership use intuition in picking ideas?

| | 59 | 78 | 50 | 62 | 77 | 78 | 56 | 75 | 75 | 70 | 50 | 67 | 89 | 50 |

4. Are questions of faith, spirituality prominent in the organization's dialogue?

| | 65 | 83 | 25 | 54 | 77 | 78 | 78 | 38 | 83 | 60 | 25 | 56 | 89 | 50 |

5. Does the leadership give permission to make mistakes?

| | 96 | 94 | 100 | 100 | 92 | 100 | 89 | 100 | 100 | 90 | 100 | 89 | 100 | 100 |

6. Does the organization enjoy its work?

| | 92 | 94 | 88 | 92 | 92 | 100 | 89 | 88 | 100 | 80 | 100 | 89 | 100 | 88 |

Organizational Attribute	Total	Subsector		Type of Innovativeness		Budget (in Millions)			Staff (Total Full-Time)			Age (in Years)		
		Non-profit	Government	How	What	<$1	$1–7	>$7	<40	40–200	>200	<15	15–30	>30
Innovation tactics														
1. Are new ideas gathered throughout the organization?	96	94	100	100	92	100	89	100	100	90	100	89	100	100
2. How are new ideas judged for adoption?														
A. Organizational capacity	96	94	100	92	100	89	100	100	92	100	100	89	100	100
B. Fit with mission	96	100	88	92	100	100	89	100	100	90	100	89	100	100
C. Dollar cost	69	56	100	77	62	44	78	88	42	90	100	89	33	88
D. Workability of idea	42	33	63	54	31	22	56	50	25	70	25	44	33	50

Organizational Attribute	Total	Subsector		Type of Innovativeness		Budget (in Millions)			Staff (Total Full-Time)			Age (in Years)		
		Non-profit	Govern-ment	How	What	<$1	$1-7	>$7	<40	40-200	>200	<15	15-30	>30
Management systems														
Mission														
1. Does the organization worry about its mission?	100	100	100	100	100	100	100	100	100	100	100	100	100	100
2. Do the staff and the board identify with the mission?	100	100	100	100	100	100	100	100	100	100	100	100	100	100
Reward														
1. Does the organization have merit pay?	38	39	38	31	46	11	44	63	17	60	50	33	22	63
2. If yes to question 1, does the organization fund merit pay?	90	100	67	100	83	100	100	80	100	83	100	67	100	100
3. Is merit pay a contributor to innovativeness?	0	0	0	0	0	0	0	0	0	0	0	0	0	0

Organizational Attribute	Total	Subsector		Type of Innovativeness		Budget (in Millions)			Staff (Total Full-Time)			Age (in Years)		
		Non-profit	Govern-ment	How	What	<$1	$1–7	>$7	<40	40–200	>200	<15	15–30	>30
Learning														
1. Does the organization pay attention to its audience, customers, clients?	89	83	100	100	77	89	89	88	92	90	75	100	78	88
2. Does the organization support training for the staff and the board?	100	100	100	100	100	100	100	100	100	100	100	100	100	100
3. Do members of the organization interact with colleagues at all levels?	73	72	75	69	77	78	56	88	83	50	100	67	78	75
4. Does the organization have a system for preventing and/or red-flagging potential problems?	85	78	100	77	92	78	89	88	83	80	100	89	89	75
5. Does the frontline staff have access to information about the organization?	42	39	50	54	33	66	33	25	73	20	25	22	78	25
6. Does the organization appear to learn from its mistakes?	100	100	100	100	100	100	100	100	100	100	100	100	100	100

Organizational Attribute	Total	Subsector		Type of Innovativeness		Budget (in Millions)			Staff (Total Full-Time)			Age (in Years)		
		Non-Profit	Govern-ment	How	What	<$1	$1–7	>$7	<40	40–200	>200	<15	15–30	>30
Budget														
1. Is budget information available in real time?	46	44	50	31	62	33	33	75	42	40	75	33	44	63
2. Is there a reserve fund or other cushion for lean times?	54	61	38	67	58	44	56	63	45	86	67	44	56	63
3. Are there strong internal financial controls?	96	94	100	92	100	89	100	100	92	100	100	89	100	100
4. Are there policies to reduce exposure to risk from high-risk projects?	73	73	63	77	69	100	56	63	92	70	25	89	78	50
5. Do program managers have budget authority?	50	39	75	54	50	56	22	75	55	40	75	56	44	50
Idea generation														
1. Is there a formal system (e.g., suggestion box) for provoking ideas?	46	33	75	62	31	22	44	75	33	40	100	22	33	88
2. Do ideas regularly arise from below?	58	50	75	69	50	56	44	75	64	50	75	56	56	63

Organizational Attribute	Total	Subsector		Type of Innovativeness		Budget (in Millions)			Staff (Total Full-Time)			Age (in Years)		
		Non-profit	Government	How	What	<$1	$1–7	>$7	<40	40–200	>200	<15	15–30	>30
Accountability														
1. Is the organization disciplined/rigorous about its systems for:														
A. Personnel	96	94	100	92	100	89	100	100	92	100	100	89	100	100
B. Budget	96	94	100	92	100	89	100	100	92	100	100	89	100	100
C. Managing time	50	44	75	77	23	56	44	50	58	40	50	44	56	50
D. Governance	100	100	100	100	100	100	100	100	100	100	100	100	100	100
2. Does the organization actively seek evaluation of its programs?	81	72	100	77	85	67	78	100	67	90	100	67	78	100
3. Does the organization actively measure outcomes?	73	72	75	69	77	89	67	63	92	50	75	78	78	63
4. Is there a role for intuition and judgment in measuring success?	81	83	75	85	77	89	78	75	83	80	75	67	78	100

| | Total | Subsector | | Type of Innovativeness | | Budget (in Millions) | | | Staff (Total Full-Time) | | | Age (in Years) | | |
Organizational Attribute		Nonprofit	Government	How	What	<$1	$1–7	>$7	<40	40–200	>200	<15	15–30	>30
Governance														
1. Does the organization trust its members?	89	83	100	92	85	78	89	100	83	90	100	89	78	100
2. Does the organization put itself at risk to the external market?	62	61	63	69	54	67	56	63	67	50	75	44	78	63
3. Does the organization worry about recruiting effective board members?	73	78	50	46	83	63	88	67	67	67	50	50	89	57
4. Is there an orientation for new board members?	84	89	71	77	92	78	78	100	83	78	100	50	100	100
5. Has the board been restructured in the past five years?	40	39	43	38	42	44	44	29	50	22	50	50	44	29
6. Does the board have subcommittees?	76	89	43	62	92	78	78	71	83	67	75	50	100	75

n = 26

Notes on Quotations

Quotes from Kathryn Roberts in Chapters One, Three, and Five are from two different stories about the Minnesota Zoo in the *Minneapolis StarTribune*, which appeared on February 1, 1988 and May 24, 1994.

Quotes from Brenda St. Germaine in Chapters Three and Five are from *The Business of Community Economic Development: A Self-Help Manual*, unpublished manuscript, last revised in 1993.

Quotes from Gloria Steinbring in Chapters Three and Six are from *VoicePrint: The Tradition of Self-Advocates as Cultural Workers*, Fall 1993, 1(1), published by Advocating Change Together.

Quotes from Kay Gudmestadt in Chapter Four are from an article about WomenVenture in the *Minneapolis StarTribune*, which appeared on December 13, 1993.

Quotes from Kathy Keeley in Chapter Four are from an article about the CHART/WEDCO merger in the *Minneapolis StarTribune*, which appeared on November 26, 1989.

Quotes from Jim Nelson and Jon Pratt about the Phoenix Group in Chapters Four and Six are from Giyard, B., "Sifting Through the Ashes," *Twin Cities Reader*, October 2–8, 1996.

All other quotes from specific individuals identified in the book came from face-to-face interviews conducted during the Surviving Innovation site visits or were made in on-the-record presentations to various University of Minnesota-Humphrey Institute classes over the life of the project.

References

Abbe, M. "Bloody Performance Draws Criticism." *Minneapolis StarTribune*, March 24, 1994, p. 1.

Aiken, M., and Hage, J. "The Organic Organization and Innovation." *Sociology*, 1971, 5(1), 63–82.

Allison, G. T. "Public and Private Management: Are They Fundamentally Alike in All Unimportant Aspects?" In J. L. Perry and K. L. Kraemer (eds.), *Public Management*. Mountain View, Calif.: Mayfield, 1983.

Altshuler, A. A. "Bureaucratic Innovation, Democratic Accountability, and Political Incentives." In A. A. Altshuler and R. D. Behn (eds.), *Innovation in American Government*. Washington, D.C.: Brookings Institution, 1997.

Altshuler, A. A., and Behn, R. D. (eds.). *Innovation in American Government*. Washington, D.C.: Brookings Institution, 1997.

Angle, H. L. "Psychology and Organizational Innovation." In A. H. Van de Ven, H. L. Angle, and M. S. Poole (eds.), *Research on the Management of Innovation: The Minnesota Studies*. New York: HarperCollins, 1989.

Angle, H. L., and Van de Ven, A. H. "Suggestions for Managing the Innovation Journey." In A. H. Van de Ven, H. L. Angle, and M. S. Poole (eds.), *Research on the Management of Innovation: The Minnesota Studies*. New York: HarperCollins, 1989.

Argyris, C. *Knowledge for Action: A Guide to Overcoming Barriers to Organizational Change*. San Francisco: Jossey-Bass, 1993.

Barzelay, M., and Armajani, B. *Breaking Through Bureaucracy: A New Vision for Managing in Government*. Berkeley: University of California Press, 1992.

Behn, R. D. "Management by Groping Along." *Journal of Policy Analysis and Management*, 1988, 7(3), 643–663.

Behn, R. D. *Leadership Counts: Lessons for Public Managers*. Cambridge, Mass.: Harvard University Press, 1993.

283

Bennis, W., and Biederman, P. W. *Organizing Genius: The Secrets of Creative Collaboration*. Reading, Mass.: Addison-Wesley, 1997.

Beresford, S. V. "Celebrating Innovations: Ten Years of Extraordinary Results for Citizens." In Ford Foundation, *Innovations in American Government, 1986–1996*. New York: Ford Foundation, 1996.

Bielefeld, W. "What Affects Nonprofit Survival?" *Non-Profit Management and Leadership*, 1994, *5*(1), 19–36.

Blinder, A. (ed.). *Paying for Productivity: A Look at the Evidence*. Washington, D.C.: Brookings Institution, 1990.

Boyte, H. C., and Kari, N. N. *Building America: The Democratic Promise of Public Work*. Philadelphia: Temple University Press, 1996.

Bozeman, B. *All Organizations Are Public: Bridging Public and Private Organizational Theories*. San Francisco: Jossey-Bass, 1987.

Bozeman, B., and Straussman, J. D. "Fostering Innovation in Government." In B. Bozeman and J. D. Straussman, *Public Management Strategies: Guidelines for Managerial Effectiveness*. San Francisco: Jossey-Bass, 1990.

Brandl, J. E. "On the New Institutionalism, Innovation, and Policymaking in Government." Paper prepared for the Innovation and Organization Conference, University of Minnesota, Sept. 18–21, 1992.

Brueggemann, W. B. *The Prophetic Imagination*. Philadelphia: Fortress Press, 1978.

Bryson, J. M. *Strategic Planning for Public and Nonprofit Organizations*. (2nd ed.) San Francisco: Jossey-Bass, 1996.

Bryson, J. M., and Crosby, B. C. *Leadership for the Common Good: Tackling Public Problems in a Shared-Power World*. San Francisco: Jossey-Bass, 1992.

Bryson, J. M., and Roering, W. D. "Mobilizing Innovation Efforts: The Case of Government Strategic Planning." In A. H. Van de Ven, H. L. Angle, and M. S. Poole (eds.), *Research on the Management of Innovation: The Minnesota Studies*. New York: HarperCollins, 1989.

Burns, T., and Stalker, G. M. *The Management of Innovation*. London: Tavistock, 1961.

Cohen, M. D., and Sproull, L. S. *Organizational Learning*. Thousand Oaks, Calif.: Sage, 1996.

Cooper, R. G., and Kleinschmidt, E. J. "New Products: What Separates Winners from Losers?" *Journal of Product Innovation Management*, 1987, *4*, 169–184.

Cotton, J. L., and others. "Employee Participation: Diverse Forms and Different Outcomes." *Academy of Management Journal*, 1988, *13*(1), 8–22.

Daft, R. L. "Dual-Core Model of Organizational Innovation." *Academy of Management Journal*, 1978, *21*(4), 193–210.

Damanpour, F. "Organizational Innovation: A Meta-Analysis of Effects of Determinants and Moderators." *Academy of Management Journal*, 1991, 34(3), 555–590.

Damanpour, F., Szabat, K. A., and Evan, W. E. "The Relationship Between Types of Innovation and Organizational Performance." *Journal of Management Studies*, 1989, 26(6), 587–601.

Delbecq, A. L., and Mills, P. K. "Managerial Practices That Enhance Innovation." *Organizational Dynamics*, 1985, 14(3), 24–34.

Dougherty, D., and Hardy, C. "Sustained Product Innovation in Large, Mature Organizations: Overcoming Innovation-to-Organization Problems." *Academy of Management Journal*, 1996, 39(5), 1120–1153.

Downs, G. W., and Mohr, L. B. "Conceptual Issues in the Study of Innovation." *Administrative Science Quarterly*, 1976, 21(20), 23–41.

Drazin, R., and Schoonhoven, C. B. "Community, Population, and Organization Effects on Innovation: A Multilevel Perspective." *Academy of Management Journal*, 1996, 39(5), 1065–1083.

Drucker, P. F. *Managing the Nonprofit Organization*. New York: HarperCollins, 1990.

Drucker, P. F. "Really Reinventing Government." *Atlantic Monthly*, Feb. 1995, pp. 49–61.

Elmore, R. F. "Paradox of Innovation in Education: Cycles of Reform and the Resilience of Teaching." Paper prepared for the Fundamental Questions of Innovation Conference, Duke University, May 3–5, 1991.

Ford, J. D., and Ford, L. W. "The Role of Conversations in Producing Intentional Change in Organizations." *Academy of Management Journal*, 1995, 22(3), 541–570.

Golden, O. "Innovation in Public Sector Human Services Programs." *Journal of Policy Analysis and Management*, 1990, 9(2), 219–248.

Goodsell, C. T. *The Case for Bureaucracy: A Public Administration Polemic*. (3rd ed.) Chatham, N.J.: Chatham House, 1994.

Gore, A. *Creating a Government That Works Better and Costs Less: Report of the National Performance Review*. Washington, D.C.: U.S. Government Printing Office, 1993.

Gulick, L., and Urwick, L. (eds.). *Papers on the Science of Administration*. New York: Institute of Public Administration, 1937.

Hage, J., and Aiken, M. "Program Change and Organizational Properties: A Comparative Analysis." *American Journal of Sociology*, 1967, 72(2), 503–519.

Hager, M., Galaskiewicz, J., Bielefeld, W., and Pins, J. "Tales from the Grave: Organizations' Accounts of Their Own Demise." *American Behavioral Scientist,* 1996, *39*(8), 975–994.

Hannan, M., and Freeman, J. "Structural Inertia and Organizational Change." *American Sociological Review,* 1984, *49*(1), 462–481.

Hatch, M. J. "The Dynamics of Organizational Culture." *Academy of Management Review,* 1993, *18*(4), 657–693.

Haveman, H. A. "Between a Rock and a Hard Place: Organizational Change and Performance Under Conditions of Fundamental Transformation." *Administrative Science Quarterly,* 1992, *37*(1), 48–75.

Herzberg, F. "One More Time: How Do You Motivate Employees? *Harvard Business Review,* 1987, *65*(5), 109–120.

Holdaway, E., Newberry, J. F., Hickson, D. J., and Heron, R. P. "Dimensions of Organizations in Complex Societies: The Educational Sector." *Administrative Science Quarterly,* 1975, *20*(1), 37–58.

Hubbard, E. "Making Sense of Public Service Partnerships: Understanding the Why and How of Interagency Efforts." Unpublished paper, 1995.

Huxham, C., and Macdonald, D. "Introducing Collaborative Advantage: Achieving Inter-Organizational Effectiveness Through Meta-Strategy." *Management Decision,* 1992, *30,* 50–56.

Kanter, R. M. *The Change Masters.* New York: Simon & Schuster, 1983.

Kanter, R. M. "When a Thousand Flowers Bloom: Structural, Collective, and Social Conditions for Innovation in Organization." *Research in Organizational Behavior,* 1988, *10*(1), 169–211.

Kaufman, H. *Are Government Organizations Immortal?* Washington, D.C.: Brookings Institution, 1976.

Kimberly, J. R., and Evanisko, M. J. "Organizational Innovation: The Influence of Individual, Organizational, and Contextual Factors on Hospital Adoption of Technological and Administrative Innovations." *Academy of Management Journal,* 1981, *24*(4), 689–713.

Larkey, P. D., and Caulkins, J. P. "All Above Average and Other Unintended Consequences of Performance Appraisal Systems." Working Paper, H. John Heinz III School of Public Policy and Management, Carnegie Mellon University, 1992.

Lawrence, P. R., and Lorsch, J. "Differentiation and Integration in Complex Organizations." *Administrative Science Quarterly,* 1967, *12,* 142–151.

Lehman, N. "Kicking in Groups." *Atlantic Monthly,* Apr. 1996, pp. 22–26.

Levin, M. A., and Sanger, M. B. "Using Old Stuff in New Ways: Innovation as a Case of Evolutionary Thinking." *Journal of Policy Analysis and Management,* 1992, *11*(1), 88–115.

Levin, M. A., and Sanger, M. B. *Making Government Work: How Entrepreneurial Executives Turn Bright Ideas into Real Results.* San Francisco: Jossey-Bass, 1994.

Light, P. C. *Monitoring Government: Inspectors General and the Search for Accountability.* Washington, D.C.: Brookings Institution/Governance Institute, 1993.

Light, P. C. "Diversity in the Faculty—'Not Like Us': Removing the Barriers to Minority Recruitment." *Journal of Public Policy and Management,* 1994, *13*(1), 163–186.

Light, P. C. *Thickening Government: Federal Hierarchy and the Diffusion of Accountability.* Washington, D.C.: Brookings Institution/Governance Institute, 1995.

Light, P. C. *The Tides of Reform: Making Government Work, 1945–1995.* New Haven, Conn.: Yale University Press, 1997.

Lynch, W. F. *Images of Hope: Imagination as Healer of the Hopeless.* South Bend, Ind.: Notre Dame Press, 1965.

Lynn, L., Jr. "Innovation and the Public Interest: Insights from the Private Sector." Paper prepared for the Innovation and Organization Conference, University of Minnesota, Sept. 18–21, 1992.

Maidique, M. A., and Zirger, B. J. "A Study of Success and Failure in Product Innovation: The Case of the U.S. Electronics Industry." *IEEE Transactions on Engineering Management,* 1984, *31*(4), 192–203.

Marquardt, M. J. *Building the Learning Organization: A Systems Approach to Quantum Improvement and Global Success.* New York: McGraw-Hill, 1996.

McKnight, J. *The Careless Society: Community and Its Counterfeits.* New York: Basic Books, 1995.

Minneapolis StarTribune, Editorial, June 12, 1991.

Mintrom, M. "Policy Entrepreneurs and the Diffusion of Innovation." *American Journal of Political Science,* 1997, *41*(3), 738–770.

Moore, M. H. *Creating Public Value: Strategic Management in Government.* Cambridge, Mass.: Harvard University Press, 1995.

Morgan, G. *Images of Organization.* Thousand Oaks, Calif.: Sage, 1986.

National Commission on the Public Service. *Leadership for America: Final Report of the National Commission on the Public Service.* Washington, D.C.: National Commission on the Public Service, 1989.

Nohria, N., and Gulati, R. "Is Slack Good or Bad for Innovation?" *Academy of Management Journal,* 1996, *39*(5), 1245–1264.

Osborne, D., and Gaebler, T. *Reinventing Government: Entrepreneurial Government.* New York: Plume, 1993.

Osborne, D., and Plastrik, P. *Banishing Bureaucracy: The Five Strategies for Reinventing Government.* Reading, Mass.: Addison-Wesley, 1997.

Perrow, C. *Complex Organizations: A Critical Essay.* New York: Random House, 1979.

Perry, J. L. "Merit Pay in the Public Sector: The Case for a Failure of Theory." *Review of Public Personnel Administration,* 1986, *7,* 56–69.

Perry, J. L., and Rainey, H. G. "The Public-Private Distinction in Organization Theory: A Critique and Research Strategy." *Academy of Management Review,* 1988, *13*(1), 182–201.

Peters, T. J. "Get Innovative or Get Dead." *California Management Review,* 1990, *33*(4), 9–26.

Peters, T. J., and Waterman, R. H., Jr. *In Search of Excellence: Lessons from America's Best-Run Companies.* New York: Warner Books, 1982.

Pew Research Center for The People & The Press. "TV News Viewership Declines." News release, May 13, 1996, p. 62.

Pfeffer, J. "Some Consequences of Organizational Demography: Potential Impacts of an Aging Work Force on Formal Organizations." In S. B. Kisler, J. N. Morgan, and V. K. Oppenheimer (eds.), *Aging: Social Change.* New York: Academic Press, 1981.

Pfeffer, J., and Salancik, G. *The External Control of Organizations: A Resource-Dependence Perspective.* New York: HarperCollins, 1978.

Pierce, J. L., and Delbecq, A. L. "Organizational Structure, Individual Attitudes, and Innovation." *Academy of Management Review,* 1977, *2*(1), 26–37.

Plagens, P. "Return of the Galisteo Kid." *Newsweek,* May 30, 1994.

Pollitt, K. "For Whom the Ball Rolls." *The Nation,* Apr. 16, 1996, p. 14.

Powell, W. W. *The Nonprofit Sector: A Research Handbook.* New Haven, Conn.: Yale University Press, 1987.

Putnam, R. D. "Bowling Alone: Democracy in America at the End of the Twentieth Century." Paper presented at the Nobel Symposium "Democracy's Victory and Crisis," Uppsala, Aug. 27–29, 1994. (Reprinted in *Journal of Democracy,* 1995, *6*(1), 65–78.)

Rainey, H. G. *Understanding and Managing Public Organizations.* San Francisco: Jossey-Bass, 1991.

Roberts, N. C., and King, P. J. *Transforming Public Policy: Dynamics of Policy Entrepreneurship and Innovation.* San Francisco: Jossey-Bass, 1996.

Roberts, N. C., and Wargo, L. "Compensating for Size: Planning in Large Public Bureaus." Paper prepared for the National Public Management Research Conference, Sept. 30-Oct. 2, 1993, University of Wisconsin, Madison.

Ruttan, V., and Hayami, K. "Toward a Theory of Induced Innovation." *Journal of Development Studies*, 1984, *20*(1), 203–223.

Salamon, L. M. *America's Nonprofit Sector: A Primer*. Washington, D.C.: Foundation Center, 1992.

Schorr, L. B. *Within Our Reach: Breaking the Cycle of Disadvantage*. New York: Anchor Books, 1989.

Senge, P. M. "The Leader's New Work: Building Learning Organizations." *Sloan Management Review*, 1990, *32*(1), 7–23.

Stevens, S. K. "Growing Up Nonprofit: Predictable Stages of Nonprofit Growth and Development." Paper published by the Stevens Group, Minneapolis, 1992.

U.S. Merit Systems Protection Board. *Working for America: An Update*. Washington, D.C.: U.S. Merit Systems Protection Board, 1994.

Vaill, P. B. *Learning as a Way of Being: Strategies for Survival in a World of Permanent White Water*. San Francisco: Jossey-Bass, 1996.

Van de Ven, A. H. "Central Problems in the Management of Innovation." *Management Science*, 1986, *32*, 590–607.

Van de Ven, A. H., Angle, H. L., and Poole, M. S. (eds.). *Research on the Management of Innovation: The Minnesota Studies*. New York: Harper-Collins, 1989.

Wagner, J. A., III. "Participation's Effects on Performance and Satisfaction: A Reconsideration of the Research Evidence." *Academy of Management Review*, 1994, *19*(2), 312–330.

Weiffering, E.J. "The Twisted Economics of Minneapolis Neighborhood Nonprofits and Low-Income Housing." *Corporate Report Minnesota*, March, 1994.

Wilkins, A. L., Perry, L. T., and Checketts, A. G. "'Please Don't Make Me a Hero': A Re-Examination of Corporate Heroes." *Human Resource Management*, 1990, *29*(3), 327–341.

Wolfe, R. A. "Organizational Innovation: Review, Critique and Suggested Research Directions." *Journal of Management Studies*, 1994, *31*(3), 405–431.

Woodman, R. W., Sawyer, J. E., and Griffin, R. W. "Toward a Theory of Organizational Creativity." *Academy of Management Review*, 1993, *18*(2), 293–321.

Zaltman, G., Duncan, R., and Holbeck, J. *Innovation and Organizations*. New York: Wiley, 1973.

Index